Evaluating the Charismatic Movement

A Theological and Biblical Appraisal

Robert H. Culpepper

JUDSON PRESS ® VALLEY FORGE

EVALUATING THE CHARISMATIC MOVEMENT

Copyright © 1977
Judson Press, Valley Forge, PA 19481

Unless otherwise indicated, Bible quotations in this volume are in accordance with the Revised Standard Version of the Bible, copyrighted 1952 and 1971 by the Division of Christian Education of the National Council of the Churches of Christ in the United States of America, and are used by permission.

Other versions of the Bible quoted in this book are:

The Holy Bible, King James Version.

The New English Bible, Copyright © The Delegates of the Oxford University Press and The Syndics of the Cambridge University Press, 1961, 1970.

Library of Congress Cataloging in Publication Data

Culpepper, Robert H.
    Evaluating the charismatic movement.

Bibliography: p. 185.
    Includes index.
    1. Pentecostalism.   I. Title
BR1644.C84   270.8'2   77-1197
ISBN 0-8170-0743-1

The name JUDSON PRESS is registered as a trademark in the U.S. Patent Office.

Printed in the U.S.A.

To Friends,
both inside and outside
the charismatic movement

Preface
and
Acknowledgments

This book was prepared with the general reader in mind. However, footnotes are included to indicate my indebtedness to many authors. For the most part, the footnotes need not concern the average reader, but, along with the bibliography, they should point those interested to sources for further study.

Now it is my great joy to express gratitude to those who have been of particular help in the preparation of this book. I wrote most of it during a recent period of study at Southeastern Baptist Theological Seminary, Wake Forest, North Carolina. Many faculty members of this seminary offered special courtesies during this time. Dr. James E. Tull kindly allowed me the use of his office. Dr. H. Eugene McLeod and the library staff of the seminary were most helpful in providing assistance in locating needed materials. Dr. J. Leo Green and Dr. John W. Eddins, Jr., read a part of the manuscript and offered encouragement. Especially am I indebted to Dr. Raymond Bryan Brown, distinguished professor of New Testament Interpretation at Southeastern, who read the manuscript chapter by chapter, making critical evaluations. This resulted in my rewriting some of the material. Likewise Dr. Leroy Seat, my colleague on the faculty of Seinan Gakuin University, Fukuoka, Japan, and Dr. E. Luther Copeland, chancellor of Seinan Gakuin, read the manuscript, offering helpful suggestions. Dr. J. Rodman Williams, President of Melodyland School of Theology, Anaheim, California, and Dr. Earl W. Morey, Pastor of St. Giles Presbyterian Church, Richmond, Virginia—both deeply involved in the charismatic movement—

provided helpful counsel. Mrs. Kathy Britt and Mrs. Yasuko Fujie did the necessary typing. My wife, Kay, provided understanding and encouragement along the way. It was a particular joy to work with Mr. Harold L. Twiss and the staff of Judson Press. None of these, however, is to be blamed for the point of view expressed or for the deficiencies in the book that remain. For these I must assume full responsibility.

All scriptural quotations, unless otherwise indicated, are from the Revised Standard Version.

Robert H. Culpepper

Seinan Gakuin University
Department of Theology

Contents

Introduction   9

PART ONE: THE CHARISMATIC MOVEMENT

Chapter 1   Profile   17

Chapter 2   Historical Background   39

PART TWO: A THEOLOGICAL APPRAISAL

Chapter 3   Baptism in the Holy Spirit   53

Chapter 4   Gifts of the Spirit and Speaking in Tongues   79

Chapter 5   Gifts of Prophecy, Healing, and Deliverance   109

Chapter 6   Other Gifts and Features of   139
            the Charismatic Movement

Chapter 7   Summary and Conclusion   159

Notes   171

Bibliography   185

Index   191

Introduction

If we, like Rip Van Winkle, were to awaken suddenly from a twenty-year slumber and try to discover what is going on in Christendom today, we would be in for some surprises. Doubtless among the things that would perplex us most would be finding here and there Anglican priests casting out demons, Lutherans speaking in tongues, Presbyterians holding healing services, and Baptists, Catholics, Methodists, Pentecostals, and Episcopalians engaged in earnest prayer together. Should we go into a Christian bookstore to investigate the kind of books being published these days, we would be amazed to find not the traditional trickle of books on the Holy Spirit, but a veritable deluge of works on that subject. Should we then seek an explanation for these phenomena, doubtless we would receive one answer: the charismatic movement.

To be sure, not all of the books about the Holy Spirit arise from the charismatic movement. Still, that movement has been the dominant catalytic agent in stimulating interest in the work of the Holy Spirit in today's world.

Why another book when there are already so many? Books related to the charismatic movement fall generally into one of three categories. On the one side, there are some arising from within the movement seeking to promote it. On another side, there are those coming from outside the movement seeking to discredit it. Finally, there are some written from a more neutral stance, attempting to understand it, evaluate it, and interpret its meaning for our day. This book falls within the third category.

There is a need for works of this type. Many of the books of the first two types come from such a highly charged emotional atmosphere that they shed more heat than light. Often books of the first type give the impression that the charismatic movement has a corner on the Holy Spirit. A large number of books of the second type attack the movement without attempting to understand it. Both sides have a tendency to adduce illustrations to prove their point of view while neglecting evidence on the other side. There is a need for a balanced presentation.

A great many books focus on a facet of the subject, treating a part for the whole. Often books deal with glossolalia or speaking in tongues as if glossolalia and the charismatic movement were synonymous. Important as this subject is, it is hardly more than the tip of the iceberg. The same is true for exorcism and healing, which also have been given special attention. Thus there is a need for a comprehensive treatment of the subject.

The charismatic movement is an interdenominational movement within Christendom seeking to promote personal and church renewal and a recovery of spiritual power by an emphasis upon the exercise of the gifts of the Spirit mentioned by Paul in 1 Corinthians 12:7-11. Historically, the movement is related to Pentecostalism, but it is not a separatist movement exercised in isolation from the rest of Christendom. Rather, it is Pentecostalism penetrating the various denominations of the Christian church, Protestant and Catholic. Generally speaking, the charismatic movement, instead of encouraging those who come under its influence to form a new Pentecostal denomination or to join an already existing one, urges its adherents to remain within their own churches and denominations and to act as spiritual leaven within them.

The older name for the charismatic movement is Neo-Pentecostalism, but most leaders of the movement now seem to prefer the term "charismatic movement" or "charismatic renewal." By avoiding the term "Pentecostalism," the charismatic movement seeks to escape the widespread prejudices against Pentecostalism that are prevalent both within the historic churches and within society in general. Traditionally, Pentecostalism has been associated with rampant emotionalism and strong anti-intellectualism and has drawn its members largely from the lower economic and social stratum of society. Though strong emotional and anti-intellectual tendencies remain within the modern charismatic movement, these are not as pronounced as they are in Pentecostalism. Moreover, the adherents of the movement come from all classes of society and from all kinds of denominational backgrounds and the Roman Catholic Church. In doctrinal matters main-line Pentecostals emphasize baptism in the Spirit as a second (salvation being the first) or third (sanctification being the second) work of grace whereby Jesus the Great Baptizer immerses the believer in the Holy Spirit and thus empowers the person for witness. They interpret speaking in tongues both as the initial evidence of baptism in the Holy Spirit and as one of the gifts of the Spirit set forth by Paul in 1 Corinthians 12:7-11. They emphasize that tongues and the other eight gifts mentioned in this passage, subject to the regulations that Paul elaborates in 1 Corinthians 14, should be a normal part of the worship services of the church.

Those within the charismatic movement usually retain the distinctive doctrinal teachings of their denominations, Protestant or Catholic. However, to a greater or lesser degree, they accept or adapt much of the distinctively Pentecostal teaching as well. Just how they do this will be discussed in chapters 3, 4, 5, and 6 of this book.

There are some outside the charismatic movement who strongly object to the adjective "charismatic" as a description of the movement. Pointing out that the word "charismatic" is derived from the Greek noun *charis,* grace, they emphasize that all of God's gifts are gifts of his grace. Thus Frank Stagg writes:

> All Christians are charismatic. . . . The "charismatic movement" is as wide as are the people of God who are exercising their God-given abilities in the service of God, whether these services are spectacular, filling stadia and headlines, or unspectacular, possibly filling empty stomachs and empty lives.[1]

There is a sense in which the validity of this criticism must be admitted. All Christians have the gift (*charisma*) of eternal life (Romans 6:23), and the Holy Spirit has been given to all who belong to Christ (Acts 2:38; Romans 8:9). Thus in the broad sense all Christians are charismatic. Still it is true that the gifts of the Holy Spirit, particularly the more spectacular ones mentioned in 1 Corinthians 12:7-11, received relatively little attention in Christendom outside of main-line Pentecostal circles until Neo-Pentecostalism or the charismatic movement appeared. Therefore, in a narrower sense, the use of the adjective "charismatic" as a description of this particular movement may be accepted.

But is "movement" a proper term? Some will object to it on the basis of the supposition that it suggests some kind of monolithic structure with one head. Quite the contrary is true, as Kilian McDonnell, eminent researcher of the Catholic charismatic

11

movement, has shown. McDonnell points out that the term comes from cultural anthropology and that "all the factors present in other movements of social change . . . are to be found in the charismatic movement."[2] These include an ideology which structures the goals and values of the movement and provides a framework for interpreting experiences and events, a commitment act, and real or imagined opposition from society at large. Other factors involved are face-to-face recruitment by persons already committed to the movement, and a loose cellular organization bound together by various personal, structural, and ideological ties. Those directly involved in the charismatic movement would doubtless place their emphasis upon a common experience interpreted from a central perspective. Nevertheless, "movement" is not an inappropriate term.

Many within the movement prefer the term "renewal" to "movement." Doubtless renewal is the goal of the movement, but for the purposes of this book "movement" is the better term. It is the more neutral term. Whether the movement is helping to bring about renewal is one of the questions to be discussed. To call it the charismatic renewal would be to answer the question before it is considered.

It is significant that the charismatic movement came to the fore during the turbulent sixties. That was the period of the Vietnam War and protest movements, of increased violence and the assassination of public figures, of the lowering of standards of morality and the acceleration of movement toward a permissive society. It was the period of women's liberation and the black power movement, of increased secularization and the "death of God" theology, of the hippie movement and the drug culture, of Jeane Dixon and horoscopes, of the flourishing of the occult and even Satanism, of Vatican II and great fermentation within the Roman Catholic Church, of the Jesus movement and a growing disenchantment with the institutional church.

How is the charismatic movement to be interpreted? Is it just a passing fad? Is it simply an emotional reaction against the denial of the supernatural, a protest movement against the tendency to frustrate the experience of the transcendent? If so, could not the same be said of spiritualism and a revival of the occult?

Various assessments of the charismatic movement are being made. On the positive side, Robert E. Terwilliger, director of Trinity Institute, New York City, has called it "a great surge of awareness of the Holy Spirit," "the most powerful force within the Church at this moment." David du Plessis, well-known Pentecostal leader noted for introducing Pentecostalism into the traditional churches, declares: "The Pentecostal movement and the charismatic renewal are creations of the Spirit of God, not an evolution of some revival somewhere." He sees in these movements evidence that "God is doing something in our generation that has no equal anywhere in all the revivals in history." Ralph Martin, internationally recognized leader in the charismatic movement in the Catholic Church, sees the movement as evidence that "God is moving to restore New Testament Christianity to all his people—that is more than renewal." John A. Mackay, president emeritus of Princeton Theological Seminary and eminent ecumenical leader, asserts:

> Despite all the aberrations that may be attached to it in certain places, neo-Pentecostalism is a rebirth of primitive, First-Century Christianity. Protestants who glory in belonging to Classical or Radical Christianity will look down their noses at Pentecostal Christianity only at their peril. For this is a phenomenon of God's springtime.[3]

On the other hand, the charismatic movement has come in for severe censure from many quarters. One Baptist group has branded it as "being of the Devil" and "unscriptural."[4] One of the basic charges brought against it is that of divisiveness. "There are churches, and today the number is on the increase, where the emergence of a charismatic group has been the occasion for hostile division, censoriousness, and the ugliness of charge and countercharge," writes James C. Logan, professor of systematic theology at Wesley Theological Seminary in Washington, D.C. The strongest opposition is leveled against glossolalia, which Robert Hamblin, Baptist pastor in Mississippi, calls "one of the most divisive influences that has ever happened in Christianity." "Experience has demonstrated that glossolalia tends to create division in the church," claims Donald W. Burdick. "Those who have it often tend to feel superior to those who don't." W. A. Criswell, past president of the Southern Baptist Convention and pastor of the largest Baptist church in the world, is even more emphatic:

13

> Wherever and whenever glossolalia appears, it is always hurtful and divisive. There is no exception to this. It is but another instrument for the tragic torture of the body of Christ. I have seen some of our finest churches torn apart by the practice.

Donald G. Bloesch, professor of theology at Dubuque Theological Seminary, takes exception to the idea that the charismatic movement is God's instrument for church renewal. He writes: ". . . it would be a gross delusion to think that this movement contains the key to the revitalization of the church in our time. Its theological basis is too weak to guarantee any kind of breakthrough in the direction of Christian renewal for which the church still waits."[5]

With opinions so sharply divided the need of a careful theological appraisal is obvious. A naive, uncritical acceptance of the movement could possibly lead individuals and segments of the church to act as though "they had swallowed the Holy Ghost, feathers and all," to borrow Luther's vivid imagery concerning the spiritualists of his day. On the other hand, an uninformed prejudgment of the movement, resulting in its total rejection, could result possibly in further spiritual impoverishment of the church, even in a quenching of the Spirit, against which Paul warned in 1 Thessalonians 5:19. Our stance should be that admonished by Paul: "Test everything; hold fast what is good" (1 Thessalonians 5:21).

In a study such as this, attempting objectivity is of the utmost importance, but real objectivity is very difficult to achieve. Personal feelings and prejudices are apt to distort the presentation and interpretation of facts. In a brilliant manner Kilian McDonnell discusses some of the factors that make an objective evaluation of Catholic Pentecostalism difficult. Since what he says is applicable to the charismatic movement as a whole, a brief summary of some of his salient ideas is in order.[6]

14

He points out that the public image of Pentecostalism is such a highly distorted one that it makes it difficult for anything related to Pentecostalism to receive a fair hearing. Moreover, many feel threatened by the kind of religious experience typified by Pentecostalism. In the minds of many people some of the common practices of Pentecostalism, such as speaking in tongues, prophesying, and interpreting utterances in tongues, violate the norms of socially acceptable behavior. Ignorance of the real issues involved leads many both inside and outside the Pentecostal movement to place an undue stress on tongues. The charismatic movement, Protestant and Catholic, often tends to take over too much of the cultural baggage of classical Pentecostalism. This cultural baggage, according to McDonnell, includes speech patterns, prayer postures, emotional expressions, and theological explanations which lose their validity when transferred from one cultural context to another. The very nature of the gifts of the Spirit, which can be appreciated only on the basis of spiritual discernment, makes an objective judgment difficult. Finally, McDonnell points out, many regard the Pentecostal movement as a threat to the structural church.

Too often movements of this kind are caricatured. A straw man, which is hardly more than a travesty of the real thing, is erected and then knocked down. It is my hope that readers of this book, regardless of their positions with reference to the movement, will recognize what is presented here as fair and accurate. A sincere effort is made to keep in mind the principle that this movement, or any other for that matter, needs to be understood in terms of its finest and most representative spokesmen. Recognizing the diversity within the movement, I seek to indicate what is representative, while at the same time pointing out variations here and there. The treatment highlights Neo-Pentecostalism or the charismatic movement within traditional Protestant churches, but along the way Catholic contributions are noted also.

The structure the book takes is itself an expression of a desire to be as objective and fair as possible. Chapter 1 deals with the movement's growth and the type of spirituality involved, while chapter 2 focuses on the historical background. The approach here is a descriptive one. This kind of treatment is used because too often writers proceed to attack the movement without ever giving a fair presentation of it.

Chapters 3, 4, 5, and 6 attempt both to set forth the basic distinctive theology of the movement and to appraise it as well. The concluding chapter summarizes some things that seem clear on the basis of this study and suggests a possible way forward out of the morass of confrontation.

The evaluations offered consist of both positive and negative appraisals. The basic criteria for evaluation of the movement which are employed throughout the latter part of the book may be set forth in three questions. First, is the matter under consideration scriptural? Does it employ sound principles of biblical interpretation and present a gospel that is in accord with the central teachings of the Scriptures? Second, is it Christ-centered? Does it focus the spotlight upon the Christ revealed in the Scriptures, or does it let other emphases steal the limelight? Third, what practical effects does it have? What kind of influence does it have upon individuals, churches, and society as a whole?

15

PART ONE: THE CHARISMATIC MOVEMENT

CHAPTER 1
Profile

When the Pentecostal movement broke out near the beginning of this century, it was soon fairly well contained, as far as the historic churches were concerned. Before long those involved in the movement dissociated themselves from the denominations to which they had belonged (mostly Holiness groups) and formed new Pentecostal denominations. At the same time the historic churches insulated themselves against what they regarded as the doctrinal aberrations and the emotional excesses of the movement. Despite the movement's rapid growth in the United States and all over the world, the historic churches were largely unconcerned. This was a movement which had begun with economically and culturally deprived people, blacks and whites. "After all, somebody needs to minister to these people, and if the Pentecostals are doing it, that relieves us of the responsibility" was the attitude often taken by the traditional churches.

Breadth of the Movement

But now all of that has changed. Pentecostalism is overflowing its Pentecostal vessels and is penetrating the traditional churches. It has moved out of the store-front meeting places to the ballrooms of the Sheraton and the Hilton. The old social, cultural, and economic pigeonholes into which the movement had been shoved no longer fit.

Those within the charismatic movement come from all walks of life. Some are doctors and lawyers; others are businessmen and large corporation executives; some are clergymen and full-time religious workers; still others are in show business or some branch of the military service. Some of them drive Cadillacs or Lincoln Continentals, and among them are people with Phi Beta Kappa keys. The presence in the movement of popular singers, like Pat Boone and Johnny Cash, and men in the high echelons of the military establishment, like retired United States Army General Ralph E. Haines, Jr., has helped to accent the movement's claim to social respectability.

Numbered among the charismatics are people who have not been Christians long, but most of the people in the movement have been active for years in their respective churches. Among them are those who have lost interest in the institutional church, but the vast majority are more active in their churches than ever before. Most of them testify concerning a deep, personal, spiritual renewal, a new fullness of life in the Holy Spirit which has come to them through their contact with the charismatic movement.

"So long as a Pentecostal worshiped in the church down the road, he could be ignored," says John Stevens Kerr. "But when your friend in the next pew calls himself a Pentecostal—and a Presbyterian as well—the problem comes directly home."[1] Reactions within the traditional churches have ranged all the way from cautious acceptance on the one hand to open hostility on the other. In between, the vast majority of Christians who show any awareness of the situation seem bewildered by it all.

Within Traditional Protestantism

It is difficult to estimate how widespread the movement is or how deep its penetration. It is safe to say that there is no major denomination within Christendom that has remained untouched. Within many of the denominations—Episcopalian, Lutheran, Presbyterian, and Mennonite—informal charismatic fellowship groups have sprung up. Most of the people in these denominational charismatic groups enjoy also some participation from time to time in charismatic fellowships of an ecumenical nature. The denominational charismatic groups enable people of the same denominational backgrounds to have spiritual fellowship in which freedom for the charismatic dimension is recognized. Over and above this is the desire of those involved to understand and interpret their Pentecostal experience in ways compatible with the doctrinal teaching of their respective denominations.

In a strong movement for renewal such as the charismatic one, tendencies toward proliferation and temptations toward starting new denominations are inevitable. So far, however, such pressures have been steadfastly resisted. Not new denominations, but Christendom renewed is the expressed objective. One articulate leader within the movement elucidates in the following way: "What the Lord wants is His whole body, His whole church renewed as the body of Christ. Small charismatic meetings and large charismatic assemblies may be transitional instruments to that end. . . ." The goal of the Pentecostal movement should be to put itself out of business. Ultimately it should not produce separate Pentecostal groups, but rather a renewed church in which the charismatic experience is readily incorporated.[2]

Here and there some of the historic churches try to deal with the "problem" of the charismatics by excluding them from their fellowship. This happened when, because of their charismatic practices, the Pat Boone family was ousted from the Church of Christ. Still such reactions may be regarded as exceptional and extreme. A number of denominations have authorized special studies on the charismatic movement and have published official reports that take a fairly positive stance toward it.

The charismatic movement is international, as well as interdenominational. The tremendous upsurge of evangelism spearheaded by the Pentecostals throughout Latin America and the African continent is a well-recognized, well-documented fact. Though this is related more directly to classical Pentecostalism than to the charismatic movement, it is not without its significance for this movement. The situation varies, of course, from country to country, but in England and Ireland, in western Europe and even eastern Europe, in Japan and Korea, in Israel and India, in Australia and New Zealand the impression which the movement makes is very much the same—that of a young, virile, growing movement which is becoming more and more a factor to be reckoned with in the life of the church.

The growth of this movement in a relatively short period of time is truly remarkable. The full story of how it came about will probably never be told, but some of the important human factors can be highlighted.

Ecumenical Acceptance

Three eminent theologians of ecumenical stature helped to pave the way for the charismatic movement through the tributes which they paid to the long-despised and largely ignored Pentecostal movement. The first was Lesslie Newbigin, missionary of the Church of Scotland, director of the Division of World Mission and

19

Evangelism of the World Council of Churches, and now bishop of the Church of South India. In 1953, in his book *The Household of God,* he recognized Pentecostalism as a third stream of Christianity to be ranked alongside of Protestantism and Catholicism. According to Newbigin, the different accents of these three streams are clarified by their basic answers to the question: "How are we incorporated in Christ?" To this question Protestantism answers: "by hearing and believing the Gospel"; Catholicism responds: "by sacramental participation in the life of the historically continuous Church." Alongside these must be placed Pentecostalism's answer: "by receiving and abiding in the Holy Spirit."[3]

Newbigin praises Pentecostalism for its sense of what is important. Not theological orthodoxy, not apostolic succession, but spiritual vitality is accented. He calls upon Protestants and Catholics alike to extend the warmest kind of welcome to Pentecostal Christians, knowing that there are in their teachings revolutionary elements which may be dangerously subversive to existing ways of thought.

John A. Mackay, formerly a missionary in Latin America and president emeritus of Princeton Theological Seminary, has also helped to bolster the prestige of the Pentecostal movement. In his keynote address as chairman of the International Missionary Council assembly in Ghana in 1957, Mackay observed that there are

> some notable cases of organized denominations in which the Church is literally the mission. This is true . . . of the Pentecostal Churches. In many parts of the world today every member [sic] of the several Churches that make up the Pentecostal World Fellowship are not only committed Christians, but ardent missionaries.[4]

Even before this in 1952 Mackay had helped prepare the way for the warm welcome which David du Plessis, world secretary for the Pentecostal World Fellowship, received at the extended assembly of the International Missionary Council in Willingen, Germany, in 1952.

In the June 6, 1958, issue of *Life,* there appeared an article entitled "The Third Force in Christendom," by the late Henry P. Van Dusen, past president of Union Theological Seminary in New York City. This followed an around-the-world trip in which he had interviewed large numbers of church leaders who had expressed their concern about the phenomenal growth of nontraditional churches. He numbered in this "third force" a broad spectrum of churches, such as the Nazarenes, Jehovah's Witnesses, and Seventh-Day Adventists, but emphasized that the largest single group was the Pentecostals.

Van Dusen highlighted some of the cardinal characteristics of Pentecostalism as he had observed them: simplicity of message, emphasis upon a life-transforming experience, aggressive evangelism, spiritual ardor, careful nurture of converts, dependence upon the Holy Spirit, and an untiring, seven-days-a-week Christianity. He went on to say that the early tendency among Protestants to ignore this movement as a temporary and passing phenomenon was beginning to be replaced by "a chastened readiness to investigate the secrets of its mighty sweep."[5]

In the early 1960s in an interview with John Sherrill, Van Dusen is reported to have called the Pentecostal movement "a revolution comparable in importance with the establishment of the original Apostolic Church and with the Protestant Reformation."[6]

These and other similar quotations from these three men— Lesslie Newbigin, John A. Mackay, and Henry P. Van Dusen—have appeared again and again in literature related to the charismatic movement, and there can be little doubt that they have contributed significantly to the movement's growth.

Outstanding Leadership

The remarkable ministry of the aforementioned David du Plessis, affectionately nicknamed by many "Mr. Pentecost," is causing many within the traditional churches to become open to the Pentecostal experience. Born in South Africa in 1905, du Plessis was converted at eleven and, according to his testimony, "baptized in the Spirit" at thirteen. He grew up in the land of his birth as a Pentecostal, hating people in the traditional churches. When the Dutch Reformed ministers preached against the Pentecostals calling them false prophets standing on street corners, he would stand on the street corners and fire back at them as "these blind leaders of the blind." In an experience similar to that in which Peter had been led to Cornelius and the Gentiles (Acts 10–11), du Plessis was led in 1951 to begin sharing the Pentecostal faith and experience in ecumenical circles, particularly within the framework of the World Council of Churches. Fully expecting that they would reject his message, he was amazed at the warm reception they accorded him. He was amazed also that the Lord took that old, harsh spirit of criticism and condemnation from his heart and flooded it instead with His own love for them.[7]

Since that time David du Plessis has traveled all over the world many times as an apostle for Pentecostalism. He has been received warmly in meetings large and small of the International Missionary Council, the World Council of Churches, and in churches of all denominations. Moreover, he has given lectures in such prominent seminaries as Princeton Theological Seminary, Yale University Divinity School, Union Theological Seminary in New York City, Southern Methodist University, Colgate Rochester Divinity School, and Fuller Theological Seminary. Pleading with people to stay in their own churches, he counsels, "Be not conformed to Pentecostalism, but be ye transformed by the renewal of your mind in your own church."[8]

The Full Gospel Business Men's Fellowship International (FGBMFI) and the worldwide ministry of its founder, Demos Shakarian, have also been human instruments for the promotion of this movement. The grandson of Armenian refugees to America, Demos Shakarian inherited a large dairy farm from his father. He sought to carry on the business, but without the success that his father had known. Committing his business to the Lord, he determined to give God first place in his life. Gradually the idea of a fellowship of Pentecostal businessmen took shape in his mind. For a long time, however, he seemed unable to translate the dream into reality. Early one morning, after hours of agonized prayer, he saw a vision of millions of men with hands upraised magnifying God. This was the stimulus that Demos greatly needed. In 1953 the Full Gospel Business Men's Fellowship International was organized with Demos Shakarian as president. It has grown steadily ever since.

This group sponsors interdenominational prayer breakfasts or dinners in ballrooms of hotels in large cities around the world. An atmosphere of praise and testimony characterizes the meetings, and often there is an altar call for those who have some special need.

Because it is a laymen's organization, the officers of the fellowship are confined to laymen. Ministers may hold membership, however, and their spiritual counsel is often sought. Though women are welcomed at its meetings, membership is confined to men who are in sympathy with its doctrinal stand. According to this group, the full gospel is the emphasis upon Jesus as Savior, Baptizer in the Spirit, the Healer, and soon coming King.

The Full Gospel Business Men's Fellowship International encourages its members to be active and loyal to their own churches and denominations. Shakarian explains the policy of the group when he says that the FGBMFI is *"not interested in starting new churches; rather we desire to be a service arm to existing ones."*[9] As of November, 1974, the FGBMFI had about a thousand chapters in the United States and another three hundred overseas, with chapters being organized on the average of one every business day. Through its monthly magazine, *Voice*, its weekly TV program, "Good News," and the ministries of its chapters throughout the world, the FGBMFI is constantly carrying on a ministry to millions.

Media Recognition

No single episode in the history of the charismatic movement has received more publicity than the events which led to the resignation of Dennis Bennett as rector of the St. Mark's Episcopal Church in Van Nuys, California, in April, 1960. Several months earlier Bennett had received the baptism in the Spirit with the manifestation of speaking in tongues. Quietly he began to share his experience with various members of his congregation, and it began to spread. This produced rumblings within the church and inquiries about what was going on. Thus he felt led to bring everything out into the open in a sermon before his congregation April 3, 1960. A tumult resulted. That day he was asked to resign and agreed without a fight. Two days later he sent a long pastoral letter to his people telling of his resignation. Without acrimony, he sought to explain the biblical basis of the experience and its basic compatibility with the teaching of the Episcopal Church that the Holy Spirit is to be received with power. He stoutly denied the rumor that was circulating that he was leaving the Episcopal Church. "What I am standing for," he said, "is to be found within the Episcopal Church. . . . But it is important that the Spirit be allowed to work freely in the Episcopal Church, and it is to this that I bear witness, and will continue to bear witness." [10]

23

Time and *Newsweek* reported the story a month or two later, and the publicity accorded the event girdled the globe. Others who had had experiences similar to Bennett's were given the courage to bring things out into the open. Until then most of Christendom had never heard of Neo-Pentecostalism or a charismatic movement. Though much of the publicity was adverse, strangely enough, the movement gained ground steadily.

Following this traumatic experience, Bennett became rector of a small, struggling church in Seattle, Washington. Here he was able to achieve what he had been unable to accomplish in Van Nuys; that is, he was able to communicate his charismatic interpretation of the gospel to his congregation. This church, St. Luke's Episcopal, which in the minds of many had been virtually written off as dead, soon became the largest Episcopal church in the diocese, and it is now something of a showcase for Neo-Pentecostalism.

Extensive use has been made of the mass media in the promotion of the charismatic movement and the type of spiritual renewal that it emphasizes. Hundreds of charismatic books grind off the presses each year. There are numerous bookstores throughout the country that specialize in charismatic literature. In addition to these, innumerable bookstands with religious literature heavily loaded toward the charismatic side are to be found in drugstores, supermarkets, and variety shops all around.

Since the movement accents personal testimony, many of its leaders have written their own spiritual autobiographies. *They Speak with Other Tongues,* by John Sherrill, deserves particular emphasis. John Sherrill, free-lance writer and staff member of *Guideposts* magazine, is the son of the late Lewis L. Sherrill of Union Theological Seminary. Starting out to write a book from an objective point of view about the tongues phenomenon in the twentieth century, this sophisticated journalist found himself in the course of his investigations becoming more and more involved until at last he passed "through the red door," to use his expression, and experienced for himself the baptism in the Holy Spirit with the manifestation of speaking in tongues. The book that he wrote not only describes his spiritual pilgrimage but also gives a good introduction to the history and theology of the charismatic movement, told in a form that reads like an exciting novel.

24

Since David Wilkerson is a Pentecostal preacher, strictly speaking, his book *The Cross and the Switchblade,* written with the help of John and Elizabeth Sherrill,[11] should be classed as Pentecostal rather than Neo-Pentecostal. Millions of copies of the book in twenty-three languages have been sold, and it has been made into a movie with the same title, starring Pat Boone. Very skillfully the Sherrills helped Wilkerson relate how, under the direct leading of the Spirit, he left a pastorate in a little mountain town of Pennsylvania to plunge into one of the worst of New York City's ghettos to start a ministry among teenage gang leaders, dope addicts, and prostitutes. Wilkerson's ministry led to the rehabilitation of many of these people and to the organization of Teen Challenge, a group that carries on a similar ministry to young people in ghetto situations across the country.

To be sure, not all of the books are spiritual autobiographies. Many of them deal with biblical subjects of a charismatic nature. Most of them are written with a light touch and are freely illustrated from life.

Magazines also have been an effective means for propagating interest in charismatic themes. In the early days of the movement, *Trinity* magazine played a significant part. That magazine is no longer published, but *Logos Journal* has come on strong to take its place. In England, *Renewal,* a bimonthly journal published by Fountain Trust, gives a rather sophisticated, theological emphasis to the movement. *Voice,* the monthly organ of the FGBMFI, features personal testimonies of men in all walks of life. With a monthly circulation of nearly a million copies, it is the most widely read charismatic magazine in existence.

The TV broadcasts of Oral Roberts in the 1950s helped to prepare the ground for the charismatic movement. To anchor himself more fully in the mainstream of historic Christianity, Roberts left the Pentecostal Holiness Church in 1968 to join the United Methodist Church. His weekly Sunday morning TV program, which originates from the multimillion dollar facilities of the Oral Roberts University, Tulsa, Oklahoma, continues to reach millions. Demos Shakarian presides over "Good News," the weekly TV broadcast produced by the FGBMFI. Featuring music, interviews, and testimonies, this program has an international outreach. The PTL (Praise the Lord) Club has a charismatic type of program which allows listeners to phone in prayer requests, and prayer time is given to them right there on the air. The Christian Broadcasting Network (CBN), the story of which is told in Pat Robertson's popular book, *Shout It from the Housetops,*[12] has a distinct charismatic emphasis. It is constantly expanding its outreach, both in the United States and abroad. These are but a few examples of the ways the airwaves are being used to carry a charismatic interpretation of the Christian message.

25

The Jesus Movement

The charismatic movement helped to spawn the Jesus movement, and the two movements have assisted in mutually strengthening each other. The origins of the Jesus movement are quite diverse, as are the different elements that compose it. Not all involved in it are charismatic, though the vast majority are. It has been characterized by one authority as a "combination of hippie culture, fundamentalist shallowness, and charismatic fervor." Another writer speaks of the Jesus people as "Bible-toting, Bible-quoting, Jesus-praising, convert-making, sin-forsaking, noisy, forward, persistent pests for Jesus' sake." Many Jesus people came from well-to-do families where they had everything they needed except love and understanding. They turned to drugs, crime, sex, and various forms of the occult in a search for "kicks." Then they got "high on Jesus" and started praising him for having rescued them from the forms of slavery that they had known.[13]

The fact that the Jesus people have received relatively little attention from the mass media during the last few years has given many people the impression that the movement was just a passing fad. While some have dropped out of the movement entirely and gone back to their old ways of life, many are still active in the Jesus houses, communes, and coffee shops. Some have joined main-line churches, particularly those churches that stress evangelical theology. Many are showing interest in serious Bible study, often seeking the help of leaders in the charismatic movement in this study. A good many have gone to other lands evangelizing. Quite a few have entered schools, swelling the enrollment of Bible schools and conservative seminaries.

Taken as a whole, the Jesus movement, despite all of its obvious excesses, has undergirded and strengthened the charismatic movement.

Personal Witness

Personal witness has been and continues to be the mightiest force in the charismatic movement. Young Christians who have just come to know Christ and Christians of long standing whose spiritual lives have recently been revitalized are telling others about Jesus. Sharing their personal testimonies and undergirding them with an appeal to Scripture, they operate on the basis of one simple assumption, "What He's done for me He can do for you." They often supplement their witness by use of the literature of the charismatic movement or cassette tapes stemming from it. In this way they are reaching many within the historic churches as well as many who have long been turned off by the institutional church. Often they show a special compassion for people with particular problems—alcoholics, drug addicts, sex perverts, and emotionally unstable people. In dealing with people of denominational backgrounds different from their own, these witnesses usually encourage their "converts" to stay within their own churches and be witnesses for Christ where they are.

Within Roman Catholicism

Remarkable as has been the penetration of the charismatic movement into the churches of traditional Protestantism, its permeation of Catholicism is even more spectacular. Having begun with four people on the campus of Duquesne University, Pittsburgh, Pennsylvania, in the spring of 1967, it spread steadily throughout the Catholic world. In less than nine years it came to involve as many as 200,000, as a conservative estimate, or perhaps, even as many as 350,000. The dramatic growth of the movement is mirrored somewhat in the attendance at the International Conference on the Charismatic Renewal in the Catholic Church held at Notre Dame, Indiana, each year. Beginning with 90 people at the first national meeting in 1967, the numbers swelled rapidly to 30,000 in 1974. Besides these annual international conferences there have been many regional Catholic renewal conferences, each of them attracting thousands. The prayer group directory in the Catholic charismatic renewal in November, 1974, listed 2,400 groups from 54 different countries. Largely a lay movement, the charismatic movement in the Catholic Church involves hundreds of priests, about ten bishops in North America, and one cardinal, Cardinal Suenens of Malines, Belgium.[14]

Catholic charismatic communities have sprung up here and there, the most famous of which is the Word of God Community in Ann Arbor, Michigan. It is from here that *New Covenant,* the Catholic counterpart of the Protestant *Logos Journal,* is issued each month. The magazine maintains a distinct Catholic focus, though from time to time it carries articles on classical Pentecostalism and Protestant Neo-Pentecostalism.

Admittedly such rapid growth could not have taken place without the knowledge of the hierarchy of the Church and, at least to a certain degree, its understanding and approval. In a meeting in Washington, D.C., November 14, 1969, the Committee on Doctrine of the National Conference of Catholic Bishops, U.S.A., submitted its report. Because of the degree of acceptance of the movement reflected in the statement and because of the wide influence the report has exercised, quotations from it should be helpful.

27

> The Pentecostal movement in the Catholic Church is not the acceptance of the ideology or practices of any denomination, but likes to consider itself a renewal in the spirit of the first Pentecost. . . .
>
> It must be admitted that theologically the movement has legitimate reasons for existence. It has a strong biblical basis. . . .
>
> It is the conclusion of the Committee on Doctrine that the movement should at this point not be inhibited but allowed to develop. Certain cautions, however, must be expressed. . . . We must be on guard that they avoid the mistakes of classic Pentecostalism. . . . In practice we recommend that bishops involve prudent priests to be associated with this movement. Such involvement and guidance would be welcomed by the Catholic Pentecostals.[15]

Most Catholic charismatics would agree, however, that the climax of all of this came when the 1975 Congress on the Charismatic Renewal in the Catholic Church convened in Rome for the Pentecost weekend. Though the 10,000 who assembled there were only a third of the number who had met at Notre Dame the previous year, to those involved in the charismatic movement in the Catholic Church the significance of this meeting far outweighed that of any previously held. It was held in Rome, and it was addressed by the pope himself!

Pope Paul VI reportedly had been "under pressure from high Vatican officials to condemn the renewal and quash it." However, when he addressed the congress on Pentecost Sunday, he did anything but that. Admitting that the Church and the world need to have the miracle of Pentecost continued in history, he set forth three biblical principles to guide discernment in authenticating the work of the Holy Spirit. First, he called for faithfulness to the authentic doctrine of the faith, calling for a more thorough biblical, spiritual, and theological formation than the movement currently possesses. "Only such a formation, the authenticity of which must be guaranteed by the Hierarchy," he said, "will preserve you from deviations, always possible, and will give you the certainty and the joy of having served the cause of the Gospel. . . ." Second, he stated that spiritual gifts are to be received gratefully, but that we are to "earnestly desire the higher gifts" (1 Corinthians 12:31), as Paul admonished. Finally, he declared, "However desirable spiritual gifts may be—and they are—only the love of charity, *agape,* makes the perfect Christian, it alone makes man pleasing to God. . . ."[16]

All of this sounds so evangelical! It has such distinct Pentecostal overtones! How does it happen that such a thing is taking place in the Roman Catholic Church? Those who are directly involved say that it is a work of the Holy Spirit. Without passing judgment on that matter, we may point to some human influences that have played their role.

Pope John XXIII helped pave the way. Elected to the pontifical office at the age of seventy-seven, he was expected by many to be a transitional, caretaker pope. Within three months after his elevation, however, he unfolded plans for the twenty-first Ecumenical Council or Vatican II. In one of his earliest public announcements concerning the council he set forth his vision that "all the bishops of the Church . . . should be gathered together as at a new Pentecost." Moreover, he composed a prayer which he enjoined Catholics all over the world to pray from the beginning of the council until its end. The prayer contained these lines: "We pray you to pour forth the fullness of your gifts upon the Ecumenical Council. . . . Renew your wonders in this, our day, as by a new Pentecost. . . ."[17]

Vatican II played its part. The council's decree on ecumenism amounted to the Church's relaxation of its previous isolation policy and laid the foundation for Protestant-Catholic fellowship particularly important in the early days of the charismatic movement in the Catholic Church. The decree emphasized the apostolate of the laity and helped make Bible reading and serious Bible study the "in thing" to do. The conciliar documents, containing 252 references to the Holy Spirit, helped inspire changes in the liturgy accenting the sanctifying role of the Holy Spirit. The documents of Vatican II also contain exceedingly important statements concerning the charismatic gifts. They state that the charismatic gifts, whatever their nature, are useful to the church and are to be received with thanksgiving and consolation. The extraordinary gifts are "not to be rashly sought after," however, and their genuineness and proper use are to be judged by those who preside over the Church.[18]

The contribution of Cardinal Suenens deserves particular emphasis. He took an active part in the deliberations of Vatican II and helped to guide it to take a positive stance toward the charismatic gifts and to express a position of openness toward the work of the Holy Spirit in our day. When Cardinal Ruffini sought to have the council relegate the charisms to the past, Cardinal Suenens pointed out that the charismatic dimension is *necessary* to the Church. "What would become of our Church without the charisms of the doctors, the theologians, the prophets?" he asked.[19]

The cardinal, who is himself charismatic, writes frequently for the *New Covenant,* and his book *A New Pentecost?,* while thoroughly Catholic in theology, is also unapologetically charismatic. His influence in the charismatic renewal in the Catholic Church is particularly strong because of his position in the hierarchy, his open and active participation in the movement, the warmth of his spirit, the theological depth that he manifests, and his dexterity as a speaker and writer.

All of the above—statements about Pope John XXIII, Vatican II, and Cardinal Suenens, with the exception of references to the cardinal's contemporary participation in the movement—constitute the background to the aforementioned beginning of the charismatic movement on the campus of Duquesne University in the spring of 1967. There in the fall of the preceding year four Catholic laymen, all members of the faculty of the university and all strongly committed to the Catholic Church and deeply concerned about personal and church renewal, began to meet together. They had all been active in a series of retreats in the Catholic Church known as the cursillo (Christ) movement which involved long hours of prayer and Bible study.

29

There is some indication that the cursillo movement laid the groundwork for the charismatic movement.[20] These four laymen read and discussed David Wilkerson's *The Cross and the Switchblade* and John Sherrill's *They Speak with Other Tongues* and wanted the kind of spiritual experience depicted in these books. This led to their seeking out a Protestant charismatic prayer group which introduced them to the charismatic dimension of renewal. Excited about what had happened to them, they began to share with others.

In mid-February a small group of students spent a weekend with these four faculty members in prayer, meditation, and study of the first four chapters of Acts. Most of them had read *The Cross and the Switchblade.* That weekend was the beginning of the rapid spread of the charismatic movement within Roman Catholicism. The interest soon spread to the University of Notre Dame and the Catholic student parish of Michigan State University. From these centers, the movement spread across the country among Roman Catholics who felt a need for a deeper experience of the Holy Spirit.

Depth

An unmistakable air of exuberance pervades the charismatic movement. Those inside the movement attribute it to the conviction that rivers of living water (John 4:13-14; 7:37-38) are flowing mightily through God's people; that such a Pentecostal outpouring of God's Spirit is in progress as has not occurred since the first century; and that new, though noncanonical, chapters in the Acts of the Apostles are being written in our day.

Characteristics of the Movement

Perhaps no one has written with more obvious excitement about this than J. Rodman Williams, formerly Professor of Systematic Theology at Austin Presbyterian Theological Seminary in Texas, now president of Melodyland School of Theology, Anaheim, California. In his book *The Era of the Spirit* and in his article "A Profile of the Charismatic Movement," which appeared in *Christianity Today,* February 28, 1975, he describes the type of spiritual experience involved. The discussion that follows is based entirely on these two works by Williams and should be interpreted as reflecting his views rather than those of the author.

There is the recovery of a vital and dynamic sense of the reality of the Christian faith. The experience of the reality of God has broken in with new freshness. Jesus Christ has become in truth the living Lord. For many the Bible has become not merely a record of what

30

happened long ago, but a testimony to God's contemporary activity.

It is as if a door had been opened, and walking through the door they found spread out before them the extraordinary biblical world, with dimensions of angelic heights and demonic depths, of Holy Spirit and unclean spirits, of miracles and wonders—a world in which now they sense their own participation.[21]

Prayer has become a joyful activity instead of an empty ritual. The Eucharist has taken on new meaning as the Doctrine of the Real Presence has become experiential fact, and for some even the administrative routine has been revolutionized.

According to Williams, a striking renewal of the community of believers as a fellowship *(koinonia)* of the Holy Spirit is occurring. The mood of praise to God, expressed in song, prayer, and testimony, is paramount in the charismatic fellowship. Joy in the Lord accompanies this praise. Ties of love are formed which transcend all human relationships, and the terms "brother" and "sister" become the natural expressions of a profoundly felt love.[22] Often in this context the sharing of material possessions takes place in varying expressions of a communal life.

The manifestation of a wide range of spiritual gifts, or *charismata,* is of striking significance. Williams avers, "There is the fresh occurrence of all the Corinthian spiritual manifestations: the word of wisdom, the word of knowledge, faith, gifts of healing, working of miracles, prophecy, discernment of spirits, tongues, and the interpretation of tongues."[23]

31

All of these are regarded as supernatural spiritual manifestations, occurring not as an expression of natural prowess but through the activity of the Holy Spirit. Not viewed as private possessions, these gifts operate within the context of the *koinonia* for the edification of the gathered group. They are earnestly sought after and prayed for, not for the sake of display or novelty, but because it is believed that the Lord wants to express himself in these ways.

"The charismatic movement lays strong emphasis on the experience described as 'baptism in the Holy Spirit' and its frequent concomitant of 'speaking in tongues.'"[24] Williams views this "baptism" as "the spiritual breakthrough out of which people move into the varied charismatic expressions and into their fresh and lively faith." The word "baptism" signifies immersion in spiritual reality. Regardless of a person's previous situation, it indicates an experience of far greater intensity than that person has known before. There is the sense of entrance into a fresh dimension of fullness of the Spirit.

In the charismatic movement "baptism in the Spirit" is wholly related to faith in Jesus Christ, representing a deepening of that faith and the experience of new life in his name. It comes in answer to a deep hungering and thirsting after God and a total yielding to Christ in such a way that he now becomes the Lord of all of life. "Prayer, often persistent and expectant, is frequently the spiritual context, and the laying on of hands for the 'fullness' of the Spirit is often the occasion when the 'baptism' occurs."

Usually the concomitant of this baptism is tongues, by which, according to Williams, the ordinary limitations of human speech are transcended and the Holy Spirit provides a new language of jubilation and praise. This new language of praise, which frequently is given at the initial moment of baptism in the Spirit, usually continues as a prayer language in the life of faith.

Frequently it happens, says Williams, that as people move into this new dimension of the Spirit's power, they experience instantaneous healings of long-suffered ailments. In addition to these initial healings, occur many other healings of diseases, some of them deemed medically incurable. Such visible answers to prayer become new occasions for praise.[25]

There is within the charismatic movement the resurgence of a deep unity of spirit which transcends denominational barriers, even those between Protestant and Roman Catholic. People from different denominational backgrounds discover that they are truly one in the Spirit, one in the Lord. This is spiritual, not organizational or ecclesiastical, ecumenism.

Williams sees the charismatic movement as representing also a fresh thrust for witness to the gospel. A witness which formerly was weak and ineffectual now has become dynamic and joyful. He also notes that the charismatic movement has led to a renewed emphasis upon eschatology. Interest in the future has been combined with a strong sense of God's activity through the Holy Spirit in the present experience of believers.

This summary of some words by Williams, a man deeply involved in the movement, should serve to communicate some of the excitement which many in the movement feel concerning what they say they see God doing in their midst.

The Charismatic Prayer Meeting

Those involved in the charismatic movement attend all kinds of charismatic conferences, conventions, and retreats. Some of these are regional; others are national or even international. Some of them are denominational, but most of them are distinctly interdenominational. Often couples, or even families, schedule their vacations in such a way as to make it possible for them to attend such meetings.

Significant as these meetings are, however, they are not central. Paramount importance must be ascribed to the charismatic prayer meetings occurring in thousands of places throughout the world. These vary greatly. Most of them are regular weekly or monthly meetings. Some, however, are called together from time to time in response to a felt need or a specific opportunity, as, for example, the visit of a well-known leader in the movement. The size of these gatherings ranges from as few as four or five to as many as five or six hundred. The smaller meetings are usually held in a home, while the larger ones require some kind of public place like a community center or the basement of a church. The meetings usually last from one and a half to three hours, with two hours being about average.

The small meetings in the homes usually attract people of the same social background, though often different denominations are represented. In these groups deep interpersonal relations develop, but, frequently, though not always, there is a tendency for the groups to become exclusive and the meetings somewhat routine. The large meetings, on the other hand, often provide variety and excitement. Though the nucleus of the meetings may not vary much from time to time, the influx of visitors, both charismatic and noncharismatic, helps to make each prayer meeting unique. Often within the large groups people of widely different backgrounds are represented: the young and the old, liberals and conservatives, men and women, clergymen and laymen, laborers and business executives, students and teachers. Frequently, Protestants, Catholics, and main-line Pentecostals are present together, though one of the first two groups usually predominates. When the groups are too large, individual participation is hampered, and it becomes difficult for those attending to know one another intimately as persons.

For a meeting of this type to be truly "charismatic," there must be an appreciation of the "gifts" and some degree of openness to them. Sometimes there are few outward manifestations, such as Paul speaks of in 1 Corinthians 12, simply an atmosphere of prayer and praise, often with a quiet undertone of tongues. In other meetings several of the "gifts" may be recognized, the most common being prophecy, tongues, the interpretation of tongues, and healing. Much depends upon the people involved, their background, and spiritual experience. Even when this does not vary much from one meeting to another, there may be considerable variety depending upon the mood of the people involved and their sense of the Spirit's leading.

33

Much emphasis is placed upon 1 Corinthians 14:26: "What then, brethren? When you come together, each one has a hymn, a lesson, a revelation, a tongue, or an interpretation. Let all things be done for edification." This passage is accepted not only as indicating what worship was like in the church at Corinth, but also as providing something of a model for worship in our day. Several times I have heard this passage read at the beginning of a prayer meeting. The significance of this for the charismatic prayer meeting consists in the fact that it enunciates five principles so important for such meetings.

The first is spontaneity. The impression which the passage gives is of a spontaneous happening rather than a planned program. This is characteristic of charismatic prayer meetings. There is no order of program. Usually there is a leader who announces the beginning of the service and the end and from time to time makes suggestions about what the group should do. Often, however, one is hardly conscious of any human leader. Those involved say that the Holy Spirit guides the group.

This suggests the second principle, participation. In the verse quoted above Paul says, "each one has a hymn, a lesson, a revelation, a tongue, or an interpretation." In the charismatic prayer meeting anyone is free at any time to make any contribution which that person feels is inspired by the Holy Spirit. Often there is someone there with a guitar or someone sitting on the piano stool ready to play the piano. Even so, one does not have to wait for another person to start the music but is free to begin a hymn or chorus at an appropriate time, and those with musical instruments, if they know the number, join in the accompaniment, and the group joins in the singing. Likewise anyone can read or quote a passage of Scripture, give a word of testimony, lead in prayer or ask for prayer, and express any of the "gifts" as one feels led. This does not mean, of course, that in every prayer meeting everyone will make some vocal contribution, but it does mean that the opportunity for free participation is there.

Variety of expression is suggested also in the words of Paul that are under consideration, and this is a third principle of a charismatic prayer meeting. In most prayer meetings there are music, prayer, Scripture, testimony, and a manifestation of some of the "gifts." Sometimes there are questions, and a brief discussion follows. Occasionally, someone brings a short talk. In the "best" prayer meetings there is usually a free flow from one type of contribution to another. For example, there are many choruses sung and many prayers uttered. These tend to be interspersed at appropriate times throughout the meeting.

An openness for the manifestation of the "gifts" is a fourth principle. Paul mentions specifically tongues and interpretation. Usually when someone speaks in tongues, there is an interpretation offered. This is understood to be in accord with Paul's injunctions in I Corinthians 14:27-28. Often there are utterances that are given and received as prophecy. This is regarded as God's word spoken directly in human language. J. Rodman Williams says that the distinctive thing about prophecy is that it occurs without premeditation. "The prophet actually does not know what he will say in advance of saying it, nor can he be sure just when the moment will come—or even *if* it will come—but he speaks when and as God wills."[26] "Singing in the Spirit" occurs from time to time in these meetings, and this is regarded by most charismatics as especially exhilarating and edifying. Williams describes it as follows:

> Occasionally words will be sung out (perhaps a bit of Scripture, maybe an ejaculation of praise) by some person in the common language but in a free manner—based on no fixed music from the past—and others soon join in the newly formed melody. Indeed, there may be long periods of joyful, lilting music, quite unplanned, moving back and forth through psalms, hymns, choruses, and the like—as the Spirit guides the meeting. But the climax is the moment when not only is the melody given by the Spirit but *also* the language, as words and music sung by the assembled worshipers blend into an unimaginable, humanly impossible, chorus of praise.[27]

Finally, Paul enjoins, "Let all things be done for edification." The edification of the members of Christ's body for spiritual warfare and witness in the world is the recognized purpose of charismatic prayer meetings. To be sure, there are times when these prayer meetings give the impression of being an assortment of this and that, when they seem to be going off in all directions without any unifying theme. More often, however, those attending go away with the feeling that from the beginning to the end the Holy Spirit was in control blending together the diverse elements into a beautiful pattern and using the singing, the prayers, the testimonies, and the special "manifestations" to minister to the various spiritual needs of those assembled.

What follows now is a composite description of a charismatic prayer meeting. It is based largely upon observation of meetings that I have attended, but it includes also elements that I have gained from conversations with people who have had much experience in this area. It is idealized only in the sense that it is hardly likely that all of these things would occur in one meeting and in that some of the distracting things that do occur from time to time are not mentioned. About forty people of various denominational backgrounds are present. Most of them are Protestant, though there are a few Catholics and one or two main-line Pentecostals. Young and old, men and women, the clergy and the laity are represented. Two of the young people have guitars. They are surrounded by several others of their age group, all of them in jeans. The group is seated in two concentric circles. About half of those present have been meeting together on a regular basis, while some have come only a few times. There are some visitors from other prayer groups and a few who have never attended a charismatic prayer group before.

The leader, a layman in his mid-thirties, starts singing, and all join together with the guitarists accompanying: "Let's just praise the Lord, Let's just praise the Lord, Let's just lift our hearts toward heaven and praise the Lord." Several times the chorus echoes through the room. Then there is silence. The leader begins to pray, thanking God for his presence and asking him to lead and bless the meeting in a special way. Two others offer similar prayers, both of them brief. All over the room quiet whispers, "Thank you, Jesus!" or "Praise God!" can be heard. Someone in the outer circle begins singing, and before the third word has been reached, most of the group joins in: "We worship and adore thee, Falling down before thee, Songs of praises singing, Alleluias ringing." Many have their eyes closed and their hands raised toward heaven. Without a break the group starts singing another chorus, "Alleluia," and more hands are raised. Most of the faces are glowing, and tears glisten in the eyes of some.

Once again there is silence, punctuated only by a very quiet undertone of praying in tongues and expressions like "Thank you, Jesus!" and "Lord, how wonderful you are!" Several men and women follow in rapid succession with brief audible prayers of awe and adoration. Silence reigns again only to be broken by an utterance understood to be a word of prophecy: "Fear not, for I am in your midst. My purposes for you are good and not evil. Open your hearts to me and to one another and I will manifest myself unto you." "Praise God!" "Thank you, Jesus!" can be heard here and there. Someone begins to read, "A new commandment I give unto you, That ye love one another; as I have loved you, that ye also love one another. By this shall all men know that ye are my disciples, if ye have love one to another" (John 13:34-35, KJV). From the other side of the room come the words, "Though I speak with the tongues of men and of angels, and have not charity, I am become as sounding brass, or a tinkling cymbal" (1 Corinthians 13:1, KJV). Several others quote passages on love, and then the leader suggests that they take time right there to express their love for one another. People move here and there about the room embracing one another and saying, "I love you, brother" or "I love you, sister." There is an atmosphere of openness and mutual acceptance, but some, particularly the newcomers, seem a bit embarrassed and ill at ease. Suddenly this all comes to a halt as all join hands and start marching around in a circle singing, "We are one in the Spirit; we are one in the Lord."

Once again there is a slight change of mood as all start clapping and swaying together as they sing, "O clap your hands, all ye people; shout unto God with the voice of triumph" (Psalm 47:1, KJV)! A festive mood prevails and several lilting choruses are sung. Among them is "Rejoice in the Lord alway: and again I say, Rejoice" (Philippians 4:4, KJV), sung several times in round-robin fashion.

Once again the group is seated, and after a brief interval of silence a newcomer speaks. "May I ask a question?" he inquires. Given the go-ahead signal, he asks, "Why do you raise your hands when you sing or pray?" "That's a good question," the leader responds. "It's scriptural, you know." Then the leader reads Psalm 63:3-4. Someone else reads 1 Timothy 2:8. Then he says, "But you don't *have* to raise your hands. You can sit, kneel, fold your hands, or worship in any way that is comfortable to you. Still, I think the time will come when you will *want* to lift your hands." Another adds, "For a long time for me that was the hardest thing in the world to do. You know there is a pride barrier about the level of the head. For me the breakthrough came when I finally got the courage to lift my hands. Then the Lord baptized me with his Holy Spirit and there poured forth from my lips a new language of heavenly praise." Hardly has this testimony ended when the group joins one of the teenagers as he begins to sing: "Thy lovingkindness is better than life, my lips will praise thee. Thus will I bless thee: I will lift up my hands in thy name" (see Psalm 63:3-4).

There follows in rapid succession a series of brief testimonies of victory and praise. A teenage boy praises the Lord for having delivered him from drugs. A housewife expresses gratitude that God has given her boldness in witness and cites some examples that have occurred during the past week. A Catholic nun in her habit praises the Lord for a new freedom in prayer that has come to her since she has experienced baptism in the Spirit. She says that formerly she had used the rosary and the prayer book but had not been able to pray spontaneously. Now, however, though she continues the former ways of prayer, she finds great joy in praying spontaneously in her own language, as well as in tongues. A middle-aged man thanks the group for having prayed for him the week before. "Since then that terrible

37

congestion in my chest that had bothered me for so long has been gone," he says. A lady asks the group to pray for her brother who is to have a very serious operation the next day. A chair is placed in the center of the room and someone suggests that this lady sit in it while those who feel so led gather around her and lay hands upon her and pray by proxy for her brother. She takes her place in the chair, and ten or twelve gather around her and lay their hands upon her. Several pray for the healing of her brother, and others offer prayers of thanksgiving because God has already heard and answered their prayers.

"Would anyone else like prayer?" the leader asks. A middle-aged man takes his seat in the chair and asks the group to pray for him that he might receive the baptism in the Holy Spirit. Again a group gathers around and several pray. Among the prayers is an audible prayer in tongues. Nothing perceptible happens, and the man thanks the group and returns to his seat. A young man in his thirties comes forward then and makes the same request. Again a group gathers about him and prays. Upon the suggestion of someone he begins to pray. He prays in his own language at first. Then he is told, "Don't pray in English! Speak whatever comes to mind!" After a bit of hesitation he begins to speak in a new tongue. His face lights up like a Christmas tree, and he continues to pray quietly in this way for several minutes.

After he returns to his seat, a bass voice speaks out in tongues. Then someone begins to interpret. "There are many hungry hearts in this neighborhood," he says. There is a pause and a lady continues, "Behold, I shall pour out my Spirit upon you in a new way." Another person concludes the interpretation, "Yea, a mighty revival shall sweep throughout the world, for my Spirit is already at work." Again whispers of praise go up from all over the room.

The leader now requests the group to stand and sing Psalm 150. Those who have brought the King James Version of the Bible share it and all sing with great joy and vigor. Then all join hands together. A few requests for prayer are voiced. Then several pray briefly in rapid succession. Now at the suggestion of the leader all begin to sing together the Lord's Prayer. When they come to the words, "For thine is the kingdom, and the power, and the glory, forever," the voices rise in a mighty crescendo and the joined hands are raised in the air. The charismatic prayer meeting has come to a close![28]

CHAPTER 2

Historical
Background

Having taken a look at the charismatic movement in its contemporary setting, we now step backward in time to trace some of its antecedents in the history of the church. It is evident that the charismatic movement sprang forth from Pentecostalism. It is also clear that Pentecostalism had its roots in early Methodism, in revivalism, and in the Holiness movement. Apart from these sources, and calling for special consideration, are some of the unusual spiritual manifestations that have occurred through the ages.

Unusual Spiritual Manifestations Through the Ages

Here we have reference to the manifestations of some or all of the gifts of the Spirit as listed in 1 Corinthians 12:7-11, strong spiritual enthusiasm, ecstasy, or what some would term Christian mysticism.

A movement of unusual spiritual enthusiasm broke out toward the end of the second century under the leadership of Montanus, who claimed the gift of prophetic inspiration, and two self-styled prophetesses, who joined themselves to him. Montanism, as the movement came to be known, claimed to be the medium for the final stage of God's revelation. In this context the Old Testament revelation represented only the infancy, and the New Testament revelation the youth of God's self-disclosure. Claiming that Christ was coming soon to set up his millennial (thousand-year) kingdom on earth, the Montanists insisted on a rigorous discipline and an ascetical life-style.

Before the Montanism movement spent its force, it claimed the allegiance of Tertullian, one of the greatest theologians of the early centuries of the church. Tertullian appealed to prophecies, visions, ecstasies, the interpretation of tongues, and the like to validate the claims of the Montanists.

Montanism was a protest against the trends toward formalism and the institutionalizing of religion, but the reaction which it provoked only succeeded in speeding these trends. It is not surprising that the church rejected Montanism. Its emotional excesses, millennial enthusiasm, and ascetical practices did not commend themselves to the church leaders of the day. More than any of these, however, it was the Montanist claim to access to a continuing revelation that was distasteful to the church. All during the second century the church had been fighting hard against heresy. In this battle it had drawn a clear line of demarcation between the apostolic and post-apostolic ages. Moreover, it had recognized bishops as the successors and representatives of the apostles. The Montanists' claims seemed to undermine the authority of the bishops. There can be little doubt that the church's strong repudiation of Montanism had the effect of putting a damper for centuries upon any similar tendencies within the church.

Some theologians of the second and third centuries manifest some hazy acquaintance with glossolalia as a contemporary phenomenon, but by the third and fourth centuries, it is referred to only in such a way as to suggest that it had not occurred for some time. Probably one of the reasons for its demise was the difficulty of determining whether inspiration of this sort was from demons or from the Holy Spirit of God.[1]

There was not much evidence of glossolalia during the Middle Ages (A.D. 500–1500) in either East or West. The fall of the western part of the Roman Empire during the fifth century helped to accentuate the development of two distinctly different traditions of Christianity. There can be little doubt, however, that experiences, such as visions, glossolalia, and the like, were more compatible with the Eastern than with the Western tradition. Forced in a large measure to take over the responsibilities of the state, the church in the West became practical-minded, this-worldly, and authoritarian. The church in the East, on the other hand, not having such secular responsibilities, developed its piety along more mystical, other-worldly lines. In the West the ability to speak in tongues or to interpret them came to be understood more as a token of demon possession than of Spirit possession. Though there is little documented evidence of glossolalia even in the East, it is quite likely that it occurred from time to time within Greek monasticism without attracting much attention.[2]

Thomas Aquinas (d. 1247), who through the centuries has been the most influential theologian of the Roman Catholic Church, seems to have had no firsthand knowledge of glossolalia. According to him the original purpose of the gift had been to enable the apostles to teach all nations, and the same gift of tongues as appeared at Pentecost can be gained even today through diligent language study.[3]

Though glossolalia seems not to have flourished during the Middle Ages, some other forms of piety did. The flowering of monasticism took place during this period, and this in turn fostered the devotional spirit. The devotional writings of such Christian mystics as Bernard of Clairvaux and Francis of Assisi are the permanent treasures of the church.[4]

With the Protestant Reformation in the sixteenth century came a new burst of spiritual life. Even so, except for an occasional outburst in the radical wing of the Reformation, glossolalia and similar spiritual manifestations seem to have been virtually unknown.

Luther understood the new tongues spoken in apostolic times as having been given as a sign and witness to the Jews. He insisted, however, that Christianity in his day no longer required confirmation by such signs. Moreover, he used the passage on tongues in First Corinthians to develop his case for preaching in the German vernacular.

According to Calvin, originally glossolalia facilitated preaching in foreign languages and served also as an adornment and honor to the gospel itself. But because it was corrupted by human ambition, as at Corinth, God removed it from the church rather than permitting it to be vitiated with further abuse.[5]

Among the Anabaptists, the so-called radical wing of the Reformation, there were those who were not content with the Reformation emphasis upon Scripture alone (sola scriptura) but maintained that "the inward voice of the Holy Spirit takes precedence over the external word of Scripture."[6] Thomas Müntzer cherished such experiences and gifts as visions, dreams, ecstatic utterance, and inspired exegesis. Among some Anabaptist Swiss Brethren at St. Gall, along with glossolalia there was lewdness and unchastity, and even the "extraordinary declaration of a deranged woman that she was predestined to give birth to the Antichrist. . . ."[7] About 1532 in Fulda, glossolalia, healing, contortions, and manifestations of mass hypnosis took place. To be sure, excesses such as these were exceptional, even among the Anabaptists. But such emotional excesses, the claim to divine revelation that goes beyond the written word, and the support of the peasant uprising by Müntzer and other Anabaptists led Luther and other Reformation leaders to oppose the Anabaptists with as much vigor as they did the Roman Catholics.

Glossolalia, ecstatic trances, and the claim to prophetic inspiration occurred among some simple Cévenol Protestant peasants in southern France in a time of extreme persecution from the Catholics in the latter part of the seventeenth century. The phenomenon of tongues also reached into Roman Catholic circles. There was an outbreak of it among the Jansenists in France in 1731, but it was soon halted through the aid of French state authorities.

In 1646 George Fox, of England, had a transforming spiritual experience that led him to affirm "that every man receives from the Lord a measure of light, and that if this 'Inner Light' is followed, it leads surely to the Light of Life and to spiritual truth."[8] For him, not the Scriptures but the Holy Spirit through which holy men gave forth the Scriptures was the touchstone and judge for testing all doctrines, religions, and opinions.

Fox founded a group called the Society of Friends or Quakers. The uncompromising stands taken by the Quakers against outward sacraments, oaths, slavery, servility in speech, and the like evoked severe opposition from seventeenth-century England. Before 1661, Fox and more than three thousand of his followers had suffered imprisonment. It is a well-known fact that in Quaker meetings all sorts of emotional outbursts, such as trembling, weeping, prophecy, and faintings, occurred. Indeed, it was because of the jerking spasms that often took place among them that they got the name Quakers. It is quite possible that glossolalia also took place in their meetings.[9]

The contribution of Pietism also is not to be forgotten in the history of significant movements. By the first of the seventeenth century Lutheran orthodoxy dominated a large part of Germany. Whereas Luther had centered religion in the heart, Lutheran orthodoxy had shifted its center to the head.

Springing up as a protest against the formalism of its day, Pietism was a reaction of the spirit against the letter. It gave the primacy to feeling in Christian experience, emphasized the role of the laity in the life of the church, and encouraged a strict ascetic attitude toward the world. The pietist movement set in motion forces which continued to exercise influence long after the movement as such had spent its force.[10]

Indirectly, Pietism gave birth to the Moravian missionary

movement and to the Methodist revival under John Wesley. The dominant personality in the early days of Moravianism was Count Zinzendorf. Reared in a background of Pietism and educated at Halle, he was ardently devoted to Jesus.

On August 13, 1727, during a Communion service led by Pastor Zinzendorf, the Holy Spirit was poured out with mighty power upon the little Moravian congregation in Herrnhut. Even before this mighty outpouring, the Spirit had kindled a spirit of prayer and supplication in the hearts of pastor and people. The congregation experienced an insatiable desire for the Word, and a round-the-clock continuous prayer meeting was started that month that literally lasted a hundred years, without interruption.[11] The piety of overflowing hearts expressed itself in innumerable hymns of lasting value. Moreover, the missionary zeal aroused by this spiritual awakening resulted in many missionaries going out from this church to various parts of the world in the service of Christ long before the beginning of the so-called Protestant missionary movement under William Carey.

That John Wesley became a new man through the experience which came to him Wednesday evening, May 24, 1738, in the Aldersgate Street Church is a well-known fact. What are not so well known are some of the spiritual antecedents of this experience: the quiet assurance of some pious Moravians during a storm as Wesley was on his way to America for missionary service, the spiritual counsel given him in Georgia by a Moravian bishop, and some deeply impressive contacts with Moravian brethren over a period of several months immediately preceding the experience. Wesley's tremendous intellectual powers and his very methodical way of doing things were never allowed to overshadow the conviction that came to him through his Aldersgate experience that in the Christian life everything that is of ultimate significance rests not upon human might or power, but upon the working of God's Spirit (Zechariah 4:6).

In some early Methodist revivals there were unusual emotional manifestations, which became the object of severe criticism on the part of many. Recognizing his own fear of regarding such demonstrations too highly, Wesley said, "Perhaps the danger *is,* to regard them too little."[12]

Wesley made no claim to the gift of tongues for himself, but he had no doubt that some of his contemporaries had it, nor that this gift had found authentic expression in other post-apostolic centuries. Still he recognized that the charismatic gifts had not been

43

commonplace through the ages. Seeking to explain the early withdrawal of the charismatic gifts, he suggested that dry, formal, orthodox men had begun to ridicule those gifts that they themselves did not possess and to decry them as either madness or imposture.[13]

During the latter part of the eighteenth century in America among a group called the Shakers the gift of tongues was widespread, while the gift of healing was manifested on a more limited basis. This group emphasized strongly Christ's Second Coming and the millennium, teaching that when Christ did come again in the near future, it would be as Mother Ann Lee Stanley, the founder of their movement.

Both Joseph Smith, the founder of The Church of Jesus Christ of the Latter Day Saints (Mormons), and Brigham Young, who led the group in its great trek to the Great Salt Lake, claimed the gift of tongues. Likewise, tongues and interpretation of tongues are mentioned several times with approval in the Book of Mormon, which is regarded as a revelation supplementary to the Bible. Mormon leaders in recent years have demonstrated a tendency toward minimizing glossolalia, while not forbidding it.

About the same time Mormonism was getting started in America, a short-lived tongues movement broke out in England (April, 1831), associated with the ministry of Edward Irving, the sophisticated Presbyterian pastor of the Newman Street Church, London. Irving himself seems not to have received the gift, though he earnestly sought it and encouraged it in others. His part in the movement led to his being deposed in May, 1832, and to his later being defrocked by the Church of Scotland. Later he became one of the founders of the Catholic Apostolic Church, "which mixed Catholic with millenarian and pentecostal tendencies."[14]

It would be difficult to demonstrate that many of the unusual spiritual manifestations which we have considered had much direct influence upon Pentecostalism. For the most part the early leaders of Pentecostalism were simple, unlearned men with no knowledge or interest in the intricacies of church history. Still a direct line of influence can be traced from the German Pietists through the Moravian Brethren to Wesley, and from Wesley through the Holiness movement to Pentecostalism. Charismatic manifestations in these movements can be compared with those in Pentecostalism.

The Immediate Background of Pentecostalism

Both the Holiness and Pentecostal movements look to John Wesley as their spiritual and intellectual father.[15] Wesley's doctrine of a second blessing bringing about instantaneous sanctification, which he defined as perfect love, was a central emphasis of Methodism in its early days. This doctrine, with adaptations, became the fountainhead not only of the Holiness movement with its stress on purity of life but of later Pentecostal theology as well.

Wesley's Doctrine of Sanctification and Methodism

In Wesley's view, entire sanctification is a gift of God which flows from Christ and his atoning work. It is based upon faith, but God gives such faith only to those who seek it. It is freedom from sin, but not sinless perfection, for errors in judgment and practice are not eradicated. In essence it is perfect love toward God and one's neighbor.

Neither infidelity from within nor great opposition from without was able to turn early Methodism away from this emphasis. The dominant influence of Methodism upon Pentecostalism was in "the centering of spiritual desire on experience and especially on *an* experience subsequent to conversion."[16]

Charles Finney and Revivalism

In terms of methodology American revivalism made an imprint upon subsequent Pentecostalism which is comparable to that of Methodism in theology. Revivalism emphasized the role of the emotions in changing the life of the individual.

45

A giant among revivalists was Charles Finney (d. 1876). Experience in teaching school and later in working in a law office while studying for the bar exam helped prepare him for his career as an evangelist and as an educator. In 1821, at the age of twenty-nine, he had an experience that made an indelible impression upon his later preaching. One day in the woods of upstate New York, while on his knees, he experienced God's gracious forgiveness. That same night, alone in his law office, he received "a mighty baptism of the Holy Spirit," which he later described as the Holy Spirit descending upon him "in waves and waves of liquid love."[17] He soon turned to preaching, using his training in law to bring the claims of Christ home to sinners with compelling logic and his sense of the Holy Spirit's presence to give his message a profound emotional impact.

He believed that revivals conform to certain divine laws and that they can be produced by discovering those laws and acting in accord with them. As part of his methodology, he deliberately sought to produce a state of emotional excitement which would sweep away opposing obstacles.

Finney's theology, too, was extremely influential in shaping Pentecostal doctrine. Emphasizing that Christ died for all, Finney stressed the freedom of every individual, under the leadership of the Holy Spirit, to respond to the gospel and be saved. He carried forward the theological legacy of Wesley by accenting Christian perfection and an experience subsequent to conversion which he called "the baptism of the Holy Ghost."

With cogent accuracy Frederick Dale Bruner declares, "In Finney were combined both the theology (essentially Methodism) and the methodology (essentially revivalism) which were later to find a permanent home in the movement called Pentecostal."[18] Armed with these two weapons, along with certain distinctive emphases acquired at the time of its birth, Pentecostalism found a ready response from many.

The Holiness Movement

Gradually within Methodism a cleavage began to develop between those who carried on Wesley's view of instantaneous sanctification received through an experience subsequent to conversion and those who objected to it, particularly the teaching on Christian perfection. The Holiness movement of the nineteenth century got its start from the former group. Becoming more and more dissatisfied with the Methodist Church because of what they regarded as its tendencies toward liberalism, its departure from the Holiness teachings of its founder in doctrine, and its compromise with worldliness in practice, many groups began to leave it before the turn of the century. Instead of forming one big, unified denomination, however, between 1895 and 1905 they fragmented into over a score of denominations.[19]

Particularly influential among the early Holiness teachers were W. E. Boardman, Robert Pearsall Smith, and his wife, Hannah. Boardman's book, *The Higher Christian Life* (1859), was widely read in England as well as America. Hannah Whitall Smith became famous through her book *The Christian's Secret of a Happy Life,* a devotional classic still in print in our day. Robert Pearsall Smith introduced the higher Christian life doctrine to England in person by teaching at a special conference at Keswick (1875). Since then the Keswick convention has become an annual affair.

The Keswick convention has carried on a Holiness emphasis, while avoiding perfectionism. Recognizing two distinct experiences in the Christian life, Keswick equates the first with the new birth and the second, the so-called "second blessing," with the fullness of the

Spirit. Generally speaking, it has carefully avoided using the term "baptism in the Spirit" as a designation for this second experience. Increasingly within the Holiness movement (apart from Keswick), the term "baptism of the Holy Spirit" or "baptism in the Holy Spirit" came to indicate the "second blessing." Toward the end of the nineteenth century in certain Holiness circles, however, a significant shift in emphasis began to appear. Largely on the basis of Luke 24:49 and Acts 1:5,8, baptism in the Spirit came to be interpreted not in terms of holiness of life, but as an empowering for service.[20] Decisive importance in this connection must be ascribed to R. A. Torrey. Torrey taught that the form which the power takes will vary from one individual to another, depending upon the diversity of gifts which the Spirit bestows.

Connecting spiritual power with spiritual gifts, certain Holiness leaders began to assert that the gifts should still be in operation in the church today. Particular stress was placed on divine healing. The ground had thus been prepared for the emergence of Pentecostalism.

Pentecostalism

It was the linking of baptism in the Spirit with speaking in tongues as the outward sign which sparked off the Pentecostal revival.[21] The first breakthrough in this connection seems to have occurred at the Bible school operated by Charles Parham in Topeka, Kansas. Before leaving on a trip Parham gave his forty students the assignment of studying the Bible in search for some common denominator in the experience of baptism in the Spirit. When he returned, they excitedly told him that they had found it, and that it was speaking in tongues. Parham accepted their explanations, and the next day, December 31, 1900, was set aside for praying for baptism in the Spirit with the expectation of speaking in tongues. When evening came and still nothing unusual had happened, Agnes Ozman recalled that according to some of the records in Acts baptism in the Spirit had followed the laying on of hands. Upon her request Charles Parham laid his hands upon her head, and she began to pray in other tongues. Soon other students of the Bible school as well as their teacher had the same experience.[22]

Later Charles Parham started another Bible school in Houston, Texas. It was here in 1905 that a one-eyed, Negro preacher named William J. Seymour came under Parham's influence and was thoroughly indoctrinated with Parham's views. Responding to an invitation from a Holiness church to preach in Los Angeles in the spring of 1906, Seymour was locked out of the church after the first

47

sermon. Using Acts 2:4 as his text, he had preached that "anyone who does not speak in tongues is not baptized with the Holy Spirit."[23] This infuriated some influential members of the congregation who were sure they had already experienced the baptism, but without tongues. At this time Seymour's preaching was purely theoretical, for he himself made no claim to having had this experience. Shut out of the church which had invited him to Los Angeles, Seymour and some of his followers continued to hold prayer meetings in the home of one of the members.

It was on April 9, 1906, in one of these meetings that "the fire fell." Seven seekers, Seymour among them, received the baptism in the Spirit and began to speak in tongues. Immediately a revival broke out. Because the house in which they were meeting was too small and the neighbors were continually protesting their noise, Seymour and his group sought larger quarters. The place which they found was an old, dilapidated, two-storied Methodist church building on Azusa Street. The floor of the meeting place was sprinkled with sawdust, and planks were placed over empty nail kegs to form benches.

Starting at about ten o'clock in the morning, the meetings often lasted until ten or eleven in the evening, sometimes even until two or three in the morning. All was completely spontaneous, with no special speakers or subjects announced ahead of time. No one knew what was coming next. Anyone who felt "moved by the Spirit" was free to preach or sing. Spiritual enthusiasm knew no bounds. Some have speculated that the revival capitalized on fears of the end of the world that followed the San Francisco earthquake, April 18, 1906.

One of the most amazing things about the revival was the integration factor. In a day when the complete separation of the races was the accepted pattern, blacks and whites sat side by side, along with Chinese and even Jews.

The Azusa Street revival provoked newspaper stories of a sensational nature. These helped to draw crowds from all over the country, and even from all over the world. The result was that the flame spread. Some who came to scoff experienced for themselves the baptism in the Holy Spirit, speaking in tongues. They returned to their homes apostles of the Pentecostal faith.

As the revival progressed, various strange manifestations like the "jerks" and "treeing the devil" came into prominence. From various occult societies came spiritualists and mediums to try to make their trances and seances a part of the services.[24] The matter of discerning the spirits became a major problem.

An intense distaste for tongues and a fear of emotional excesses provoked strong reactions of oppositions and persecution from society in general and the traditional churches in particular.[25] Fear that this kind of emotional enthusiasm would penetrate the churches led many of these churches to close their doors and shut their ears to the message of Pentecostalism. This, in turn, hastened the formation of new denominations. Still Pentecostalism grew. It made its strongest appeal to the uneducated, economically deprived classes of society. Many denominations began to lose members to the Pentecostals, and this caused them to brand the Pentecostals "sheep-stealers."

Before long, doctrinal differences began to appear within the Pentecostal movement itself. One of the earliest doctrinal disputes had to do with the relation of sanctification to baptism in the Spirit. Another centered around the question of whether or not a revelation based on a contemporary prophecy or interpretation of tongues should be regarded as having the same authority as Holy Scripture. Still a third involved the doctrine of the Trinity.[26] These controversies, along with variances in church polity, personality conflicts, and racial differences, soon led to the formation of a number of Pentecostal denominations. Among the leading ones are the Assemblies of God, Church of God (Cleveland, Tennessee), Church of God in Christ (black), and the Pentecostal Holiness Church.

49

Within ten years of the beginning of the Azusa Street revival, Pentecostalism had become a worldwide movement with thriving Pentecostal communities in Europe (the Scandinavian countries, Great Britain, Germany, and Switzerland), in Asia (India and China), in Africa (Union of South Africa and the vast central African territory), and in Latin America (Chile and Brazil), as well as the United States.

The growth of the worldwide Pentecostal movement is one of the most remarkable stories in the history of the Christian church. Taken as a whole, it is the fastest growing segment of the Christian community. A little over sixty years after the outbreak of the Azusa Street revival classical Pentecostalism was estimated to embrace a community of between twelve and fourteen million believers, four-fifths of these living outside the United States.[27] In some countries Pentecostalism is growing at a rate nine to fifteen times as fast as the historic churches.[28] Over 80 percent of the evangelicals of Chile are Pentecostal, and in Brazil the two and a quarter million Pentecostals comprise two-thirds of the total evangelical force of the nation.[29] There are about a million Pentecostals in Indonesia,[30] where for some years a truly remarkable, though highly exaggerated, Pentecostal style revival has been raging. Currently in Africa there is a large growth of "independent" churches with a Pentecostal style worship and piety. One American historian and statistician predicts that by the year A.D. 2000 Africa and Latin America will have more Christians than the rest of the world combined, and that most of these will be of a Pentecostal type.[31]

How can one account for the phenomenal growth of the Pentecostal movement? Pentecostals themselves account for it in terms of their faithfulness to the New Testament experience of the Holy Spirit. Emphasizing that the spiritual manifestations recorded in the New Testament, such as speaking in tongues, prophecy, healing, and miracles, should be continued in our day, David du Plessis says: "The New Testament is not a record of what happened in one generation, but it is a blue-print of what should happen in every generation until Jesus comes."[32]

Students of church growth, while recognizing the spiritual vitality of the Pentecostal movement, emphasize the indigenous nature of the movement in each country as one key to its growth. Not being tied financially or institutionally to churches in other parts of the world, Pentecostal churches, with some exceptions here and there, are able to express the Christian faith in a way that is natural and compatible with the background of the people.

Pentecostals, generally speaking, are aggressive in their evangelistic outreach. Not waiting for the people to come to the churches, they go to them where they are on the street corners or in the homes. They preach a simple, experience-centered message which is easily explained and easily understood. They seek to minister to the needs of people where they are. They pray for the sick to be healed, for the alcoholics to be delivered, for the sinsick that they might find the Savior. Assimilating the new members into a warm Christian community, they seek to nurture them in the faith. They try to provide jobs for those who are unemployed. They trust their laymen, using them in witness from the time they first become Christians. Their pastors usually emerge from among these laymen who have had on-the-job training in giving their testimonies on street corners, in teaching Sunday school classes, in preaching in worship services, and in helping at new preaching points. Helping their members discover their spiritual gifts and use them for the glory of God is a top priority for Pentecostals. They regard church going not as a dull duty, but as a joyful privilege. They use music that is lively and rhythmic, and they encourage those who can play instruments to use them in the worship services. They give opportunities for congregational participation through clapping, singing, dancing, praying, testifying, and the exercise of spiritual gifts. They widen their outreach by starting new congregations in other areas.[33]

Not all Pentecostal churches are growing. Those which have not had the necessary leadership or evangelistic thrust have lagged behind. The growth rate varies, too, from country to country. This is evident even in Latin America, where, generally speaking, the climate is conducive to Pentecostal church growth. Whereas in Chile Pentecostals constitute over 80 percent of the evangelicals, in Bolivia they comprise less than 8 percent.[34]

Pentecostals in Latin America are greatly concerned about the departure of second- and third-generation Pentecostals from the church. "Usually, Pentecostal children overcome the cultural limitations of their parents and rise on the social ladder."[35] With this change in social status often there comes a disenchantment with Pentecostalism. Here Pentecostals face a dilemma. If they follow the route that other denominations have taken in the course of their historical development, becoming increasingly sophisticated, they will lose their appeal to the masses. On the other hand, if they continue on the same cultural and intellectual level, they will lose many of their children, who, through the impetus received from their faith or the faith of their fathers, have learned to "get ahead" economically and socially.

Sociologists of religion have long pointed out that there is a tendency for churches of the sect type that minister largely to economically and culturally deprived peoples (Pentecostal churches fit into this category) to become increasingly respectable as they climb the social ladder.[36] Thereupon, other sects arise at the bottom as a protest against the liberal tendencies of groups which were previously less sophisticated. This trend can be observed within Pentecostalism. This movement within Pentecostalism from the sect type to the church type is discernible in such trends as beautiful church buildings supplanting store-front or second-floor meeting quarters, less charismatic emotional ardor and more liturgical order in the worship services, a growing interest in education, particularly an educated ministry, a deepened concern for social problems, a growing ecumenical involvement, and a new capacity for self-criticism. At the same time, new ultraconservative, highly fanatical sects are arising at the bottom.

What is the relation between Pentecostalism and the modern-day charismatic movement? The current charismatic movement is the offspring of Pentecostalism. Had there been no Pentecostalism,

51

probably there would have been no charismatic movement. Many of the thought forms, worship patterns, and theological ideas of Pentecostalism have been brought over into the movement. This movement has stimulated a new interest in Pentecostalism, heretofore largely ignored and often scorned by the historic churches. Some Pentecostals have been bewildered or even resentful that the charismatic gifts, which previously they had thought of as their exclusive monopoly, are being manifested within the historic churches. Other Pentecostals have gladly joined with Protestant and Catholic charismatics in services of prayer and praise.

Pentecostal leaders like David du Plessis and Pentecostal Bible teachers like Judson Cornwall and Derek Prince have been warmly welcomed in Protestant and Catholic churches that are beginning to move in the direction of charismatic expression. At the same time, Neo-Pentecostals like Dennis Bennett and Larry Christenson and Catholic charismatics like Kevin Ranaghan have also ministered in classical Pentecostal churches. Sometimes in charismatic meetings planned mainly for Christians within the traditional churches, Pentecostals have tended to try to take over to show everyone how it is done. Still, there have been wise statesmen within Pentecostal circles who have warned Protestant and Catholic charismatics against some of the mistakes of Pentecostalism in its early history, especially its unbridled emotionalism.

In this chapter we have observed that throughout the history of the church there have been occasional outbreaks of spiritual enthusiasm, which either in their emotional tone or spiritual manifestations suggest some parallels to Pentecostalism and the current charismatic movement. Moreover, we have noted that a certain historical continuity can be traced from German Pietism, through the Moravian Brethren to Wesley and from Wesley through the Holiness movement to Pentecostalism, the mother of the modern-day charismatic movement. We have given attention to the phenomenal growth of Pentecostalism and the spiritual vigor of this movement, which in a large measure carries over into the modern-day charismatic movement.

Leaders of Pentecostalism and the charismatic movement alike maintain that they are simply returning to the pattern of New Testament Christianity. In the next chapters we will be examining the biblical and theological basis of the charismatic movement, trying to determine to what extent, if any, it deviates from the biblical witness. Primary emphasis will be focused upon the current charismatic movement rather than upon classical Pentecostalism.

PART TWO: A THEOLOGICAL APPRAISAL

CHAPTER 3

Baptism
in the
Holy Spirit

As a rule, charismatics adhere to basic Christian theology such as is expressed in the Apostles' Creed, as well as to the particular teachings of their own churches and denominations. In addition to these, normally they have some distinctive doctrines which are related to their charismatic experience. Most leaders of the charismatic movement claim to ground such doctrinal views, not on their experience, but on the teachings of Holy Scripture. They insist that in all cases Scripture provides the norm. They believe that the interpretation of Scripture should not be weakened in order to conform to contemporary experience; rather contemporary Christian experience should be blessed and empowered until it conforms to the pattern of Scripture.

In a movement as broad as the charismatic one a great variety of interpretations is to be expected. This study attempts to delineate some of the main distinctive emphases of Protestant Neo-Pentecostalism. At the same time it takes note of some of the variations within this spectrum. It gives attention to some areas in which the accents of Protestant and Catholic charismatic leaders run parallel, while pointing out some distinctive Catholic interpretations as well.

Charismatic Interpretations

Neo-Pentecostalism continually highlights the contrast between the tremendous spiritual dynamic of the early church and the relative powerlessness of most churches and Christians today. The churches of today have their fine buildings, beautiful liturgies, learned scholars, and a variety of professional ministers. While having few of these, the early church had something vastly more important—spiritual power. Christians in those days saw God daily moving in response to their prayers. Mighty miracles attended prayer and the preaching of the Word. Not only were the lost saved, but also the blind received their sight, the lame walked, and those suffering from demonic oppression were delivered from their bondage. However much Christians may have evoked hostility from the society around them, they could not have been regarded as boring, dull, or dead. The church on the day of Pentecost provoked from the crowds reactions of amazement and perplexity. People may possibly be perplexed at the church today, but they are seldom amazed at what is happening, because the wonder and sparkle of those early days is usually missing.

"But," the charismatics ask, "why should it be so?" Does not the New Testament tell us that "Jesus Christ is the same yesterday and today and for ever" (Hebrews 13:8)? And does not Jesus promise his disciples: "He who believes in me will also do the works that I do; and greater works than these will he do, because I go to the Father" (John 14:12)?

The New Testament associates spiritual power with the work of the Holy Spirit. All power has been delivered to the risen Lord in heaven and on earth (Matthew 28:18), and he pours it out on the disciples through the Holy Spirit (Acts 1:8; 2:33; 4:31). Paul can say that his words and deeds were attended "by the power of signs and wonders, by the power of the Holy Spirit" (Romans 15:19; cf. 1 Corinthians 2:4). He reminds the Galatians that by hearing with faith God supplies the Spirit to them and works miracles (Galatians 3:5). Obviously what is lacking in the church today, say the charismatics, is the same kind of experience of the Holy Spirit which the early church had.

The starting point for a recovery of spiritual power, they say, is in the rediscovery of what the New Testament calls baptism in or with the Holy Spirit. Referred to variously as the Pentecostal experience, receiving the Spirit, the release of the Spirit, the outpouring of the Spirit, or the Spirit falling upon someone, it is a distinct, recognizable experience. Not a gradual or passive thing, it has the nature of an event, a dramatic endowment with power and energy, as the Holy Spirit comes to one in a decisive way!

Most Protestant Neo-Pentecostals follow Pentecostalism in distinguishing baptism in the Spirit from conversion. This baptism does not relate to an experience of salvation, but is one in which the

Christian is empowered for ministry in Christ's name. In conversion the Holy Spirit comes to dwell in the believer (Romans 8:9), and through his indwelling presence life is imparted. Through the baptism in the Spirit there is a release of the Spirit so that rivers of living water flow out from the believer (John 7:37-38). Long ago R. A. Torrey made the crucial distinction when he said:

> In regeneration there is the impartation of life by the Spirit's power, and one who receives it is saved: in the baptism with the Holy Spirit, there is the impartation of power, and the one who receives it is fitted for service. . . .[1]

Michael Harper, British Neo-Pentecostal, says that the failure to understand this important differentiation is the main hindrance to people claiming the promise of the Father and receiving it.[2]

Though baptism in the Spirit is a door to new fullness of life in the Spirit, it is not a magic wand by which all of life's problems are solved. According to charismatics, while baptism in the Spirit does lift the spiritual life to a new dimension and opens the door to the operation of the gifts of the Spirit, it is not a shortcut to spiritual maturity. It boosts growth, but it does not render continued growth unnecessary. It does not bring about instant holiness. It makes one more aware than ever of one's own perversity, while at the same time giving one a power to cope with it more adequately. Thus it is completely compatible with moral struggle. Moreover, the fact that one has been baptized in the Spirit does not mean that one automatically remains Spirit-filled for the rest of one's life. There is a need for being continuously filled with the Spirit (Ephesians 5:18) by always keeping the doors of the heart open to the Holy Spirit.

Neo-Pentecostals say that the importance of this experience is underscored by the fact that it is mentioned in all four Gospels (Matthew 3:11; Mark 1:8; Luke 3:16; John 1:33). The Triune reference is unmistakable. It is the promise of God the Father (Luke 24:49; John 1:33), but it is also promised by God the Son (Acts 1:5), and by God the Holy Spirit, the Inspirer of Scripture. John the Baptist first refers to it in contrasting his baptism with that of the one who is coming after him (Matthew 3:11; Mark 1:8; Luke 3:16). Jesus makes John's promise his own when he says, "John baptized with water, but before many days you shall be baptized with the Holy Spirit" (Acts 1:5).

The fulfillment comes at Pentecost when all are filled with the Holy Spirit and begin to speak in tongues as the Spirit gives them utterance (Acts 2:4). On this occasion in his mighty sermon Peter explains that it is the crucified and risen Jesus who has poured out the

55

promise of the Father (Acts 2:32-33). Later Peter recognizes the same pattern of the Spirit's activity in the outpouring of the Holy Spirit upon the Gentiles in Cornelius's house. In explaining to Jewish Christians in Jerusalem why he has dared to baptize the Gentiles, Peter interprets the outpouring of the Spirit upon them as of the same kind which the church had experienced on the day of Pentecost and recognizes in both experiences the fulfillment of Jesus' prophecy that they should be baptized with the Holy Spirit before many days (Acts 11:15-17; cf. 1:5).

First Corinthians 12:13 poses a problem for the Pentecostal, Neo-Pentecostal interpretation of baptism in the Spirit because it seems to teach that all Christians are baptized in the Spirit and to relate this experience to initiation into the Christian life. Paul writes: "For by one Spirit we were all baptized into one body—Jews or Greeks, slaves or free—and all were made to drink of one Spirit." Most Neo-Pentecostals recognize a basic difference between this passage and the six passages in the Gospels and Acts which speak of baptism in the Spirit. They point out that the Greek preposition *en* is usually translated "in" or "with," as in the six passages already considered, but that in 1 Corinthians 12:13 the correct translation is "by."[3] The baptism *by* the Spirit in 1 Corinthians 12:13, they say, is not to be confused with the baptism *in* the Spirit in the other six passages. The former denotes the Spirit's work in conversion or regeneration, making the sinner a member of the body of Christ under the sign or seal of water baptism. The latter denotes the activity of Christ the great Baptizer in immersing the believer in the Spirit and empowering him for service.[4] According to this interpretation, the Holy Spirit baptizes us into Christ and his body (conversion), and Christ baptizes us into the Holy Spirit (Pentecost).

According to many Protestant charismatics, the Scriptures bear witness to a twofold experience. This is suggested first by the analogy between Jesus' experience and our own. They point out that Jesus was born of the Holy Spirit (virgin birth) and was guided, we may believe, by the Holy Spirit throughout his infancy, youth, and young manhood. Nevertheless, before he began his public ministry, it was necessary for him to receive an enduement with power from on high as the Holy Spirit descended upon him and abode with him (Matthew 3:13-17; Mark 1:9-11; Luke 3:21-22; John 1:32-33). Here Jesus himself was baptized in the Holy Spirit. It would seem that before this experience Jesus performed no miracles and issued no great teachings. Following this experience, however, we are told that he was led by the Spirit into the wilderness for an encounter with Satan

(Luke 4:1), that he returned in the power of the Spirit into Galilee (Luke 4:14), that he announced in Nazareth, "The Spirit of the Lord is upon me" (Luke 4:18), and that he cast out demons by the Spirit of God (Matthew 12:28). Charismatics say that in their experience the new birth corresponds to Jesus' having been born of the Spirit and their baptism with the Spirit corresponds to Jesus' having been filled with the Spirit following his baptism in water. If the Son of God needed an enduement with power, surely all who minister on his behalf need the same, it is urged.

In his witness to Jesus, John the Baptist pointed to him not only as "the Lamb of God, who takes away the sin of the world," but also as the one "who baptizes with the Holy Spirit" (John 1:29, 33). The problem with the church today, says Michael Harper, is that while proclaiming Christ as the Lamb of God who takes away the sin of the world, it has failed to lift him up as the one who baptizes in the Holy Spirit.[5]

Many Neo-Pentecostals also point to a twofold experience of the apostles. On the first evening after his resurrection Jesus appeared unto his disciples and breathed on them saying, "Receive the Holy Spirit" (John 20:22). With this the disciples experienced new life in the Spirit, but they were still in need of the enduement with power from on high which came at Pentecost.[6]

This twofold pattern appears again and again in the book of Acts. The Samaritans "believed Philip as he preached good news about the kingdom of God and the name of Jesus Christ," and they were baptized (Acts 8:12). Nevertheless, there was something lacking in their experience, for the Holy Spirit had not yet fallen upon them. However, when Peter and John came down and laid hands on them and prayed for them, they received the Holy Spirit (8:14-17). Saul, the persecutor of the church, met Jesus on the Damascus Road and bowed the knee to him, but it was not until three days later, when Ananias laid hands on him and prayed for him, that his sight was restored and he was filled with the Holy Spirit (9:1-18). It is clear that there was something lacking both in the experience and theology of the disciples at Ephesus. At any rate, when Paul instructed them more fully, baptized them in the name of the Lord Jesus, laid his hands on them, and prayed for them, the Holy Spirit came upon them and they spoke in tongues and prophesied (Acts 19:1-7).

But not all Protestant charismatics accept this two-stage, or "second blessing" theology. It is rejected decisively by Thomas A. Smail. He says that it obscures the centrality and sufficiency of the Lord Jesus Christ. It leads us to glorify the Spirit when the Bible

57

specifically says that it is the business of the Spirit to glorify Christ. Moreover, according to Smail, it is "in danger of dividing the Christian life into a salvation which is gift to the sinner, and the fulness of the Spirit which is reward of the saint. . . ."[7]

Both Protestant and Catholic charismatics often use the word "Pentecost" to refer not simply to an event in the past but to a pattern of God's action which is always valid. Jesus' promise to baptize his disciples with the Spirit was fulfilled on the day of Pentecost, but this does not preclude the possibility that he would so baptize others in the future. Quite the contrary, the charismatics say, for Peter on the day of Pentecost specifically said: "For the promise is to you and to your children and to all that are far off, every one whom the Lord our God calls to him" (Acts 2:39). Moreover, Peter interpreted a subsequent experience of a similar nature as a fulfillment of Jesus' promise (Acts 11:15-17; cf. 1:5). Thus charismatics say that just as Acts 2 records the Jerusalem Pentecost, Acts 8 sets forth the Samaritan Pentecost; Acts 9, Paul's personal Pentecost; Acts 10-11, the Gentile Pentecost; and Acts 19:1-7, the Ephesian Pentecost.

The emphasis upon Pentecost is especially attractive to Catholic charismatics. They like to repeat the part of the prayer of Pope John XXIII which says: "Renew Thy wonders in this our day, as by a new Pentecost." They also point out that in the general audience of November 29, 1972, Pope Paul VI said: "The Church needs an eternal Pentecost." In their view, the charismatic renewal is one manifestation of this Pentecost. Near the close of his widely read book, *A New Pentecost?*, Cardinal Suenens says: "John XXIII and Paul VI have not prayed in vain for a new Pentecost. It is here, before our eyes, like the first rays of dawn."[8]

Is the baptism in the Holy Spirit intended for all Christians? May any Christian receive it? Here Protestant charismatics are almost unanimous in answering with an emphatic "Yes!"

How is the baptism in the Spirit to be received? Classical Pentecostalism tended to elaborate various formulas or conditions for receiving the baptism. Often the conditions set forth seemed to imply some kind of worthiness on the part of the recipient. Most Protestant Neo-Pentecostals repudiate this type of approach. J. Rodman Williams emphasizes the gift quality of this experience, with God's part being the giving and man's part the receiving. Man does nothing to earn it, for it is God's gracious gift. He says: "There are no conditions or requirements to be met, no stairs to climb or hoops to jump through, but simply the reception of a freely offered gift." What is required is simply openness and readiness.

Michael Harper explains the way the baptism is received in terms of Jesus' invitation, "If anyone thirst, let him come to me and drink" (John 7:37). As *thirst* is the condition for our coming, *drinking* is the means of our appropriation. Larry Christenson says that it is received in the same way as salvation, that is, by faith. Most Protestant charismatics emphasize the importance of asking for the baptism, using Luke 11:9-13 as scriptural support. In this context often what is expected is that God will demonstrate that he has answered the prayer by the evidence of tongues. Continual appeal is made to Acts 2:38, where it is said that the normal order is: repent, be baptized as an expression of faith, receive the gift of the Holy Spirit (generally thought of as verified by the evidence of tongues). Dennis and Rita Bennett emphasize in this connection the importance of renouncing every form of the occult, and they attempt to explain how the baptism is received in terms of making suggestions about how one may begin speaking in tongues.[9]

What is the relation of water baptism to baptism in the Spirit? Here charismatics are sharply divided. Most classical Pentecostals practice water baptism (usually by immersion), but deny that it has saving significance. In their view the normal recipient of baptism in the Spirit is one who has already been saved and received water baptism. The distinction between water baptism and Spirit baptism given by David du Plessis (classical Pentecostal) has been accepted by many Protestant Neo-Pentecostals. According to him, in water baptism the church is the agent, water is the element, and the new Christian is the object. In Spirit baptism, however, Christ is the agent (baptizer), the Holy Spirit is the element, and the believer is the object. Dennis and Rita Bennett (Episcopalian charismatics) speak of three baptisms: spiritual baptism into Christ, which takes place as soon as Jesus is received as Savior; baptism with water, symbolic of inner cleansing from sin and death and resurrection to newness of life; and baptism with the Spirit, in which the indwelling Holy Spirit is poured forth to manifest Jesus to the world.[10]

Arnold Bittlinger, a German Lutheran charismatic professor of theology, will not accept the differentiation of two or three baptisms or even two distinct experiences. According to him, there is only one baptism, baptism by water and Spirit. Every Christian has been baptized in both or he or she is not a Christian in the full sense of the word. In baptism one receives potentially everything one will ever receive in Christ. But God's purpose in baptism must be actualized through the appropriation of its potential in the life of the individual Christian.[11]

59

Thus far little reference has been made to the way Catholic charismatics understand baptism in the Spirit. The reason is that, generally speaking, they feel rather uncomfortable with the whole concept. They believe that it represents too much of a theological hangover from classical Pentecostalism. To those not involved in the charismatic renewal, they say, it suggests another baptism, thus another sacrament to be placed alongside the seven already recognized in the Catholic Church. They insist that there is but "one Lord, one faith, one baptism" (Ephesians 4:5). In the Catholic view, to be baptized in water is to be baptized in the Holy Spirit, for the sacrament of baptism mediates the Holy Spirit. Cardinal Suenens suggests that because of the ambiguity of the phrase it would be better to avoid speaking of "baptism in the Spirit" and look for another expression.[12] When Catholics do use the term "baptism in the Spirit," they mean that the Holy Spirit given in initiation (the sacraments of baptism and confirmation) is now breaking forth into personal conscious experience. They insist that theologically the fullness of the Spirit belongs to the beginning of the Christian life rather than to a later stage.

Catholic charismatics are open to the operation of the gifts of the Holy Spirit within the context of the body of Christ, and they like to think of the charismatic renewal in terms of Pentecost. To express what Protestant charismatics mean by "baptism in the Holy Spirit," they generally prefer terms like "discovery of the Spirit," "release of the Spirit," "manifestation of baptism," or "renewal of . . . spiritual life."[13]

60

Appraisal

Six questions call for discussion: (1) the meaning of being baptized with the Spirit and being filled with the Spirit according to the New Testament, (2) the nature of Christian experience: two-staged or not? (3) Pentecost: a once-for-all event or a pattern of God's activity, (4) how baptism in the Spirit is received, (5) the relation of water baptism and Spirit baptism, and (6) the question of spiritual power.

New Testament Meaning of Baptism in the Holy Spirit

Though the expression "baptism in the Spirit" never occurs in the New Testament, there are seven instances in which the verb "to be baptized" is used in connection with the Holy Spirit. Five of the passages are predictive in nature (Matthew 3:11; Mark 1:8; Luke 3:16; John 1:33; and Acts 1:5). As such, they point forward to

Pentecost and were fulfilled in the events of that day. Instead of referring to some post-conversion experience to be sought earnestly by every Christian, they refer to the historic experience of the outpouring of the Holy Spirit.

The sixth passage of importance is Acts 11:16. Historical in nature, this verse in its larger context relates how Peter recounted to Jewish Christians in Jerusalem what happened to Gentiles in the house of Cornelius as he was speaking to them. Here we do have a repetition of what happened at Pentecost, but not in the sense that is taught in Pentecostal and Neo-Pentecostal circles. Here baptism in the Spirit, far from being distinguished from conversion as a subsequent experience, occurs simultaneously with conversion and is an integral part of this experience.

The seventh passage, 1 Corinthians 12:13, is didactic or doctrinal in nature. Since it gives a theological interpretation of Christian experience, it is crucial for an understanding of what the New Testament means by being baptized in the Holy Spirit. This passage supplies the key for the understanding of this doctrine, for it is a sound principle of biblical interpretation that, in the formulation of doctrine, passages of a predictive or of an historical nature are to be understood in terms of the doctrinal ones which give a theological interpretation of the issues under discussion.

61

As we have seen, the Greek preposition *en* is normally translated "in" or "with," but it can, as an exception to the rule, be translated "by." In the other six passages that we have been considering, the RSV translates *en* "with," but there it uses "by." This supports the typical Pentecostal, Neo-Pentecostal interpretation that we have already considered. But there is no good reason why the normal translation should not be employed here as well as in the other six passages. When "by" is used, it forces the interpretation that the baptizer here is the Spirit rather than Christ, as is clearly the case in the Gospels, and as is generally assumed to be the case in the two passages in Acts. When the passage is translated "with one Spirit" or "in one Spirit," however, its meaning becomes consistent with that in the other six passages. This lends itself to the interpretation that in this passage, as in the other six, Christ is the baptizer. Its meaning would then be that "Christ (the subject) baptizes the believer (object) with the Spirit (element) into the body of Christ (purpose)." [14]

The context of the passage speaks of the unity among Christians. The passage itself speaks of "one Spirit" and "one body." Paul appeals to baptism in the Spirit as an experience that unites Christians, not one that divides them. It is not an experience of which it can be said that some Christians have had it, while others have not. The New Testament nowhere speaks of baptism in the Spirit in this way. Paul can say in "one Spirit we were all baptized into one body . . . and all were made to drink of one Spirit." Twice he uses the word *all*. The use of the aorist tense in both of these verbs indicates an accomplished action that took place at a particular point in time. It was the time when the Holy Spirit came to dwell in them and they were incorporated into the body of Christ. No second-stage experience for *some* Christians, baptism in the Spirit is an initiatory experience for *all* Christians, without which they are really not Christians at all.[15]

Many Neo-Pentecostal teachers have not moved far enough away from Pentecostal theology at this point. They claim that baptism in the Spirit is distinct from the initial experience of receiving Christ. This view is unsatisfactory on two counts. First, it implies that there are some who have received Christ as their Savior who have not received the Holy Spirit. On the contrary, anyone who has received Christ as Savior *has* received the Holy Spirit (Romans 8:9). Second, it implies that the first part of our Christian experience is related to Christ, but the second and better part comes through the Holy Spirit. Rather, all the blessings that God has for us, he has for us in Christ, but they are mediated to us through the Holy Spirit.

It is significant that the New Testament never enjoins Christians to be baptized in the Spirit. The reason seems to be that the fundamental presupposition is that they have already been so baptized. To become a Christian is itself to receive the Holy Spirit or be baptized in the Spirit (Acts 11:16; Romans 8:9; 1 Corinthians 3:16; 6:19; 12:13; 2 Corinthians 3:5-6).

Paul said of the Christians at Corinth that they had all been baptized in the Spirit (1 Corinthians 12:13) and that they were not lacking in any spiritual gift (1 Corinthians 1:7). Nevertheless, he said that he could not address them as spiritual *(pneumatikois)* but as carnal *(sarkinois,* 1 Corinthians 3:1). The distinction which he made was not between those who have received the baptism in the Spirit and those who have not, but between spiritual Christians and carnal Christians, between Christians filled by the Spirit and those dominated by the flesh.[16] It is not surprising then that while Paul (or the rest of the New Testament for that matter) never enjoins Christians to be baptized with the Spirit, he does command them to be filled with the Spirit (Ephesians 5:18).

The term "full of the Holy Spirit" is sometimes used in the New Testament to indicate the characteristic or distinguishing mark of a person. Thus Jesus was "full of the Holy Spirit" not only when he was led into the wilderness (Luke 4:1) but also throughout his ministry. When a dispute arose in the church at Jerusalem, the congregation was admonished to seek out seven "full of the Spirit and of wisdom" to help in the daily distribution (Acts 6:3). Stephen is characterized as "a man full of faith and of the Holy Spirit" (Acts 6:5; cf. 7:55), and Barnabas as "a good man, full of the Holy Spirit and of faith" (Acts 11:24).

On the other hand, the book of Acts also indicates that being filled with the Spirit was something that recurred in the lives of the same believers (Acts 2:4; 4:8, 31; 9:17; 13:9, 52). Usually it is associated with a particular boldness for witness.

On the basis of this study a clear distinction can be made between baptism in the Spirit and being filled by the Spirit. The baptism in the Holy Spirit is initial; it is a once-for-all experience that marks the reception of the Holy Spirit and the beginning of the Christian life.

As an initiatory event the baptism is not repeatable and cannot be lost, but the filling can be repeated and in any case needs to be maintained. If it is not maintained, it is lost. If it is lost, it can be recovered. The Holy Spirit is grieved by sin (Eph. 4:30) and ceases to fill the sinner. Repentance is then the only road to recovery.[17]

63

Paul commands: "And do not be drunk with wine, for that is debauchery; but be filled with the Spirit . . ." (Ephesians 5:18). It is because drunkenness involves a loss of self-control that it is contrasted with the fullness of the Spirit, for Paul clearly states that the fruit of the Spirit is self-control (Galatians 5:23). Three things are to be noted about the verb in this command. First, it is a plural verb in the imperative mood. Both the prohibition and the command are universal in their application. None of us is to get drunk, but all of us are to be filled by the Spirit. Being filled with the Spirit is not a privilege reserved for the few, but a duty resting upon all. Second, it is the passive voice. The meaning is thus: "Let the Holy Spirit fill you." We are filled with the Spirit by yielding to him. As drunkenness comes from drinking, the fullness of the Spirit comes from a different kind of drinking (John 7:37). Third, the verb is in the present tense, meaning that the action is continuous, requiring continuous appropriation. Paul's meaning is not that one should "get filled with the Spirit" in one experience, but that one should "keep on being filled with the Spirit" in all experiences and daily living.[18]

And what are the evidences of being filled with the Spirit? They are a right relation to God and a right relation to others (Ephesians

5:19-20). The Holy Spirit leads us to praise the Lord and give thanks at all times. He causes us to establish spiritual communication with one another and to submit to one another. Thus the fullness of the Spirit manifests itself in worship and fellowship (Ephesians 5:17-21).

The Nature of Christian Experience

The fact that Jesus' experience of the Holy Spirit was marked by two decisive stages—born of the Spirit (virgin birth) and anointed or baptized with the Spirit (baptism)—is no satisfactory basis for arguing that the experience of the Christian should follow this two-stage pattern. One could as easily argue that because Jesus' baptism in the Spirit came at the time of his baptism in water, ours should also. There are many things about Jesus' experience which are not analogous to ours. The important thing is that our experience is based upon his and mediated through him. Indeed this is the significance of calling him the baptizer. At the time of his baptism "God anointed Jesus of Nazareth with the Holy Spirit and with power" (Acts 10:38). According to John, the Holy Spirit not only descends upon him but also remains upon him (John 1:33). He can baptize in the Spirit only because he was baptized in the Spirit. He can mediate this Spirit to others because he permanently possesses the Spirit. Through the Holy Spirit believers receive both new birth or life and new power. These are best understood, however, not as distinctly different stages of Christian experience, but as different aspects of it.

Likewise, John 1:29 and 33 point to two aspects of Christian experience rather than to two distinct stages. Becoming a Christian always involves these two things: cleansing from sin and the gift of the Holy Spirit. Jesus is both "the lamb of God, who takes away the sin of the world" and "he who baptizes with the Holy Spirit." Jeremiah spoke of a day when God would not only forgive sin but also would write his law upon the hearts of his people (Jeremiah 31:31-34). Moreover, Ezekiel prophesied: "I will sprinkle clear water upon you, and you shall be clean. . . . And I will put my spirit within you, and cause you to walk in my statutes . . ." (Ezekiel 36:25, 27). Both of these prophecies are fulfilled in Christ, who takes away sin and who baptizes with the Spirit. But there is no evidence either in the Old Testament prophecies or in John 1:29 and 33 that two different stages of experience are indicated. Likewise the apostles promised the forgiveness of sins and the gift of the Holy Spirit through Jesus without any suggestion of two different experiences (Acts 2:38; Titus 3:4-7).

There are three main interpretations of John 20:22, where the resurrected Lord, on the evening of Easter Sunday, breathes on the disciples and says to them: "Receive the Holy Spirit." One interpretation, which we have already considered, is that at this time the disciples received new life in the Spirit, but that it was not until fifty days later, the day of Pentecost, that they received an enduement of power from on high. A second interpretation is that the bestowal of the gift at this time was provisional, a mere anticipation of the decisive gift at Pentecost. A third interpretation is one followed by most critical scholars. They point out that each group of New Testament writings must be interpreted from the context of its own perspective: Lucan writings from the Lucan perspective and Johannine writings from the Johannine perspective. Since John records that Jesus has promised the Spirit (John 7:37-39; 14:16-18, 26; 15:26; 16:7-15) but gives no other fulfillment of this promise, this is John's equivalent of Pentecost.

Regardless of the interpretation we give to this passage, one thing is clear: our experience can never be the same as that of the apostles. They lived through a great change between the ages. There had been a time when they had not known Jesus. Then, they had been with him in the days of his flesh. They had experienced the desolation of the cross, the hope that came with the resurrection of Jesus, and the empowerment that came with the descent of the Spirit at Pentecost. We simply cannot put ourselves back in their position and make their experience normative for ours. Before Pentecost the hundred and twenty were waiting in obedient, expectant faith. On the day of Pentecost they were empowered by the Spirit and gave joyous witness to Jesus as Lord and Christ. They could not receive the Pentecostal gift before Pentecost. The three thousand who were converted that day apparently received the forgiveness of their sins and the gift of the Spirit simultaneously. It was not the experience of the apostles, who lived through this change of dispensations, but that of their converts which provides the norm for ours.[19]

But what about the passages in Acts that are adduced by charismatics to support a two-stage view of Christian experience? At least two of the three will not support the weight they place upon them. It is *possible* to conceive of Paul's conversion experience as a two-stage one, since he met Christ on the Damascus Road but, presumably, was not filled with the Holy Spirit until three days later (Acts 9:1-19). But since baptism is a normal part of becoming a Christian, it is *more natural* to think of Paul's conversion as one single experience beginning on the Damascus Road and lasting to the

65

ministry of Ananias. Who can calculate what it meant to Paul for him to have one among those whom he had been persecuting lay hands upon his head and call him brother?

It would appear that the twelve disciples in Ephesus were not really Christians before Paul's encounter with them (Acts 19:1-7).[20] They did not even know that the age of the Spirit had dawned; they had little knowledge of Jesus; and their understanding and experience were so deficient that Paul rebaptized (or baptized) them, laid his hands upon them, and prayed for them, and the Holy Spirit came upon them with charismatic manifestations. This is the only case in the New Testament where it is specifically stated that someone who had previously been baptized was baptized again.

Luke's story of the Samaritans to whom Philip witnessed does seem to fit into the two-stage pattern (Acts 8:1-24). Probably they were true believers even before Peter and John came down from Jerusalem and laid hands upon them. The account says that they gave heed to what Philip said; that they believed and were baptized; and that there was great joy in that city. It appears that what had been lacking were the charismatic manifestations that the book of Acts highlights. Why then was there no dramatic outpouring of the Spirit until the apostles from Jerusalem came down? Various theories have been offered. Some see this as just another instance of Luke's emphasis upon Jerusalem as the center of redemptive history. There can be no doubt that this is an important Lucan perspective, but it is hardly an adequate answer to this question. Others emphasize the role of the apostles, particularly in the laying on of hands. In fact, the whole rite of confirmation has been built largely upon this passage. But Luke records other cases in which the gospel is communicated effectively by Christians other than apostles (Acts 8:26-40; 11:19-26), and he recounts various examples of the Holy Spirit being given where there is no mention of the laying on of hands (Acts 2:4; 10:44). The most plausible view is that this experience was the means the Holy Spirit used in healing an age-old breach between Jerusalem and Samaria, his method of making sure that converts from two sides of the "Samaritan curtain" would find each other in finding Christ.[21]

Will Paul's theology support a two-stage view of salvation? Paul never argues for a personal identity between the risen Christ and the Holy Spirit, but throughout his epistles he assumes the closest possible association between the two. In 1 Corinthians 15:45 he says the "last Adam became a life-giving spirit." In another place he says, "the Lord is the Spirit," but he falls short of completely equating the two, for immediately he makes a differentiation, saying; "where the

Spirit of the Lord is, there is freedom" (2 Corinthians 3:17). For Paul the Holy Spirit is "the Spirit of the Lord" (2 Corinthians 3:17), "the Spirit of Christ" (Romans 8:9), or "the Spirit of Jesus Christ" (Philippians 1:19). The Holy Spirit is the mode by which Christ indwells his people. There is no distinction in his view between being "in Christ" and "in the Spirit." He can speak of "the Spirit," "the Spirit of God," "the Spirit of Christ," "Christ . . . in you," and "the Spirit . . . in you" without any distinction (Romans 8:6-11).

One searches in vain in the epistles of Paul for support for a two-stage view of salvation. Galatians 4:4-7, which is sometimes interpreted in this way, simply differentiates different points in salvation history, the sending of the Son and the sending of the Holy Spirit. When one becomes a Christian, one receives the Spirit as a seal or downpayment, assuring one's complete salvation (Romans 8:9; Ephesians 1:13-14; 4:30; 2 Corinthians 1:22; 5:5). Receiving the Holy Spirit is no second blessing beyond that of receiving Christ. All of God's treasures are centered in Christ (Colossians 1:27-28; 2:9), but they are mediated to us through the Holy Spirit.

Still we have not said all that needs to be said. In the New Testament, baptism in the Spirit is related to what Dunn calls "conversion-initiation," to all that is involved in becoming a Christian.[22] The *appropriation* of all that is latent in this relationship, however, is the process of a lifetime, and it is never fully accomplished in this world. It is at this point that confusion arises. This process of appropriation requires an openness to the Spirit's leadership and a constantly deepening discovery of what is involved in the lordship of Christ. It necessitates living by the Spirit, walking by the Spirit, and being constantly filled with the Spirit. It may come through a series of dramatic crisis experiences, or it may be mediated quietly, almost imperceptibly in undramatic, steady growth.

The important thing to recognize is that one cannot program the work of the Holy Spirit. He is not a computer subject to human control. Christians must not try to put the Spirit in a box, fence him in, or circumscribe the method or pattern of his operation. He is sovereign, and he demonstrates a mysterious freedom that is comparable to the blowing of the wind (John 3:8). The book of Acts, to which charismatics make such frequent appeal, demonstrates this point beautifully. Sometimes the Spirit is given after baptism, sometimes before it. Sometimes his coming is connected with the laying on of hands; sometimes it is not. Sometimes it is a two-stage experience, more often not. In the light of such facts, John Taylor points out how fruitless it is to try to harness the freedom of the Holy

Spirit to some sort of preconceived scheme as to how he should operate. "The Holy Spirit does not appear to have read the rubrics! He will not and cannot be bound." Protestant charismatic Thomas Smail grasps the point quite well when he says, "The Holy Spirit is always doing the same things, but he is always doing them differently, in an endless creativity that has no need to repeat itself." [23]

What has been said thus far may seem to be a repudiation of the Pentecostal experience. Such is not the case. The Pentecostal experience is expressed in terms of a defective theology. At this point, generally speaking, Catholic charismatics, apart from their strong insistence that the Holy Spirit is mediated through what they call the sacraments of initiation (baptism and confirmation), are theologically more correct than their Protestant counterparts. They usually see more clearly than Protestant charismatics that what is involved in the Pentecostal experience is a deeper appropriation of that which is given through the "in Christ" relationship which begins when one becomes a Christian.

Unquestionably, many charismatics (classical Pentecostals, Protestant Neo-Pentecostals, and Catholic Pentecostals) have had an experience that has revitalized their relationship to God in Christ, deepened their devotional lives, opened their hearts to the teachings of Scripture, given them a new joy and peace, a new love and openness to others, a new confidence in the promises of God, and a new boldness in witness. There is no reason for repudiating this experience. There are strong reasons for praising God for it. On the other hand, there is no theological basis for them to assume that everyone must have the same kind of experience which they have had. To do so is to try to put the Holy Spirit in a box, to program his operation. We are to be witnesses to Christ, not to an experience. We should stand in awe of the variety of the Spirit's operations, while maintaining "the unity of the Spirit in the bond of peace."

There are many Christians whose relationships to Christ have become clouded, whose spiritual lives have grown dry and stale. Often to them a one-stage theology sounds like a counsel of despair rather than a message of hope. It sounds as though we are saying: "Things are not going to get any better. You've got all you are going to get, so be satisfied with it!" What a misunderstanding! To them the message needs to be sounded: "There are riches in Christ that you haven't begun to appropriate. It is time for you to start possessing your possessions. Reach down, brother or sister, and draw fresh water from the well of salvation. Open your heart to the movement of Christ's Spirit that rivers of living water may ever flow through you."

The Nature of Pentecost

Charismatics do not deny the once-for-all aspect of Pentecost, but they place their emphasis upon what they call the pattern of Pentecost. How are we to evaluate this approach?

Each time the name "Pentecost" appears in the New Testament, it has reference to the Jewish Feast of Weeks, one of the three most important festivals in the Jewish calendar. The term has special significance for Christians because it was on this festival day fifty days after the first Easter that the Holy Spirit was poured out in mighty power upon Jesus' expectant disciples (Acts 2).

In Christian theology Pentecost designates a once-for-all historical event.[24] According to the record in Acts, on that day 120 followers of Jesus were empowered for effective witness, three thousand new converts were made, and the first Christian community, a conscious fellowship of caring and sharing, came into being.

In Old Testament times the Spirit of God was poured out sporadically upon particular individuals to empower them for a special task. For example, the Spirit of the Lord came upon Samson and he slew a lion with his bare hands (Judges 14:6), upon Micah and he proclaimed God's word (Micah 3:8). Not an abiding presence, but the sudden inspiration of a moment was described in these cases. Also not all of God's people, but only a select few, were subject to such inspiration. As the hope of a coming deliverer began to develop, the view took shape that the expected Messiah would not just have temporary moments of inspiration from time to time but that the Spirit of the Lord would abide upon him (Isaiah 11:2). Moreover, in the Golden Age toward which the prophets looked, the Spirit would be poured out on all of God's people and not only upon special individuals (Joel 2:28-29).

The outpouring of the Spirit upon Jesus at the time of his baptism constituted the fulfillment of the first prophecy. The Spirit worked mightily in him throughout his ministry. Still, for the disciples, the age of the Spirit did not begin until Pentecost, when the Holy Spirit descended upon them in mighty power. John 7:39 says tersely of this period prior to Pentecost: "The Spirit had not been given, because Jesus was not yet glorified." The glorification of Jesus through his death and resurrection was, in John's view, the necessary condition for the giving of the Spirit. There is an inseparable link between Calvary and Pentecost. The outpouring of the Spirit is dependent upon the glorification of Jesus (John 7:39), his going away (John 16:7-8), and his being lifted up (John 3:14; 12:32, 34). All three

69

terms designate the same series of events: "his being lifted up on the cross to die, his being lifted up from the grave to live, his being lifted up to the Father to reign."[25] Seen in this light, the outpouring of the Spirit is not in competition with Calvary, but the fruit of it (John 16:7).

The gift of the Spirit at Pentecost meant that the risen Christ was present with his disciples. It was the exalted Lord who had poured out the Spirit (Acts 2:33), but it was the presence of the Lord himself which they experienced through the Spirit. From now on the Holy Spirit was indissolubly connected with Jesus. The Holy Spirit was the Spirit of Jesus (Acts 16:6-7) or the Spirit of Christ (Romans 8:9). Just as Jesus illumines the face of the Father, he casts light also on the character of the Holy Spirit. The holiness of Jesus defines and gives content to the holiness of the Holy Spirit. It was necessary for the standard to be established before any universal outpouring of the Holy Spirit took place. That standard is Jesus. The Holy Spirit is a spiritual presence, but so is the devil. How may we differentiate the work of the Holy Spirit from the work of the devil? The test is the resemblance to Jesus. The Holy Spirit exalts Christ (John 16:14-15), leads us to confess that Jesus is Lord (1 Corinthians 12:3), and works to produce within believers the character of Jesus (Galatians 5:22-23). Because the presence of Christ through the Spirit is a spiritual presence, it is not limited as Jesus was during the days of his flesh. Thus the departure of Jesus and the coming of the Spirit was for the disciples a great gain (John 16:7-11).

The fact that the Holy Spirit comes to us now is based upon the fact that he was given then. The promises concerning the last days were fulfilled at Pentecost. "This means that the Spirit is given, and permanently given, to all members of the community."[26] We do not have to wait for him to come. He is already here. This is what we mean when we refer to Pentecost as a once-for-all event.

But is this all? May we also speak of Pentecost as designating a pattern of the Spirit's operation? Are we justified in speaking of a Samaritan Pentecost, a Gentile Pentecost, an Ephesian Pentecost, of Paul's Pentecost, and of your Pentecost and mine, as those involved in the charismatic movement so frequently do?

To keep a proper perspective, we need to bear in mind that this sort of interpretation is not confined to charismatics, but that many reputable, noncharismatic biblical scholars also speak of a Samaritan Pentecost, a Gentile Pentecost, and the like.[27] We need to remember also that the Bible never alludes to these experiences in this way. Are we thereby justified in saying that such a manner of speaking is unbiblical, however? The term "trinity" never occurs in the Bible, but this does not mean that the doctrine of the Trinity is without biblical foundations. We have already called attention to the fact that in the New Testament "Pentecost" always designates a Jewish festival. Nevertheless, Christian theology can use the term to refer to the descent of the Spirit, because on a particular day of Pentecost long ago the Spirit did come. Since the book of Acts chronicles other subsequent outpourings of the Spirit, is it proper to associate the term "Pentecost" with these also?

At this point some analogies may be of value. In Christian theology the incarnation refers to the Word becoming flesh, God coming into human history in the person of Jesus Christ (John 1:14). As such, it is a once-for-all, unique event. Nevertheless, Paul can tell the Galatians that he is in travail, like a woman in labor at the birth of a child, until Christ be formed in them (Galatians 4:19). Moreover, he can speak of the church as the body of Christ, which is animated and directed by Christ, who is the head. Thus we have a scriptural basis for saying that the only effective means of communicating the gospel is by the Word becoming incarnate in the lives of believers. Likewise the cross and the resurrection are once-for-all, historical events. They really happened. Nevertheless, we can speak of the principle of the cross and the principle of the resurrection as valid in our lives. The first three Gospels all indicate that Jesus admonished his disciples to deny themselves and take up the cross and follow him (Luke 9:23, and parallels). And again and again Paul speaks of our dying and rising with Christ (Romans 6:1-14; Colossians 3:1-4).

May we speak in a similar way about Pentecost? When we speak of the principle of incarnation, or the principle of the cross or of the resurrection, this kind of language is suggested by the biblical witness. But the New Testament never speaks of recurring Pentecosts, except with reference to the Jewish feast (Acts 20:16; 1 Corinthians 16:8). For example, Luke does not associate the term "Pentecost" with the outpourings of the Holy Spirit upon the Samaritans, upon Cornelius and his household, upon the Ephesians, or upon Paul. When Paul wants to speak about the presence of God in Christian experience, he speaks of the Holy Spirit or of being "in Christ" or "in the Spirit," never of Pentecost. Pentecost is a once-for-all historical event. It can never happen again. But the Holy Spirit makes all that is associated with the Christ event contemporary in our experience. Apart from the work of the Holy Spirit, the New Testament is no more than a chronicle of past events and a record of ancient moral and religious teachings. Because of the work of the

Holy Spirit, we, like the early Christians, can know the presence of the risen Christ in our lives, forgiving, cleansing, comforting, guiding, strengthening, and working within us to stamp Christ's likeness upon us.

The intention of those who speak of recurring Pentecosts is good, but the theological form that it takes is unbiblical. The intention is to raise the level of our expectations, to indicate that the kind of moral and spiritual transformation wrought in the lives of the disciples by the coming of the Holy Spirit at Pentecost can and should occur in our lives. The focus is taken off the past and placed on the present. It is not just something that happened *then* and *there;* it can occur *here* and *now.* Church history bears out the fact that when personal renewal or church renewal comes, it occurs usually where there is an attitude of open expectancy, "Lord, do it again!" Pentecostalism and the charismatic movement should be praised for focusing the spotlight on the importance of Christian experience. At the same time the biblically inaccurate, theologically incorrect form which this emphasis often takes should be pointed out and corrected. Our need is for the reality of the living Christ in our lives through the presence and power of the Holy Spirit. Never should our denial of recurring Pentecosts be understood as our saying: "That leaves us safe. We don't have to be concerned about the Holy Spirit in our lives today because his coming was a once-for-all event in the ancient past." No, the fact that he came then means that we can know the blessedness of his presence here and now, and this presence is none other than that of the risen Lord himself! John Taylor reminds us that every Christian is meant to possess his or her possessions, but many never do. It is better to speak incorrectly of a second blessing or a second Pentecost and "lay hold of the reality of new life in Christ than to let the soundness of our doctrine rob us of its substance." [28] But we are not faced with an either/or situation, either correct doctrine or vital experience. Why not both/and? A correct understanding of the Scriptures opens the way for the richness of the New Testament life in the Spirit. Anything which does not measure up to the New Testament standard should be discarded.

How Baptism in the Spirit Is Received

If our interpretation thus far is correct, to become a Christian is to receive the Holy Spirit or to be baptized in the Spirit. One receives the Spirit when one receives Christ, and one receives Christ through the Spirit. The conditions are repentance and faith, a turning away from sin and a turning to the Savior (Mark 1:15; Acts 20:21). Peter's

72

words in Acts 2:38 are clear: "Repent, and be baptized . . ." (faith expressed in action). The promise is "And you shall receive the gift of the Holy Spirit." Paul makes it clear that the Holy Spirit is received, not by the works of the law, but "by hearing with faith" (Galatians 3:2, 14). According to John's Gospel, one receives the Spirit by coming to Jesus and believing in him (John 7:37-39; cf. 1:12).

Water Baptism and Spirit Baptism

Ephesians 4:5 speaks of "one Lord, one faith, one baptism." In light of this the differentiation of three baptisms by Dennis and Rita Bennett, as previously mentioned, is theologically unacceptable. Lutheran charismatic teacher Arnold Bittlinger is right. Since Pentecost there is only one baptism, and that is baptism by water and Spirit.[29] Of course, it is possible to be baptized in water without being baptized in the Spirit (Acts 19:1-7). In such a case baptism is an empty rite, and the most important element involved in becoming a Christian is missing. On the other hand, it is possible to be baptized in the Spirit before being baptized in water (Acts 10:44-48). However, Spirit baptism does not render water baptism superfluous. Rather it constitutes the solid basis for following through with water baptism. As the rite of initiation into Christ, water baptism "symbolizes Spirit baptism."[30]

73

The Bible frequently refers to baptism in a nonliteral sense (Mark 10:38; Luke 12:50) even as it refers to circumcision sometimes in the same way (Romans 2:28-29; Colossians 2:11-13). Without literal circumcision there would have been no circumcision analogy; without a literal crucifixion there would have been no crucifixion analogy; and without literal baptism there would have been no baptism analogy. Paul's references to baptism in Romans 6:1-11; 1 Corinthians 12:13; Galatians 3:27; and Colossians 2:11 are like those of Jesus in Mark 10:38 and Luke 12:50, nonliteral in character. Paul's emphasis is upon faith (Galatians 3:26-27; Colossians 2:11-13), the spiritual experience of dying and rising with Christ (Romans 6:1-11), and of receiving the Spirit and being incorporated into Christ's body (1 Corinthians 12:13), not upon baptism in water, however much the ritual act may lie behind his analogies. "Paul would be an enigma indeed," Frank Stagg correctly observes, "if after holding that circumcision of the flesh was not necessary to salvation he would conclude that water baptism was."[31] Paul does not make this mistake; neither should we.

Receiving water baptism is a dramatic means of expressing faith in Christ through an act of obedience to him. It usually serves to deepen one's commitment and sometimes is the occasion of a richer experience of the Spirit. The mere fact that one has received water baptism should not be taken in itself as proof that one has received the Spirit. In such a case the inner experiential element involved in becoming a Christian is obscured, and water baptism, which in itself is a human act, becomes confused with the gift of the Spirit, which is a divine one.[32]

In the New Testament water baptism is believers' baptism, administered only to those who have faith.[33] Those who practice infant baptism usually speak of it as the sacrament of God's prevenient grace (meaning that God moves toward us before we move toward him) and proclaim the necessity of the individual's personally ratifying later the decision which was made long before in the act of baptism. While the New Testament clearly proclaims God's prevenient grace, that God moves toward us before we move toward him, it connects this not with water baptism but with God's coming into our human situation in Christ and his giving himself for us upon the cross. In the New Testament people come to baptism themselves and are not brought to it by others. Those who practice infant baptism usually speak of the Spirit's being given in baptism, apart from the personal faith of the recipient. This appears to contradict Paul's clear teaching that the Spirit is not given through the works of the law (circumcision or, by analogy, baptism) but "by hearing with faith" (Galatians 3:2).

Conversion-initiation, or all that is connected with becoming a Christian, involves the church, the individual, and God. The church proclaims the saving grace of God in Christ. The church's involvement is still there even when one accepts Christ simply by reading the Bible, when there is no direct human witness. The Bible was given through the church, not only in the writing of it, but in the preservation, translation, and dissemination of it as well. The Holy Spirit uses the Word of God to open the hearts of those who hear. Though the individual cannot come to Christ apart from the ministry of the Spirit, one can use one's freedom to resist the Spirit and reject Christ. Thus becoming a Christian involves the personal decision of faith, accepting the Savior. The church endorses this decision of faith by administering baptism to the believer upon request. The Christian is then recognized as incorporated into the church. God keeps his promise by giving the Holy Spirit. Along with the gift of the Holy Spirit, God offers the forgiveness of sins, eternal life, and a new relationship as his child. The order given above in the enumeration of these elements is a logical one and does not indicate a necessary

74

sequence. The gift of the Holy Spirit is always contingent upon faith, but it may be received before baptism, at the time of baptism, or after baptism. The gift itself is not dependent upon anything which a person feels or any charismatic manifestations, but simply upon God's keeping his promise.

Spiritual Power

The contrast which the charismatics highlight between the tremendous power of the early church and the relative powerlessness of many churches and Christians today is not to be passed off lightly. It was said of Paul and his companions that they had turned the world upside down (Acts 17:6), but most Christians today hardly create a ripple in the water. In many areas of the world, Christianity evokes little opposition, and the attitude of the world toward the church is that it couldn't care less whether the church exists or not.

To be sure, there are Christians today who are aglow with the Spirit, and there are churches both inside and outside the charismatic movement where great spiritual power is manifest. But these are the exception and not the rule. Speaking generally, one may say that the biggest difficulty with Christianity today is that it lacks credibility. We Christians usually profess in words far more than we express in life. We profess Christ as Lord, but we live as though we ourselves are in control. We claim to have the Spirit, but we make most of our decisions without reference to his guidance. We talk about sports, politics, the weather, and even the church, but we are tongue-tied when it comes to talking about Jesus Christ as Lord.

Jesus promised his disciples that they would receive power when the Holy Spirit came upon them (Acts 1:8). We claim to have the Spirit. Where then is the power? This question should disturb us and cause us to cry out to God for a new and more profound appropriation of the Holy Spirit in the totality of our experience. When the battleship *Missouri* was stuck in the sands of the Chesapeake Bay, it took the rising tide to get it floating again. The mighty German tanks came crushing through the strongest defenses of the allied lines in the Battle of the Bulge during World War II, but when they ran out of gasoline, they came grinding to a halt. The best-conceived plans, strategies, and programs, apart from the blessing and power of the Holy Spirit, will not win the world to Christ.

Still there is some question about the way charismatics usually pose the problem. There is too much emphasis upon the bizarre, the unusual, the dramatically miraculous elements, as if power is to be identified with these and these alone. Whenever through the crucified

75

and risen Christ lives are cleansed, victory over sin is given, patience and courage in the face of adversity are demonstrated, the kind of love seen at Calvary is expressed, a winning witness to Christ is given, and Christlikeness of character is manifest—there the power of the Holy Spirit is revealed.

The salient contribution of Paul to the doctrine of the Holy Spirit is not his treatment of the *charismata,* the gifts of the Spirit, as important as that is. Rather, it is the inseparable way in which he links the Holy Spirit to Christ and interprets the work of the Holy Spirit in ethical terms, his description of the Spirit producing within us the character of Christ (Galatians 5:22-23). The power of the Holy Spirit is demonstrated not only in reference to the faith that removes mountains but also in terms of the love that suffers long and is kind. The Spirit guides us in our daily lives, inspires in us a consciousness that God is our Father and that we are his children, and helps us in our prayers (Romans 8:14-17, 26-27). He also enables us to put to death the deeds of the flesh (Romans 8; Galatians 5) and causes us in ever-increasing measure to reflect the glory of the risen Christ by working within us to refashion our lives into Christ's image (2 Corinthians 3:17-18).

The reason Christianity lacks credibility in the world today is not so much that we Christians are unable to work miracles as that our lives bear so little resemblance to Jesus Christ. Long ago Nietzsche sneered: "You Christians are going to have to look more redeemed for me to believe in your redeemer." The world speaks in a similar way to us today. In our churches we have placed all too little emphasis upon living by the Spirit, walking by the Spirit, and being filled with the Spirit. We have made also too much of a dichotomy between personal and social ethics. We have been content with poverty in the midst of affluence, with overstuffing ourselves while a large part of the world starves to death. We have talked about peace while preparing for war. We have mouthed platitudes about all people being created equal, while practicing discrimination on the basis of race and sex. We have sung, "This is my Father's world," while wantonly wasting its resources and polluting our environment. We seem more interested in preserving the status quo than in changing the world when our own material prosperity is at stake. Even when we try to do good on a world scale, too often it is with the obvious motive of trying to save ourselves by saving the world from communism, rather than seeking to minister to the world's needs.

There are no easy solutions to these problems, but when and if they are found, I feel sure they will involve accepting the lordship of

Christ with all of the radical implications involved, in really being open to the Spirit's leading and sensitive to human need, in forming Christian communities in which people are accepted as they are and thereby liberated to become what they ought to be, communities in which Christlike virtues are inculcated and spiritual power is manifest in all of the personal and social dimensions of Christian experience.

> O Spirit of the living God,
> Thou light and fire divine,
> Descend upon thy Church once more,
> And make it truly thine!
>
> Fill it with love and joy and pow'r,
> With righteousness and peace,
> Till Christ shall dwell in human hearts,
> And sin and sorrow cease.[34]

77

CHAPTER 4

Gifts of the Spirit
and
Speaking in Tongues

The charismatic movement gets its name from the Greek word *charismata*, grace gifts. It is one of the terms which Paul uses in 1 Corinthians 12 in a discussion of spiritual gifts in the body of Christ. Until recent years traditional Christianity (Protestant and Catholic) gave relatively little attention to spiritual gifts in either theology or worship. Now, largely because of the charismatic movement, the question of spiritual gifts has come to the forefront in the life of the church. The questions with regard to these gifts are so important to an understanding and evaluation of the charismatic movement itself that three chapters will be taken to deal with them. Throughout these next three chapters the charismatic interpretations related to the various topics will be set forth first, and then an appraisal of these interpretations and the issues involved will be made.

The Place of the Gifts

Charismatics of nearly every stripe are generally agreed with their Pentecostal forebears that baptism in the Spirit or the Pentecostal experience, by whatever name it may be called, is the gateway into a new dimension of life in the Spirit in which the gifts of the Spirit become operational. By the gifts of the Spirit they generally mean largely, though not always exclusively, the nine gifts of the Spirit enumerated by Paul in 1 Corinthians 12:8-10. They associate the operation of these gifts with the power that Jesus promised his disciples in Luke 24:49 and Acts 1:8. They regard them as supernatural, but not abnormal. They regard as subnormal any group or church which claims to be the body of Christ, but which is not open to these gifts.

They recognize that the supreme gift is the Holy Spirit and not any of the gifts that he bestows. But how, they ask, can you really be open to the Holy Spirit and his marvelous ministry without being open to his manifestations? Wherever the Holy Spirit is, he wants to manifest himself, and he manifests himself through the fruit he grows and the gifts he bestows. In their view, to say "I'll take the fruit, but you can have the gifts" is to quench the Spirit (1 Thessalonians 5:16-22) by trying to circumscribe the area of his operation and the manner of his manifestation.

Main-line Pentecostals have had a tendency to mix human works with divine grace (unmerited favor) in setting up preconditions for receiving baptism in the Spirit. Thus, when the breakthrough comes and one is "baptized in the Spirit," the gifts that are expressed are often accepted, either consciously or unconsciously, as merit badges that God pins on one's lapel to mark one off as "spiritual." Most leaders of the charismatic movement, both Protestant and Catholic, generally speaking, are aware of this pitfall and seek to avoid it themselves and warn others against it. They point out repeatedly that spiritual gifts are not merit badges or rewards for good behavior. Neither are they an evidence of special spiritual maturity, nor the measure of it. Rather they are gifts freely bestowed by God upon those who will receive them in childlike faith.

Charismatics are agreed that the context in which the gifts operate is the body of Christ, and the purpose for which they are given is the building up of the body for effective witness in the world. By the body they mean not just the local church, but any assembled group in which the recognition of the lordship of Christ breaks down barriers to fellowship and there is a real caring and sharing on a deep personal level. They think of the operation of the gifts not as solo performances that call attention to the individual through whom they flow, but as manifestations of the Spirit that exalt Christ and strengthen the brotherhood.

British charismatic author Michael Harper calls attention to the five words used in 1 Corinthians 12 to designate spiritual gifts. They are *pneumatika,* literally, "spirituals" (12:1). That is, they are spiritual endowments and as such are to be distinguished from natural gifts. They are *charismata* (12:4) and are thus gifts of God's grace and unmerited favor *(charis),* having nothing to do with human merit. The reference to them as *diakoniai* "services" (12:5), indicates that they are avenues of service for helping others. The term *energemata,* "powers" (12:6), designates them as momentary bursts of spiritual power or energy, rather than permanent endowments. They are also called a *phanerōsis,* "manifestation" (12:7). This means that unlike fruit of the Spirit, which are invisible graces, the gifts can be seen, heard, or felt.[1] Throughout this passage Paul emphasizes that there are varieties of gifts, but they all have one divine source, and the purpose that God has in manifesting them is the common good.

Many within the charismatic movement highlight the supernatural character of the gifts, distinguishing them sharply from ordinary human endowments or anything one learns on one's own. They understand them as direct channels for the Spirit of God, tools which the Lord uses to equip his people to do his work. On the other hand, there are charismatics who think that distinctions between the natural and the supernatural are imposed upon Paul, rather than endemic to his thought patterns. They say he shows neither a miracle-mongering preference for the more spectacular gifts of 1 Corinthians 12 nor an anti-supernaturalist bias toward the more commonplace gifts of Romans 12.[2] Many within the Catholic charismatic renewal seek to guard against interpreting the gifts as mere psychological states or sociological functions on the one hand and oversupernaturalizing them on the other. Still they emphasize that the Spirit is sovereign in his gifts and operates through these in mighty power.

Most charismatics recognize that the gifts can be abused and sometimes are. Michael Harper sounds a warning against what he calls "charismania," saying that there are charismaniacs everywhere. He deplores the fact that within the charismatic movement all kinds of extremists have been allowed to minister with little attempt being made to curb them for fear of being thought intolerant or unloving. He thinks the difficulty lies in the apparent inability of some charismatic leaders to distinguish between a critical spirit and the gift of discernment.[3]

According to Paul, charismatic gifts that are genuine will exalt Jesus as Lord (1 Corinthians 12:3). They should also express love and edify the Christian community (1 Corinthians 12-14). One German charismatic says that every gift, no matter how natural it may seem, is a *charisma,* grace gift, if it serves to exalt Christ and build up the community. On the other hand, every gift, no matter how supernatural it may appear, is stripped of its value if it serves to exalt the bearer of it and split the community.[4]

Charismatics tend to emphasize the gifts enumerated in 1 Corinthians 12:8-10, because they believe that these are the gifts that

81

traditional Christianity has neglected. They see the neglect as stemming partly from a false teaching which distinguishes between temporary and permanent gifts, regarding the more spectacular ones as never intended by God to be permanently expressed in his church. They think that this distinction has no solid basis in Scripture and that it is contradicted by their own experience. They recognize, however, that part of the problem has been the fear of abuse. The corrective for this, they believe, is not disuse, but proper use.

With these problems in mind charismatics frequently attack attitudes within traditional Christianity which make no room for the more spectacular gifts. They point out that many Christians who reject the gifts that Paul delineates in 1 Corinthians 12 stress the love which he sets forth in 1 Corinthians 13, as if gifts were an immature or inferior expression of Christianity to be displaced by love. Charismatics sometimes explain that love is not an alternative to the use of spiritual gifts, but a motive for striving for them. Far from being a substitute for love, the gifts are the medium which the Spirit uses for bringing love to concrete expression. In what better way, they ask, can love be expressed concretely than when the Spirit uses a word of wisdom to minister to someone struggling with a personal problem or when the gift of healing is manifest through the community to restore health to the sick? In 1 Corinthians 14:1 Paul says: "Make love your aim, and earnestly desire the spiritual gifts." As some charismatics see it, however, many Christians seem to read this passage as if it said; "Make love your aim and earnestly reject spiritual gifts." [5]

To a group of spiritual virtuosos in Corinth who were puffed up over their spiritual gifts Paul addressed the questions: "Are all apostles? Are all prophets? Are all teachers? Do all work miracles? Do all possess gifts of healing? Do all speak with tongues? Do all interpret?" (1 Corinthians 12:29-30). If Paul were addressing our churches today, we are told, probably he would ask rather: "Do *any* possess gifts of healing? Do *any* work miracles? Does *any* speak with tongues? Do *any* interpret?" [6]

Less in a spirit of confrontation, in a document in Malines, Belgium (hereafter referred to as the Malines Document), some Catholic charismatics point out that the difference between Christians in the early church and a community of Christians in the contemporary church is basically a difference of awareness, expectation, and openness. Recognizing that the Spirit usually does not manifest himself beyond the level of openness and expectation within the community, they suggest that the problem has been that often Christian communities have not been aware that such charisms (gifts) as prophecy, healing, working of miracles, speaking in tongues, and interpretation of tongues were real possibilities for the life of the church today. They interpret the charismatic renewal as saying that every local church and the church universal should be open to the full spectrum of the gifts. They emphasize the positive statements concerning the gifts in the documents of Vatican II, stating again and again that the church is basically charismatic, for church and charisms (gifts) go together. They see the goal of renewal as being the whole church renewed charismatically so that it no longer needs a distinct movement.[7]

Cardinal Suenens sounds some of the same views in his book *A New Pentecost?* He maintains that the charismatic dimension is vital to the very existence of the church. Without it the church would not be merely impoverished; rather its very being would be negated. He sees in the current charismatic renewal an evidence of the renewal of the church and calls the manifestations of the Spirit that are burgeoning everywhere "the buds that tell us spring has come." Likewise, he compares the charisms to a pipe organ played by the Holy Spirit. The melody that the organist desires cannot be produced unless each key responds properly to the organist's touch.[8]

83

Appraisal of Spiritual Gifts

The first task is that of seeking to discover if there is any sound basis for distinguishing some gifts as temporary and others as permanent. We should note that this type of thinking has never been a part of Catholic thought. Indeed, one of the prerequisites for the canonization of a saint in Catholic life is that there must be strong attestation that the person so canonized has worked miracles. Catholics, then, have not ordinarily rejected offhand the possibility of contemporary miracles. Rather, they have tended to think of the medium through which they operate as being not ordinary Christians, but "saints" in their special understanding of the word.

When we come to Protestantism, however, we find a different picture. There is a tendency to stress the temporary character of some of the gifts. One view is that the purpose of the miracle or sign gifts was to authenticate the Christian message in the days before the completion of Scripture. Now that the canon of Scripture has been completed, there is no longer a need for further display of the miraculous gifts. In the Pauline sense, they say, we no longer have apostles and prophets in our day. Neither are the gifts of miracles, healing, tongues, interpretation of tongues, and discerning of spirits in evidence. All these were temporary gifts never intended for the permanent life of the church. Those who take this view usually cite 1 Corinthians 13:8-9 in its support. Here it is said that Paul maintains that tongues and prophecy will pass away when the perfect is come. They usually interpret "that which is perfect" as referring to the Bible.[9]

Another view is that the purpose of the special supernatural gifts was the authentication of the apostles. Thus, we are told, some of those upon whom the apostles laid their hands received miracle-working power, but they were not able to pass this along to others. Miracles then inevitably passed from the scene with the death of the apostles and their disciples. In support of this view passages that emphasize miracles as authenticating the apostles are cited (Acts 14:3; Romans 15:18-19; 2 Corinthians 12:12; Hebrews 2:3-4). Those who take this view sometimes assert that nowhere does the New Testament tell us that we are to continue to manifest the miraculous gifts. Sometimes the proponents of this theory fuse it with the first view in saying that the disappearance of the miraculous gifts is no great loss to the church, because we now have the complete Bible. To insist that the church still needs miraculous signs today, they say, is to overlook the finality of the Scriptures.[10]

In at least one of these gifts the distinction between the temporary and the permanent is valid. We no longer have apostles today in the sense of those who as witnesses to the resurrection and recipients of God's primal revelation laid the foundation for the Christian church for all ages (Acts 1:22; Ephesians 2:20). The recognition of this fact, however, does not provide a solid basis for making the type of broad distinction between the so-called miraculous and nonmiraculous gifts that is outlined in the theories described above.

It seems to me that these theories will not stand for two reasons. First, they are not well grounded biblically. It is poor exegesis to appeal to 1 Corinthians 13:8-9 in support of the idea that tongues and prophecy are temporary, for in the context of that passage "that which is perfect" refers not to the completed Scriptures, but to the complete revelation of Christ which will come when we see him "face to face." A misunderstanding is manifest also in the interpretation of the purpose of miracles and spiritual gifts that is expressed. Not only did the miracles of Jesus bear witness to the fact that he was the Christ, the bearer of the kingdom, but also they gave expression to the compassion of Jesus. Such compassion was manifest also in most of the miracles performed by the apostles through the Spirit. The

84

New Testament affirms that the new age has dawned, that the kingdom is a present reality. If that is true today, we have no basis for dismissing miracles out of court. Paul speaks of the spiritual gifts that are in dispute as having been given by the Spirit for the edification of the body of Christ. If those gifts served to edify the body then, what basis do we have for thinking they could not bring edification in our day? Some interpreters who insist on the temporary character of the miraculous gifts say that the New Testament nowhere promises that these gifts will continue. This argument can be turned around. Nowhere does it say that they will not continue. Rather, the implication is that they will, for, according to John 14:12, Jesus promised that his disciples would continue his works and do even greater ones, and Hebrews 13:8 says that "Jesus Christ is the same yesterday and today and forever."

A second reason for rejecting the theory of the temporary nature of the gifts is that there is good evidence for believing that the Holy Spirit still bestows his gifts upon his people when there is an attitude of openness and expectancy. I once viewed the miraculous manifestations of the Spirit as temporary in design and expressed this view in an article on "The Problem of Miracles" in the April, 1956, issue of the *Review and Expositor*. However, what I have seen, heard, read, thought, felt, and experienced since then has convinced me that I was wrong. When fact and theory collide, the better part of wisdom is to revise or discard the theory in the light of the facts rather than stubbornly to hold to the theory in defiance of the facts. In my judgment, views of the temporary nature of the gifts should be buried.

This does not mean, however, that one should accept as a genuine gift of the Spirit everything that purports to go under that name. There are too many obvious counterfeits around for that. It does mean that in principle one should not reject the full spectrum of the gifts mentioned in Scripture as a live possibility in our day and, if strong evidence indicates that they are still operational, one should acknowledge the presence of spiritual gifts.

Problems still exist, however, even when the theoretical hurdle is eliminated. The fear of abuse lingers on. The kind of candor that Michael Harper demonstrates in talking about "charismaniacs everywhere" is refreshing. Indeed among the most hopeful signs that are appearing within the charismatic movement these days is a growing evidence of the capacity for self-criticism and the ability of the movement, to a certain extent, to correct itself in the light of obvious mistakes. But if there is charismania on the one hand, there is charisphobia (to coin a word) on the other. Perhaps fear of the gifts, because the expression of them is unpredictable and because they are not easily subject to human control and are subject to abuse, accounts for a lack of openness to the gifts in many quarters. All of God's gifts can be abused—administration and teaching as well as tongues and healing. Paul was fully aware of the abuse to which the gifts are liable, but this never led him to repudiate the gifts as such. The remedy for abuse, as some of our charismatic brethren have reminded us, is not disuse, but correct use.

In the charismatic movement the stress falls upon the gifts enumerated in 1 Corinthians 12:8-10. We need to remember, however, that this is only one of several lists found in the New Testament. Other lists are to be found in 1 Corinthians 12:28, 29-30; Romans 12:6-8; Ephesians 4:11-12; 1 Peter 4:9-11. There is a good deal of overlapping in the lists. Since all of the gifts mentioned in one place do not appear in all the other places, not even in Paul's letters, it is reasonable to conclude that the lists are merely examples of the Spirit's operation, not fixed formulas. It is true that, generally speaking, the church in the past has neglected the more spectacular or miraculous gifts. This fact, however, should not lead us to overemphasize them in the present. This would be trying to correct one distortion by introducing another.

How are we to view the gifts? They are genuine gifts from God, sovereignly bestowed. He is the source. Every Christian has at least one gift. It is implied that no particular gift is had by all (1 Corinthians 12:29-30) and that no one has all of the gifts. Paul's point in the analogy of the body and its members is the diversity of gifts within the body. The ear does not have the gift of seeing, nor the eye the gift of hearing. Each member of the body has a function and is needed for the healthy operation of the body. Each member needs the others. To change the analogy, what God wants is not a one-man band, but an orchestra in which each member makes a contribution to the music produced by the group. Since the gifts are sovereignly bestowed, and each has a divinely appointed function, there is no basis for a sense of superiority on the part of some, nor of a sense of inferiority on the part of others. Twice Paul enjoins the Corinthians earnestly to desire (literally, to be zealous for) spiritual gifts (1 Corinthians 12:31; 14:1). He qualifies this injunction, however, by specifying the higher gifts in the first case and emphasizing prophecy particularly in the second. This seems to imply that an openness for certain gifts or even a zeal for them might have something to do with their becoming operational in one's life.

The gifts are not to be regarded as something one has, like a boy

86

having a certain number of marbles in his pocket. The gifts are not static but are evidences of the Spirit coming to expression through various members of the body. A charism has the character of an event, "the experience of grace and power *in a particular instance and only for that instance.*"[11] The gifts are not to be confused with natural talents or abilities, though they may not be completely unrelated. The charisms are not examples of God blessing the efforts of his people. Rather, they are instances of God expressing himself through his people.

The charismatic movement rightly emphasizes the body as the context for the operation of the gifts and the building up of the body for effective witness in the world as the purpose for their manifestation. Indeed one of the greatest contributions of the movement is the profound sense that expresses itself within it of Christians ministering to one another through the gifts that the Holy Spirit inspires. Here you do not have the clergy ministering to the laity, but all ministering to each other through the manifestations of the Spirit given to the body. Despite this, within the movement there are a lot of "lone ranger" charismatics, running here and there, seeking to minister to anybody and everybody, whether there is an openness for their ministry or not.

Since all Christians have spiritual gifts, all Christians are charismatics. In this sense we have to recognize that the reference made throughout this book to certain people as charismatics in distinction from others has a nonbiblical ring. It is a concession to current usage. It is employed because of the lack of a better way of expressing the distinctions intended.

Charismatics connect the operation of the gifts with spiritual power, often saying that as the character of Christ is demonstrated through the fruit of the Spirit (Galatians 5:22-23), so the power of Christ is manifest through the gifts (1 Corinthians 12:8-10). There is a connection between the gifts and power; otherwise they would have no value in edifying the body. Moreover, the operation of the gifts can be a powerful force in evangelism, as many stories in the book of Acts clearly show (for example, the healing of the lame man at the gate of the temple, Acts 3–4). But there are different kinds of power. There is the power of love, the power of a Christlike character, the power of truth, and the power of the cross. The assumption that only certain gifts are evidence of divine power is a false assumption. Think what a loss the world would have suffered had Christ used supernatural power to overwhelm his enemies and come down from the cross! The wisdom of God is much more profound than human understanding. Sometimes God's power is demonstrated in what appears to be human weakness.

Tongues and Interpretation of Tongues

As we have already taken note, it was the linking of tongues to the experience of baptism in the Spirit that touched off the Pentecostal movement. Through Pentecostalism the experience of tongues passed over into main-line Protestantism and through the resulting Protestant Neo-Pentecostalism into Catholicism. The importance that is attached to this experience varies among Neo-Pentecostals (Protestant and Catholic), but, generally speaking, speaking in tongues does not have quite the centrality in the experience of Protestant and Catholic charismatics as it has in main-line Pentecostalism. Indeed some highly respected Catholic charismatics say that the central issue in the renewal is not speaking in tongues but fullness of life in the Holy Spirit. Accordingly, they say that the purpose of the renewal is not to get everybody speaking in tongues but to have the whole church become so open to the full spectrum of the charisms that a separate movement will no longer be needed. They think that the centrality ascribed to tongues comes more from people outside the renewal than from those inside.[12]

Most charismatics would agree with Larry Christenson's definition of tongues as "a supernatural manifestation of the Holy Spirit, whereby the believer speaks forth in a language which he has never learned, and which he does not understand."[13] They appeal to Acts 2:4 and 1 Corinthians 14:13-14 for the basic ingredients of this definition. They interpret Acts 2:4 to mean that the believer does the speaking while the Holy Spirit supplies the words. In this process there is a disengagement of the mind and the speech apparatus so that the speaker's mind neither chooses the words that are spoken nor understands what is said. They believe, moreover, that this understanding of tongues accords with the teachings of Scripture and is verified in their own experience.

They often speak of this as an example of divine-human cooperation. The tongues speaker is not compelled to speak but chooses to do so. The words he or she speaks, however, are not spoken under his or her own power but through the ability which the Holy Spirit supplies. Charismatics sometimes express it this way: "Without the Holy Spirit you can't, but without you the Holy Spirit won't."[14]

In this light it is not difficult to understand why charismatics almost with one accord object to tongues being labeled "ecstatic utterance." They believe that such terms as "ecstatic utterance," "the language of ecstasy," "tongues of ecstasy," "ecstatic speech," and "ecstatic language" in the *New English Bible* (1 Corinthians 12–14) are not real translations of the original, but interpretations, and inaccurate ones at that. They think that the term "ecstasy" connotes one's being swept away in extreme emotion so that one loses personal control. In 1 Corinthians 14 Paul speaks of tongues as being subject to the control of the speaker. Those who claim to have this gift say that they can start and stop speaking at will; they can speak softly or loudly, as they so desire. Often no emotion at all accompanies this sort of speech. To describe it in terms of "ecstatic utterance," they think, is to confuse tongues in the Bible and in the contemporary charismatic movement with similar pagan manifestations, ancient and modern.

Most charismatics believe that in the practice of tongues real languages, human or angelic, are spoken, though there are some charismatics who take exception to this view.[15] Charismatics say that unless the exercise of tongues is a public utterance which calls for the companion gift, interpretation of tongues, it makes no difference that no one understands. The speech is prayer inspired by the Holy Spirit and addressed to God. It is sufficient that God understands. However, many charismatics point out that on certain rare occasions someone who hears the tongue recognizes it as an identifiable language, just as on the day of Pentecost. There are numerous stories of this kind, some of them involving miraculously given messages coming at some crucial point in the life of the hearer.[16] These cases, however, are unusual, and most charismatics agree that the normal use of tongues, except in a public meeting when it is accompanied by the gift of interpretation, is to communicate with God, not to convey a message to others.

Sometimes critics of tongues say that, if through this gift real languages are spoken, missionaries who have the gift of tongues ought to be able to communicate with those to whom they are sent without learning the language. Charismatics object strongly to this kind of reasoning. They say that it reflects a basic misunderstanding of the nature of tongues and the purpose for which the gift is given. One does not choose one's own tongue; it is given by the Holy Spirit. Moreover, the tongue is given to enable one to praise God more effectively, not to make it possible for one to escape the drudgery of having to learn a new language.

Charismatics often distinguish between tongues as a sign and tongues as a gift. In referring to tongues as a sign, they usually interpret it as the initial evidence or one of the initial evidences of the experience of baptism in the Spirit. With this distinction they do not mean to imply that this sign is not given by the Holy Spirit, but they refer to it as the gift of tongues only if it remains as a continuing part of the life and experience of the believer. There are many, they say, who experience tongues in connection with their baptism in the Spirit who are never able to speak in tongues again.

What biblical basis do charismatics have for interpreting tongues as a sign that one has received the baptism in the Spirit? Charismatics usually explain this along the following lines: When Paul asked the Ephesians, "Did you receive the Holy Spirit when you believed?" (Acts 19:2), he expected them to be able to answer very clearly one way or the other. For the early church, receiving the Holy Spirit was a very definite experience normally accompanied by charismatic manifestations, the most conspicuous of which was speaking in tongues. Speaking in tongues was one of the outward manifestations of the coming of the Holy Spirit at Pentecost (Acts 2). It was the sole manifestation mentioned in connection with the Gentile Pentecost (Acts 10), and it appeared along with prophecy when the disciples at Ephesus received the Holy Spirit (Acts 19:1-7). Tongues are not mentioned specifically in Acts 8, but there must have been some dazzling manifestation of the Spirit because of the impression made upon Simon the magician. There is no more plausible suggestion than that it was tongues. We are not told in Acts 9 that Paul spoke in tongues. However, Paul himself says in 1 Corinthians 14:18 that he spoke in tongues more than any of the Christians at Corinth. He may have begun this practice when he was filled with the Spirit (Acts 9:17-18). Thus, the argument goes, the pattern is established in Acts. Definitely in three cases, probably in four, and possibly in five, speaking in tongues was the initial evidence of baptism in the Spirit.

90

Most Protestant charismatics, like their Pentecostal forebears, interpret tongues in the early church and in contemporary experience as a fulfillment of the prophecy of Jesus: "And these signs will accompany those who believe: in my name they will cast out demons; they will speak in new tongues . . ." (Mark 16:17). Usually they omit the rest of the passage, as we have done here, and they make no mention of a textual problem in regard to the ending of the Gospel of Mark. Catholic charismatics in the Malines Document, to which reference has already been made, refer to the passage as canonical, though probably not Markan.[17]

Generally speaking, the nearer charismatics stand in their basic charismatic theology to classical Pentecostalism, the more they insist upon tongues as the sign of baptism in the Spirit. There are some Protestant charismatics who insist that tongues, and nothing else, is, according to the New Testament, the indubitable proof of baptism in the Spirit. On the other side of the spectrum are those charismatics, Protestants and Catholics, who regard such a position as religious fanaticism. They think it does untold harm by trying to impose a law of tongues upon the interpretation of the New Testament. In between are all kinds of fine shades of interpretation. For the most part, Catholic charismatics place less emphasis upon tongues as a sign of the Holy Spirit's operation in one's life than their Protestant counterparts. The Malines Document, for example, says: "It is now generally recognized that what is called 'baptism in the Spirit' is not in any necessary way tied to tongues."[18]

Many charismatics acknowledge that often when Christians begin speaking in tongues they have doubts as to whether the experience is authentic, whether the Spirit is giving the words, or whether they are just making them up. Frequently, charismatics of long standing seek to quell these doubts that newcomers to the experience have by pointing out that after Jesus was baptized in the Spirit, he was thrust into the wilderness to be tempted of the devil. They reassure those who have doubts by appealing to Luke 11:9-13. No human father would give his child a serpent instead of a fish, or a scorpion in place of an egg. Neither will God, they say, give a counterfeit when you ask for the real thing.

So far we have been discussing tongues as a sign or evidence of baptism in the Spirit. Now we come to consider it as a continuing gift of the Spirit. The gift manifests itself, we are told, in two ways. By far the more common way is as a devotional gift to enrich one's personal prayer life. According to one prominent Protestant charismatic, it accounts for 99.99 percent of all speaking in tongues.[19] Often referred to as one's private prayer language, it is largely a gift of exalted praise (Acts 10:46; 1 Corinthians 14:2). Those who have had the experience say that it enables them to break the language barrier and express the inexpressible. It has the nature of a response to the wonder and glory of God. Far from being a substitute for prayer in one's own language, they say, it stimulates such prayer in warm, spontaneous, heartfelt praise.

Charismatics frequently call praying in tongues "praying in the Spirit" (Ephesians 6:18; Jude 20). Prayer in the Spirit, they say, may also take the form of intercession. Charismatics point out that often we face situations in which for one reason or another we do not know

91

how to pray as we ought. In such cases, they say, when one prays in tongues, the Holy Spirit helps one to pray, interceding for the saints according to the will of God (Romans 8:26-27).

A second use of tongues is in public worship, when, according to Paul in 1 Corinthians 14, an interpretation is required. This usage may be prayer in a public meeting which needs interpretation so other believers can express their agreement (1 Corinthians 14:13-16). Or it may come in the form of a message which, when coupled with interpretation, has the value of prophecy (1 Corinthians 14:5, 27-33). Thus, speaking in tongues in a worship service is different from praying in tongues in private when no interpretation is needed. According to Paul, the interpretation may come from the one who speaks or from someone else (1 Corinthians 14:13, 27). If one speaks without interpretation, one will be simply speaking into the air, and it will have no edificatory value (1 Corinthians 14:6-9). Therefore, if there is no one to interpret, according to Paul, one should "keep silence in the church and speak to himself and to God" (1 Corinthians 14:28). With these words of Paul in mind some charismatics emphasize 1 Corinthians 14:13 where Paul puts the responsibility on the one who speaks in tongues in public to be prepared to interpret. Paul limits the number of manifestations of this kind in a single service to two or three, and these are to be given in turn, not simultaneously (14:27). As is the case when any prophecy is given, those who hear have the responsibility of weighing what is said (1 Corinthians 14:29). Charismatics understand these regulations given by Paul as not intended to suppress speaking in tongues and prophecy but to regulate them (1 Corinthians 14:33, 40).

In emphasizing the value of speaking in tongues, charismatics appeal to all of the positive things Paul says about this gift in 1 Corinthians 12-14. This charism is clearly spoken of as a gift of God (12:8, 10, 28). If it had no abiding value, God would not have ordained it. When one speaks in tongues, one utters mysteries in the Spirit and edifies oneself (14:2,4). Paul says that he will pray with the Spirit and that he will pray with the understanding, that he will sing with the spirit and with the understanding (14:15). Obviously, they say, Paul sees value in both kinds of praying and singing. He says to the Corinthians, "I want you all to speak in tongues" (14:5). He places a special value on the private use of tongues, for he says, "I thank God that I speak in tongues more than you all . . ." (14:18). And to avoid being misunderstood, after setting forth some regulations for tongues in public worship, he says clearly: "Do not forbid speaking in tongues" (14:39).

There are several other values which charismatics frequently ascribe to speaking in tongues. Many of them think of it as a doorway that leads to the other gifts. Countless are the testimonies of those who say that by yielding to this gift they entered into a new dimension of life in the Spirit. Many charismatics think of it as a means by which the Holy Spirit is able to bypass the censor of the conscious mind and have new access to the depths of the subconscious. Often, we are told, there is the healing of profound psychological wounds, along with the welling up of spontaneous praise. Great stress is laid upon a new experience of freedom that often attends the exercise of this gift. Many Jesus people testify that through the deep sense of the presence of God in their lives which came in connection with their speaking in tongues they were able to break the drug habit. They emphasize that a power not their own enabled them to do this without the terrible withdrawal symptoms called "cold turkey," which most people who have been hooked on drugs experience when the drugs are withdrawn.

Is the experience of tongues then intended for everyone? Most charismatics say that it is open to everyone. They believe that the gift of prayer and praise through tongues is not intended for an elite group but that it is meant to be "a normal experience for all Christians."[20] Paul could say, "Now I want you all to speak in tongues" (1 Corinthians 14:5). They say this suggests that tongues is a charism granted in principle to all Christians. How, then, can 1 Corinthians 14:5 be reconciled with 1 Corinthians 12:30 where Paul in asking, "Do all speak with tongues?" obviously expects a negative reply? The answer that most charismatics give to this is that in 12:30 Paul is speaking about the exercise of the gift in public meetings, not its use in private devotions. Some suggest that in 12:30 Paul is not talking about the gift of tongues, which is open to all, but about a public ministry of speaking in tongues, which is limited in scope.

Charismatics frequently lay their hands upon people when they pray for them to receive the baptism in the Spirit with the manifestation of tongues. They justify this practice by citing Acts 8:14-17 and 19:6. They believe that this is often an aid in helping others have this experience, but not a necessary precondition (Acts 10:44-48). There are many testimonies of people having received this experience at the time of being prayed for in this manner or shortly thereafter. There are also many testimonies of people having begun to speak in tongues when no one had laid hands upon them.

Interpretation of tongues, as we have already seen, is described by Paul and understood by charismatics as a companion gift to the

93

gift of tongues used in public worship. The purpose of the gift is to render the tongue intelligible, and the value of the gift is that through it a message is communicated for the edification of the body. Charismatics understand this to mean that the two gifts when exercised together have the same value as prophecy (1 Corinthians 14:5, 27-33). They understand this not as a translation in the sense that one first understands the words individually and their grammatical connection in a sentence and then translates. Rather they explain it as a gift of inspiration by which one is able to express the meaning of an utterance in tongues without reference to the meaning of individual words and rules of grammar. The basic accuracy of the interpretation is often confirmed, charismatics say, by the fact that within a given congregation several people frequently receive the same basic impression of the meaning of the message in tongues as the one which is later given by someone else in a public interpretation. Among charismatics, however, there are relatively few people who ever receive or manifest this gift.

Agnes Sanford relates a story of a woman in a meeting speaking out in perfect Hebrew and having it translated accurately in English by another woman, when neither the tongues speaker nor the interpreter understood Hebrew. She says that the story was related to her by a seminary professor who understands Hebrew and was in the meeting when this took place. He had gone to the meeting not as a charismatic but simply as one interested in the operation of the Holy Spirit.[21]

Appraisal of Tongues and Interpretation of Tongues

The technical term for speaking in tongues is glossolalia. It is formed from two Greek words, *glossa* and *lalein. Lalein* means "to speak." *Glossa* can mean "tongue" in the sense of the organ of speech (Mark 7:33) or it can mean "tongue" in the sense of a language (Revelation 5:9). Some think a third meaning, that of inspired or ecstatic utterance, is indicated in the New Testament passages that refer to speaking in tongues (for example, throughout 1 Corinthians 12-14). There are passages which speak of "new tongues" (Mark 16:17), "other tongues" (Acts 2:4), and "kinds of tongues," (1 Corinthians 12:10, 28). The New Testament never speaks of an "unknown tongue," though the word "unknown" is inserted before "tongue" in some passages in the King James Version in 1 Corinthians 14. The word "unknown" is printed in italics to indicate that it is not in the original language.

Speaking in tongues is mentioned explicitly in only three books in the Bible, Acts (2:4; 4:13 form the broader context; 10:46; 19:6), 1 Corinthians (chapters 12-14), and Mark (16:17). There is a serious question as to whether Mark 16:9-20 is to be regarded as a part of Mark, a textual problem that we will consider later. Many think a reference to tongues is implicit in Romans 8:26-27; 1 Thessalonians 5:19-20; Ephesians 6:18; Jude 20; Ephesians 5:19; and Colossians 3:16.

A question immediately arises about the relationship between tongues in Acts and First Corinthians. It is clear that in Acts 2, Luke intends for us to understand that a miracle took place which involved communication, either through the disciples speaking foreign languages or dialects unknown to them, or through people hearing them, or both. It is probable that Luke thinks of this as the reversal of what occurred when there was a confusion of tongues in connection with the building of the Tower of Babel (Genesis 11:1-9). There is no indication that the tongues mentioned in Acts 19:6 are to be thought of as a form of intelligible speech. The situation is not so clear in Acts 10:46, but the probability is that the experience was essentially the same as that in Acts 19:6.

Three main theories have been advanced to indicate the relationship between tongues in Acts 2 and in 1 Corinthians 12–14. One view is that the tongues are basically the same. In both cases they are genuine foreign languages (whether languages of earth or heaven). The main difference is that on the day of Pentecost the Spirit simply gave to the believers languages that could be understood by their hearers. The opposite view is that the tongues in Acts 2 and First Corinthians are decidedly different. The tongues at Corinth were a cheap imitation of the real thing. At Pentecost the tongues were real languages, intelligible to the hearers, and speaking in tongues united the people. At Corinth the tongues were a meaningless gibberish, and their exercise brought disunity. A third view is that the tongues on the day of Pentecost and later at Corinth were essentially the same, but this is obscured by the way Luke treats the sources that lie behind his narrative. According to this view, Luke, for theological reasons of his own, weaves a "language source" into an account of Pentecost in which originally the foreign language idea was not involved. By eliminating Luke's "language source" (the word *heterais,* "other," in Acts 2:4 and all verses of 2:6b-11), a picture of glossolalia remains, we are told, which is fully consistent with that in Acts 10:46 and 19:6 and First Corinthians. Most glossolalists support the first view; many conservative scholars who reject modern-day glossolalia advocate the second; and a majority of critical scholars agree basically with the

95

third.[22] A fourth possible view is that the phenomenon of glossolalia in 1 Corinthians 12–14 is different from that in Acts 2, but that both passages bear witness to valid workings of the Holy Spirit. This view seems to be the best explanation of the scriptural evidence.

The only detailed discussion of glossolalia to be found in the New Testament is in 1 Corinthians 12–14; so we are dependent upon this source for our fundamental understanding of this phenomenon. In Corinth it was obviously a problem, but so was the Lord's Supper. Did the problem lie in the nature of glossolalia itself, or in the basic character of the Corinthian church, where immorality was not frowned on, the Lord's Supper was abused, and the resurrection was denied by some and misunderstood by others? There spiritual gifts which had been intended by God for the edification of the body had become the occasion for strife and divisions.

In the church at Corinth there were some who prided themselves on the spiritual gift which they possessed and made others feel worthless and inferior, as though they had nothing to contribute to the body. They ranked tongues as the most important gift and ostentatiously exercised the gift before others. There seems to have been an almost endless number of tongues speakers, many of them speaking simultaneously and without interpretation. The result was bedlam in services of worship intended for the glory and praise of God. Paul wrote to correct this situation. He made a number of concessions to the tongues speakers. He acknowledged tongues as a genuine gift, admitted that he himself spoke in tongues more than any of them, conceded that in one's personal devotional life the exercise of the gift brings edification, and expressly said that speaking in tongues should not be forbidden and that he wanted them all to speak in tongues. If Paul's intention was to quash the practice, he chose a strange method to arrive at his objective! Paul was writing to regulate abuse rather than to encourage disuse of this gift.

Nevertheless, none of his concessions was an unqualified one. He acknowledged speaking in tongues as a genuine gift (1 Corinthians 12:10), but whereas the Corinthians placed it at the head of the list, he placed it at the bottom (12:8-10, 29-30). He admitted that he spoke in tongues more than any of them but said, "nevertheless, in church I would rather speak five words with my mind, in order to instruct others, than ten thousand words in a tongue" (14:18-19). He said that speaking in tongues edifies the individual, but contrasted it with prophecy which edifies the church (14:4). He said that he wanted them all to speak in tongues, but that more than this he wanted them to prophesy (14:5). He said, ". . .

earnestly desire to prophesy, and do not forbid speaking in tongues" (14:39). In other words he accepted tongues, but showed a strong preference for prophecy. His criterion for evaluation was that prophecy edifies the congregation, but the exercise of tongues without interpretation does not.

Implicit in Paul's thinking is a distinction between the private devotional use of tongues and the exercise of tongues in public. Without this distinction, verses 18 and 19 of chapter 14 do not make sense. In verse 18 he says that he is thankful that he speaks in tongues more than any of them. Then in verse 19 he says that he had rather speak five words with his understanding than ten thousand words in a tongue, a proportion of one to two thousand. The key to the interpretation is found in the words "nevertheless, in church" with which he prefaces the latter statement. Obviously he speaks in tongues in private rather than in public. Paul has nothing to say against the use of tongues in one's private devotions. He does not try to regulate this in any way. The whole burden of his argument is directed against abuse of tongues in public worship, because the practices of tongues speakers are not only sowing the seeds of dissension within the congregation but are disrupting the public worship services as well. Even so, Paul does not forbid the use of tongues. Rather, he specifies that the companion gift of interpretation is to be exercised along with it so it will have some edificatory value for those who hear. He insists that not more than two or three are to speak in this way in one service, and that these are to speak in turn, not simultaneously. Paul's fundamental premise is that since God is not a God of confusion but of peace, everything is to be done decently and in order (14:33, 40).

97

Now we are in a position to evaluate some of the claims made for glossolalia by modern-day glossolalists. What about the claim of many charismatics that glossolalia is a sign of baptism in the Holy Spirit, *the* initial evidence or one of the initial evidences that indicates that one has entered a new dimension in one's spiritual life? Our survey of this problem has indicated that charismatics themselves vary widely in their interpretation of this question. There seems to be a move among charismatics away from the hard line of the Pentecostal position. This is a hopeful sign. Unfortunately, among Protestants the more liberal attitude seems not to have penetrated very deeply at the grass roots level. The situation among Catholic charismatics is brighter at this point.

The interpretation of glossolalia as the sign or initial evidence of baptism in the Spirit is to be rejected. The first and fundamental reason is that this doctrine lacks the biblical support that it needs. In the Pentecostal system of doctrine this interpretation of tongues ranks in importance with the doctrine of justification by faith, that one's standing before God is based not upon any works of one's own but upon God's grace (unmerited favor) received in simple childlike trust. Now there can be no question about the secure biblical foundation of the doctrine of justification. The interpretation of tongues as the evidence of the coming of the Spirit simply does not have this kind of biblical support.

Here at this point we find some of the worst examples of biblical interpretation to be found among charismatics. Too many of them have simply borrowed from classical Pentecostalism at its weakest points—biblical exegesis and theology. The doctrine in question is based solely upon three or four incidents in the book of Acts and upon the long, controversial ending of the Gospel of Mark. In Acts the doctrine is not anchored in any clear teaching. It is simply a human inference from some incidents recorded by Luke. This inference is then treated as a doctrine. The problem with this procedure has been pointed out again and again by able interpreters of the Scriptures. Christian doctrines should be rooted in the didactic or teaching sections of Scripture rather than in the historical parts. The historical sections are to be understood as recording what happened, not necessarily what should or must happen.

98

James D. G. Dunn provides some valuable insights into the problems connected with relying too much upon Luke's accounts at this point. He concedes that in Luke's presentation glossolalia was *a* manifestation of the Spirit's coming, but so was praise of God (Acts 10:45), prophecy (19:6), bold speech (4:8ff., 31), and powerful speech (13:9ff.). He strongly denies, however, that in Luke's view, glossolalia was *the* manifestation of the Spirit. Dunn thinks that the type of glossolalia indicated in Acts was "ecstatic speech, a veritable torrent of utterance." Luke manifests a strong interest in various forms of charismatic, ecstatic, and miraculous phenomena, but he shows little awareness that similar phenomena occurred frequently in those days in non-Christian settings. He makes no effort to show the distinctiveness of the Christian phenomena, manifests no awareness that glossolalia, prophecy, and other charismatic gifts are subject to abuse, and gives no criteria for differentiating the true from the false. He fails to relate the experience of the Spirit to the experience of Sonship, an emphasis which was so important both in the experience of Jesus and in the interpretations of Paul. He should have known the limitations of these charismatic phenomena because the problems involved with glossolalia, false prophecy, and the like were evident in the church at the time Luke wrote. In short, according to Dunn, Luke gives a lop-sided historical account. And, says Dunn, "To draw theological conclusions from a lop-sided historical account is to saddle oneself with a lop-sided theology."[23] This is the basic mistake, I believe, that Pentecostals and many other charismatics have made.

A second example of a faulty use of Scripture is seen in the way charismatics frequently appeal to Mark 16:17-18 to support their view that Jesus foretold and desired the use of tongues among his followers. Again and again they quote this passage to indicate Jesus' endorsement of tongues, but they omit the part of the passage which speaks of handling serpents and drinking poison. Obviously, they do not want to be identified with the snake handlers! But they cannot have it both ways. They cannot claim Jesus' support for speaking in tongues without at the same time recognizing his approval of snake handling.

Most charismatics show no recognition of the textual problem involved in Mark 16:9-20. The Malines Document, produced by reputable Catholic charismatics and noncharismatics in sympathy with charismatic experience, is an exception here. The fact of the matter is that verses 9-20 of chapter 16 do not stand in the oldest and most reliable manuscripts of the Gospel of Mark. There is a high degree of unanimity among textual critics that the Gospel of Mark either ends with verse 8 or that the original ending of the Gospel has been lost. Two shorter endings and various combinations of obviously spurious endings are found among the manuscripts. What we have in Mark 16:9-20 is a reflection of second-century theological interests in baptismal regeneration, exorcism of demons, speaking in tongues, handling of serpents, drinking poison, and healing the sick.[24] In recognizing this fact, we are not tampering with the Word of God. We are showing respect for it by pointing out the secondary nature of these verses. Thus, it is not legitimate to appeal to these verses to give speaking in tongues the authority of Jesus. There is no evidence either that speaking in tongues was a part of Jesus' experience. The closest one can come to connecting tongues with Jesus is to say that the risen Lord was the source of that which occurred at Pentecost, and this included speaking in tongues (Acts 2:33).

Paul never treats glossolalia as an indication of any kind of higher spirituality. Rather there are suggestions that Paul looked upon the undue importance and significance that some Corinthian glossolalists attached to this gift and the undisciplined use which

99

they made of it as an evidence of spiritual immaturity (1 Corinthians 14:20). He did speak of glossolalia as a sign, but not in the same way that Pentecostals and Neo-Pentecostals do. He spoke of it as a sign not to the believer but to the unbeliever, and the context of the passage seems to indicate that he thought of it as a judgment which would confirm the unbeliever in unbelief (1 Corinthians 14:22). If Paul does not support the interpretation in question, neither does any other part of the New Testament.

The conclusion then is inevitable. Nowhere in the New Testament is there a secure support for the Pentecostal, Neo-Pentecostal view which interprets glossolalia as *the* sign or initial evidence of the entrance of the Spirit into one's life.

Our second objection to recognizing tongues as the sign of Spirit baptism is that this interpretation is the incubator of spiritual pride. The conclusion inevitably follows that those who speak in tongues have the Spirit, while those who have not had this experience do not have him. The least of the gifts is treated as the most important because it becomes the criterion for separating the "haves" from the "have nots." It sows the seeds of division within any Christian community by arbitrarily dividing Christians into two classes, first-class citizens who have had this experience and second-class ones who have not.

A third reason for rejecting the Pentecostal, Neo-Pentecostal interpretation of tongues as a sign is that, if it is a sign, it is certainly not self-authenticating. Glossolalia is not a phenomenon that is peculiar to the Christian faith. It appears in many non-Christian religions. Most charismatics recognize that glossolalia can be counterfeited. Many of them admit that when they began the practice of glossolalia, they had doubts about whether the experience was genuine. Then someone reassured them, they say, by quoting Luke 11:11-13 and saying that our heavenly Father would not give a stone to his children instead of bread, nor a scorpion in place of an egg. The parallel passage in Matthew, which is probably more original, has "good things" where Luke has "the Holy Spirit." The context says nothing about tongues. This is another instance of faulty use of Scripture in seeking to equate speaking in tongues with receiving the Holy Spirit.

When the question of how true Christian glossolalia can be distinguished from false glossolalia is raised, many charismatics answer "by the spiritual fruit that is manifest" (see Galatians 5:22-23). This is a good answer, but it leaves the glossolalist in a strange position if he wants to defend glossolalia as a sign. The reason is that glossolalia which itself is supposed to be *a* sign or *the* sign authenticating baptism in the Spirit has to be authenticated by another sign. This reinforces our conclusion: if glossolalia is a sign, it is not a self-authenticating one. It either has to be accepted on faith or authenticated by another sign. If it has to be authenticated by another sign, it is of little value as a sign. If it has to be accepted on faith, why can one not accept the presence of the Holy Spirit in one's life without any such sign? The Holy Spirit himself is self-authenticating. Paul says: "The Spirit itself beareth witness with our spirit, that we are the children of God" (Romans 8:16, KJV).

Closely related to the question of whether or not glossolalia should be interpreted as a sign are several other problems: Are we dealing with real languages, ancient or modern? Is it proper to refer to glossolalia as "ecstatic utterance"? How is glossolalia to be understood from a psychological standpoint?

Is glossolalia to be understood as a real language? We have already indicated that Luke manifests this understanding of it in Acts 2. What can be said of Paul's understanding? There are some arguments that can be used to support the idea that Paul is thinking of real languages unknown to the speaker. The term *glossa* normally conveys the meaning of language when it does not refer to the organ of speech. Moreover, the term *hermeneuein,* "to interpret," and words based on this stem have the meaning of translating or giving the essence of a foreign language. This would suggest that when Paul uses the words in 1 Corinthians 12 and 14, he is thinking of tongues as a real language which requires interpretation or translation.

However, there is much to be said for the idea that Paul is thinking of an entirely different category and that he uses such words as *glossa* and *hermeneuein* because there were no other ready-made words at hand. He does refer in one place to the "tongues of men and of angels" (1 Corinthians 13:1), and perhaps this gives us a clue to his meaning. Tongues then would be a heavenly language, a Spirit-inspired utterance normally unintelligible to the speaker and his hearers. When Paul thought of interpretation of tongues, he did not have in mind something that could be done by a linguistics expert. The tongues used on the day of Pentecost were intelligible because God made them so through a special miracle (assuming, of course, that the Acts 2 account is historically reliable). The tongues employed at Corinth could become intelligible only through the gift of interpretation because it was only normal that the language inspired by the Holy Spirit had to be interpreted by the Holy Spirit.

It is significant that though linguistic experts have studied

101

hundreds of hours of tongues recorded on tape, they have never been able to identify any of them as a known human language.[25] They say that glossolalia has a rhythm or cadence that is similar to that of a language, and that they can tell when someone tries to simulate tongues. However, the examples of tongues they have studied seem to lack the basic ingredients of an earthly language. Linguistic experts cannot break the code because, it appears, there is no code to break. Even with the same tongues speaker there is no evidence that words are used with fixed meanings as in normal human language. There is no grammar or syntax to study.[26]

What then are we to make of the many testimonies about tongues being recognized as actual human languages? Of course, each testimony needs to be studied and analyzed carefully. Often it is only a few words or a short phrase that is recognized. These could have been words heard at some earlier period which had lodged in the subconsciousness of the glossolalist and were expressed in the form of glossolalia. This would be highly remarkable, if not miraculous. In some cases, it is conceivable that otherwise nonsense syllables are imbued with special meaning in the subjective consciousness of the hearers. When the meaning conveyed ministers to a particular need in the life of the one who hears, it could be understood as a direct result of the work of the Holy Spirit. It may even happen that at times the same type of miracle occurs which Luke reports in Acts 2. If God did it before, there is no theoretical reason why he could not do it again if it fit in with his purpose to do so. But if so, why does he not repeat the tongues of fire and the rush of the wind as well?

If we accept the explanation of linguistic experts that the glossolalia which has been examined thus far does not have the basic characteristics of a language, does that mean that we are to conclude that contemporary glossolalia is different from that which Paul describes? No, that conclusion is not necessary. We have no tape recordings of Paul's glossolalia or that of his Corinthian contemporaries. We cannot analyze these linguistically. In speaking of glossolalia, Paul does so not as a linguistics expert, but as one talking about a form of inspiration which he recognizes as a *bona fide* gift of the Spirit and which he himself practices.

Are charismatics correct in objecting to tongues being spoken of as ecstatic utterance? This depends largely upon the understanding of ecstasy. Is it appropriate to speak of a young man as in ecstasy when his girl friend accepts his marriage proposal or when his favorite football team makes that last-minute touchdown necessary to win the game? If so, in a comparable way glossolalia may sometimes be

102

regarded as an ecstatic experience. Evidently it was so at Pentecost, for some present at the feast even thought the disciples were drunk (Acts 2:13). Modern-day glossolalists, however, say that often in the exercise of glossolalia there is no particular emotional experience involved.

The main reason charismatics object to tongues being called "ecstatic utterance" is that it seems to suggest that one has gone "off his rocker" and lost control of oneself. The first meaning which *Webster's New Collegiate Dictionary* (1975) assigns to ecstasy is that of "a state of being beyond reason and self-control." Glossolalists make the point that Paul assumes that the glossolalist can control his or her speech. This, they say, is exactly what they experience. The point is well taken! The influence of the history of religions school of thought is strong in the minds of many biblical scholars and commentators. The basic assumption is that we can understand better what the Bible means in reference to certain experiences and phenomena it mentions by comparing them with what would appear to be analogous experiences in other religions of the ancient world. What is frequently overlooked in this process is the basic uniqueness of the Christian faith. Very often in non-Christian religions phenomena such as prophecy and glossolalia took place when the subject of the experience was in a trance or when he had worked himself up into a frenzy like the prophets of Baal in 1 Kings 18. The type of glossolalia which Paul describes in First Corinthians and which present-day charismatics claim to experience bears no resemblance to this.

103

How is glossolalia to be interpreted from a psychological point of view, and what is its relation to mental health? These are two different questions. With regard to the first, the most widely accepted view is that the ability to throw the mind in neutral and make sounds that resemble language without the conscious control of the brain is a capacity that is latent in the human brain. Some have applied the thought of the famous Swiss psychiatrist, C. G. Jung, to the problem and interpreted glossolalia in terms of Jung's views of the "collective unconscious." Others have observed that there is a close correlation between the practice of glossolalia and belief in demons. With this in mind they interpret glossolalia as an expression of love in the child-parent relationship and demonology as the projection of fear and hate in the same relationship. Still others have interpreted it in terms of the babble of infants or small children before they really learn how to talk.[27]

Most psychologists agree that in Pentecostal, Neo-Pentecostal experience glossolalia is a behavior that is "caught" or even learned. Often before one starts speaking in tongues, one has some personal or family crisis that opens one to the experience. The individual then comes into contact with some group that practices glossolalia, and within the context of this group one is given some explanation of this phenomenon which causes one to seek the experience. Frequently there is a strong relationship of trust or dependence with a particular member of the group. There may be some exceptions to this in particular cases, but this, we are told, is the general pattern. One psychologist concludes on the basis of his research that anyone who can be hypnotized can learn to speak in tongues.[28]

There is no unanimity among psychologists with regard to the relationship between glossolalia and mental health. In one of the pioneer works on glossolalia George Barton Cutten in 1927 associated the experience with abnormal mental states such as hysteria and schizophrenia. A number of psychologists in the sixties published studies that strongly repudiated Cutten's conclusions. Some even indicated that speaking in tongues might in many cases have a positive influence in the direction of the integration of personality. One research team in this period concluded on the basis of field data that Pentecostals are normally well-adjusted people and that there is no basis for thinking of them as psychologically imbalanced or emotionally unstable. In the same period another research team spoke of Pentecostals as "uncommonly troubled people." One of the latest and most competent studies concludes that "glossolalists are neither more nor less emotionally disturbed than equally religious non-tongue speakers." It states that glossolalists are characteristically less depressed than nonglossolalists, but that they generally show much more dependence upon an authority figure.[29]

What then are we to conclude about the relationship between glossolalia and mental health? Probably the best we can do is to avoid quoting psychological research to make extravagant claims about the dangers of glossolalia on the one hand or the benefits to be derived from it on the other.

We return to the basic question: Theologically, how are we to regard glossolalia? Here we must do battle on two fronts. On the one hand, we must oppose the extravagant, unbiblical claims of many contemporary glossolalists. When some of them suggest that if you do not speak in tongues, there is something wrong with your experience and you need the Holy Spirit, they are going beyond the biblical evidence. There is nothing in the Bible to indicate that Jesus spoke in tongues, and Mark 16:17 should not be used to say that he commanded it or expected it of his followers. When glossolalists appeal to passages like Romans 8:26, Ephesians 6:18, and Jude 20 to say that the Bible encourages us to speak in tongues, they are going beyond the biblical evidence. The practice of glossolalia may be one of the ways in which the Spirit helps us in our prayers, but it is certainly not the only way, and probably not the most important one. Praying in the Spirit may include speaking in tongues, but it is by no means limited to this type of prayer. The Corinthians took the least gift and tried to make it the most important one. The Corinthian error should not be repeated.

On the other hand, we must oppose the intolerant attitudes of many who do not speak in tongues. When nonglossolalists suggest that glossolalists should be thrown out of the church, they should be asked to demonstrate the biblical basis for such an attitude. When those who do not speak in tongues indicate that those who do are really not loyal to their denomination, they should be asked if the criteria for evaluating denominational loyalty are biblical or nonbiblical. If the criteria are recognized as biblical, then the nonglossolalists should be asked to show where the glossolalists fall short as far as the biblical witness is concerned. Paul recognizes glossolalia as a genuine gift of the Spirit, though he places it at the bottom of the list. The biblical command is not "Forbid speaking in tongues," but "Do not forbid speaking in tongues."

This, however, is not an open-ended license to practice glossolalia and force it on everyone else. It presupposes Paul's very clear teaching in 1 Corinthians 12–14. Paul's great concern in this passage is the unity and the upbuilding of the body, and it is not by accident that his great hymn of love, chapter 13, stands between chapters 12 and 14. In chapter 12 Paul teaches that the gifts are sovereignly bestowed by the one Spirit and that there is no basis for a feeling of superiority on the part of some or of inferiority on the part of others. In chapter 14 he uses the criterion of whether or not a gift edifies the body as a basis for placing a high value on prophecy but a relatively low value on tongues. In chapter 13 he sets forth love as the motive and the atmosphere in which all of the gifts are to be exercised. He defines love in terms of its likeness to Jesus on the one hand and its absence of self-seeking pride on the other.

Glossolalia should not be regarded as a status symbol to pin on one's lapel as an indication that one has made the commitment act and that now one is "in" because one qualifies as a super Christian. Neither should glossolalia be regarded as a stigma that brands the bearer as an outcast, that indicates that one has crossed the line which marks off that which is acceptable from that which is unacceptable. Both attitudes are unbiblical. We are not to try to program the Holy Spirit or fence him in. To say that he must manifest himself through tongues is to do it in one direction. To say that he must not so manifest himself is to do it in another.

The above statement should answer the question of whether tongues are for all or not. That is not for us to decide. Should we seek tongues? Long ago A. B. Simpson set forth the dictum: "Seek not; forbid not." It is safe to say that if there were less seeking, there would be less forbidding. The teaching of the Bible is that we are to seek the Lord. We are to be open to his gifts and express gratitude for them, not only for the ones the Spirit has given to us, but for the ones he has given our brothers and sisters as well, insofar as they use them for the edification of the body.

What should we say about the gift of interpretation of tongues? It also should be accepted as a genuine gift, and tongues should not be used in public worship without it. The message conveyed in this way should pass the test of conforming to the lordship of Christ, as is the case with all charismatic manifestations (1 Corinthians 12:3). On the analogy of what Paul says about prophecy, we may suggest that it should edify, encourage, and console (1 Corinthians 14:3-5).

106

But how may we know if the interpretation offered is really what the tongues speaker says? As a rule we cannot. The accuracy of the gift of interpretation in expressing the content of an utterance in tongues cannot be said to have been demonstrated scientifically. John Kildahl tells of having played tape recordings of tongue speech privately for people who claim to have the gift of interpretation to give the meaning. He says that in no case did the different interpreters of the same message suggest anything like the same meaning.[30]

We recall Agnes Sanford's story of a service in which one woman spoke in Hebrew and another interpreted the message when neither one understood the language. There are not many seminary professors who know enough Hebrew to interpret a message in it accurately if they were to hear it. But perhaps the best answer to that is to leave that story alone and simply relate another one. John Kildahl tells of the son of a missionary to Africa attending a tongue-speaking meeting where he was a complete stranger. At one point in the service he rose and recited the Lord's Prayer in the African dialect that he had learned as a child. Thereupon someone interpreted it as a message of the imminent Second Coming of Christ.[31]

Perhaps the call for demonstration is out of order. God's gifts are not intended as showpieces. However, the exaggerated claims of tongues speakers about the linguistic qualities of their gifts call forth such counterdemonstrations. If tongues speakers were content to interpret their gift in terms of 1 Corinthians 12–14 instead of ascribing to it the same type of miraculous linguistic qualities suggested by Acts 2, perhaps this kind of call for demonstration could be avoided.

CHAPTER 5

Gifts of Prophecy, Healing, and Deliverance

In this chapter we will take up the other three gifts of the Spirit that have come to the forefront in reports of the charismatic movement. These are the gifts of prophecy, healing, and deliverance. In each case, we will follow the pattern set in chapter 4 by examining the reports of the spiritual gift and then appraising it from a biblical and theological point of view.

Prophecy

Charismatics understand Paul as saying that when tongues are used in public, an interpretation is always required so the utterance will have meaning and value for the congregation. However, they say, since prophecy is an utterance under the inspiration of the Holy Spirit which is intelligible both to the speaker and the hearers, no interpretation is needed. What is accomplished in two steps through tongues and interpretation occurs directly in one step through prophecy, they say.

According to the well-known Protestant charismatics Dennis and Rita Bennett, "The gift of prophecy is manifested when believers speak the mind of God, by the inspiration of the Holy Spirit, and not from their own thoughts." In this definition the words "and not from their own thoughts" are especially important. As charismatics understand it, one who prophesies does not decide first to say something, then think out what to say and how to say it, and finally stand up and speak it. Rather, one gets an "anointing," an inner urge that comes from the Holy Spirit. Often when one begins to speak, charismatics say, the one exercising the gift of prophecy does not know what one is going to say. Usually one has received only the first few words or the first sentence or so but launches out on faith and speaks these words, finding that others follow. Thus the gift of prophecy is not a special ability which one can use at any time at will. It is bestowed by the Holy Spirit at a particular moment for a definite purpose.[1]

One who bears a message of prophecy is essentially one who speaks for God (Exodus 4:14-16; 7:1). In Old Testament times, charismatics remind us, only a relatively few of God's people were used in this way. However, Moses expressed the desire that God should put his Spirit upon all his people so they might prophesy (Numbers 11:26-30). What Moses longed for is expressed in clear prophecy in Joel 2:28-29:

> "And it shall come to pass afterward,
> that I will pour out my spirit on all flesh;
> your sons and your daughters shall prophesy,
> your old men shall dream dreams,
> and your young men shall see visions.
> Even upon the menservants and maidservants
> in those days, I will pour out my spirit."

110 Charismatics never tire of pointing out that this is the passage that Peter quoted on the day of Pentecost and declared was being fulfilled through the things that were then taking place (Acts 2:17ff.). Since the day of Pentecost, they say, the gift of prophecy is no longer confined to a select few. It is open to all without respect to age, sex, or social condition. The fact that Paul urged the Corinthians to aspire to this gift and be zealous to receive it is taken by charismatics to mean that the gift is open to all Christians (1 Corinthians 12:31; 14:1; cf. 14:24). He states specifically that women may prophesy (1 Corinthians 11:5).

Charismatics point out that, according to Paul, there is a difference between the gift of prophecy, which is open to all, and the ministry or office of prophet, which is open to relatively few. When Paul asks, "Are all apostles? Are all prophets?" obviously expecting a negative answer, he was thinking about the ministry or office of prophet. Those who have a ministry of prophecy are the prophets whom God has given to the church (Ephesians 4:11). Now, as then, say charismatics, many exercise the gift of prophecy from time to time, but relatively few have a ministry of prophecy. In the life of a prophet, we are told, the gift of knowledge is often conjoined with the gift of prophecy. For example, when Jesus told the Samaritan woman she had had five husbands and the man with whom she was living then was not her husband, she said: "Sir, I perceive that you are a prophet" (John 4:18-19).

Prophecy in the New Testament sense, charismatics stress, is not primarily foretelling, but forthtelling. It may take the form of prediction, as some of the stories in Acts indicate (11:27-30; 21:10-11). However, it is normally speaking forth God's word in a particular situation. Paul places special stress on prophecy because it is of great value in edifying believers. God works through it for building up, urging on, and consoling the congregation (1 Corinthians 14:3). But it also has value to bring unbelievers to God. When all prophesy under the leadership of the Holy Spirit, unbelievers are convicted, judged, and caused to fall down in worship of God, acknowledging his presence in the congregation (1 Corinthians 14:24-25). Some think that Paul's words, "the secrets of [the] heart are exposed," mean that the gift of prophecy is combined with the gift of knowledge.[2]

Charismatics point out that there are various mistakes that one can make with respect to prophecy. One mistake is that of holding it in low esteem and thus neglecting it. Doubtless this is what the Thessalonians were doing and Paul had to remind them: "Do not quench the Spirit, do not despise prophesying" (1 Thessalonians 5:19-20). Another mistake, perhaps one closely related to the first, is that of failing to speak out a word of prophecy for fear of making a mistake even when such a word is laid upon the heart. Of course, charismatics say, mistakes will be made. Paul tells the Corinthians: "For our knowledge is imperfect and our prophecy is imperfect" (1 Corinthians 13:9). He does not for this reason suggest, however, that they should desist from prophesying. Rather, he urges those who have not yet started exercising this gift to desire it earnestly (1 Corinthians 12:30; 14:1). The responsibility for what is said rests not upon the speaker alone, but upon the congregation as well, for the congregation must weigh what is said (1 Corinthians 14:29). Another mistake is continuing to speak after the special "anointing" is gone. In this way prophecies sometimes start out in the Spirit but end up in the flesh, thus spoiling what God intended.

Charismatics commonly voice two strong words of caution with regard to prophecy. First, prophecy must always conform to the biblical witness. Opposition to prophecy is often based upon the fear that prophecy will be more highly regarded than Scripture and that it will go beyond Scripture. The community in which prophecy is accepted must recognize this danger and always be on its guard against it. Second, one should be careful about using prophecy to tell other people what to do or depending upon prophecy to discover the

111

will of God for oneself. Offering personal guidance is not the purpose of prophecy.

Charismatics are mindful that prophecies usually reflect the limitations of the channels through which they come. Pure water may pick up some of the rust which comes from the pipe through which it flows. One who normally uses poor grammar will do the same when speaking a word of prophecy. Likewise, "a man's attitude and opinions, his theological beliefs and social prejudices all may color the content of his prophecy."[3] Protestants who have been nurtured on the King James Version of the Bible often use such expressions as "Thus saith the Lord" and "Yea, I say unto thee." Catholics, on the other hand, more normally say, "Don't you know?" or "The Lord would say. . . ."[4]

Charismatics recognize the responsibility of the congregation for weighing prophecy (1 Corinthians 14:29; 1 Thessalonians 5:20-21). The danger of one speaking when the Lord has not spoken or even speaking under demonic inspiration rather than divine is not discounted (1 John 4:1-3). They point out that it is not by accident in the enumeration of the gifts that Paul lists discerning of spirits between prophecy on the one hand and tongues and interpretation of tongues on the other (1 Corinthians 12:10). This gift, they say, is of particular value in detecting any demonic influences that may lie behind utterances that purport to be true prophecy.

With these things in mind charismatics have suggested various tests that need to be applied in weighing prophecy. True prophecy, they say, will conform to the teachings of Scripture (2 Timothy 3:16). It will exalt and glorify Christ (John 16:14; 1 Corinthians 12:13; 1 John 4:1-2). It will edify the congregation (1 Corinthians 14:3-4). If it is given in the form of a prediction, the truth or falsity of the prophecy will be indicated by whether or not the prediction comes to pass (Deuteronomy 18:20-22). Even if the prediction comes to pass, the prophecy may be judged as spurious if it has the effect of turning people away from the one true God (Deuteronomy 13:1-5). Prophecy is to be judged not only by its content, but also by its tone and the fruit it produces (Galatians 5:22-23; Matthew 7:21-23). True prophecy will be both liberating and life-giving in its effects (2 Corinthians 3:5-6, 17). Finally, the Spirit dwelling within believers will enable them to distinguish true prophecy from that which is false (1 John 2:20, 27; 1 Corinthians 12:10).

Appraisal of Prophecy

The word "prophecy" means different things to different people.

To some it suggests prediction, a kind of fortune-telling or reading of the crystal ball. This kind of forecasting may range all the way from picking the winner in the Super Bowl to predicting who is going to be the next president. For others it connotes applying the Christian message to urgent social problems in something of the tradition of Martin Luther King, Jr., or Clarence Jordan. Still others think of prophecy as inspired preaching, often with a preacher like Billy Graham or Norman Vincent Peale in mind. What does the Bible mean by prophecy?

There is a tremendous breadth in what the Scriptures have to say about prophets and prophecy. Limitations of time and space will not permit us to explore the richness of scriptural teaching on this subject. Fortunately, this is not necessary because our immediate concern is to discover what Paul means by the gift of prophecy. This objective can best be accomplished if we confine our study to a Pauline context, focusing particularly upon 1 Corinthians 12–14. With this in mind let us give attention to the following observations.

Our first observation is that Paul assigned tremendous importance to prophecy. "Prophecy" or "prophets" appears in all of Paul's lists of the gifts of the Spirit or discussions of these gifts (Romans 12:6-8; 1 Corinthians 12:8-10, 28-30; 1 Corinthians 13:1-3, 8-12; 14; Ephesians 4:11-12; 1 Thessalonians 5:19-21). It is the only gift which is mentioned with such invariable constancy. Though Paul recognizes that one day prophecies will pass away, he thinks of this in terms of the time when the perfect has come and we see the Lord face to face (1 Corinthians 13:8-12).

113

Second, prophecy is an intelligible utterance, and this is the primary thing that distinguishes it from tongues which become intelligible only through the companion gift of interpretation (1 Corinthians 14).

In the third place, Paul recognizes the Holy Spirit as the source of true prophecy (1 Corinthians 12:8-11). Not a product of human wisdom, it is a gift of the Spirit.

Fourth, we note that Paul's primary reason for esteeming prophecy so highly is that it has great value in edifying the congregation of believers (1 Corinthians 14), but he recognizes that it may also have the effect of turning unbelievers to the Lord (1 Corinthians 14:22-25).

Our fifth observation is that there is strong evidence that Paul distinguishes between the gift of prophecy and the office or ministry of prophet. Three times Paul lists prophets among the recognized leaders whom God has placed in the church to foster its spiritual growth (1 Corinthians 12:28-29; Ephesians 4:11-12). In each case he mentions prophets second only to apostles. It is clear that Paul did not think of all Christians as apostles. Neither did he regard all believers as prophets, evangelists, pastors, or teachers. He recognized these as special ministry gifts to the body of Christ. On the other hand, Paul urges all the Corinthians to desire the gift of prophecy (1 Corinthians 12:31; 14:1; cf. 14:12). It appears that Paul has this distinction in mind in 1 Corinthians 14:29-31. He says in verse 29 that in a service of worship two or three prophets are to be permitted to speak, but in verse 31 he says, "You can all prophesy one by one." In other words, he is saying that the recognized prophets should not dominate the service. They should let those who are not esteemed as prophets have an opportunity to prophesy under the inspiration of the Spirit.

Our sixth observation is that Paul appears to regard prophecy as a spontaneous inspiration coming from the Holy Spirit, and not something which one thinks out. This does not mean that one cannot think out something under the leadership of the Holy Spirit. It simply means that this kind of utterance is not what Paul has in mind when he speaks of prophecy. In 1 Corinthians 14:26 he does not mention prophecy, but the word "revelation" *(apocalupsis)* apparently carries for him this meaning in its particular context. In verse 30 of the same chapter he says that if one receives a revelation while another is speaking a prophecy, the first person is to be silent and let the second one speak. He follows this by saying, "For you can all prophesy one by one" (verse 31). Verse 30 highlights the spontaneous nature of prophecy and suggests also that it is not supposed to be interminable. Paul has in mind not a long discourse, but a short, direct message from the Lord.

Seventh, though Paul thinks of prophecy as spontaneous, this does not mean that it is not subject to the control of those who prophesy. "The spirits of the prophets are subject to prophets," he says (14:32). They are to speak in turn and exercise common courtesies in starting and stopping.

Finally, according to Paul, the church has the responsibility of evaluating what is said (1 Corinthians 14:29; 1 Thessalonians 5:20-21).

The preceding observations may be summarized in the following description of prophecy. According to Paul, prophecy is a spontaneous, intelligible utterance, inspired directly by the Holy Spirit. It may be spoken by any Christian so inspired. It is given within the context of the church's worship and is directed toward a particular need. It is subject to the control of the one who speaks it and to the evaluation of the congregation which receives it. If this interpretation of Paul is correct, it means that charismatics are basically correct in their fundamental understanding of prophecy as a spontaneous speaking of the mind of God under the leadership of the Holy Spirit.

No doubt this interpretation of prophecy raises a red flag in the minds of many. Most of us in the main-line churches, Protestant and Catholic, have little or no experience with this kind of prophecy. The whole idea sounds strange to us, perhaps even a bit weird. We have doubts as to whether God speaks directly to people in our day so they can become mouthpieces of the Holy Spirit. Moreover, many of the sermons we have heard and some of the books and commentaries we have read have led us to think of prophecy largely in terms of inspired preaching.

Now it is quite clear that Paul places a high premium on preaching and claims to preach under the inspiration of the Holy Spirit (1 Corinthians 2:4-5; 1 Thessalonians 1:5-6; 2:13-14; Romans 15:18-19). The message which he preaches is the word of the cross, which is a stumbling block to the Jews and foolishness to the Greeks (1 Corinthians 1:18-25). Paul recognizes that when the Lord uses his preaching to produce changes in the lives of others, this is not due to his skill as an orator or preacher, but to the power of the Holy Spirit which attends the proclamation (1 Corinthians 2:4-5; 1 Thessalonians 1:5-6). Mindful of the importance of the work of the Holy Spirit in relation to preaching, Paul asks the Ephesian Christians to pray for him that he might be given boldness in proclaiming the mystery of the gospel (Ephesians 6:18-19). But nowhere does Paul refer to his own preaching or that of anyone else as prophecy. 115

The interpretation of prophecy as inspired preaching, however, is not without biblical foundations. The Old Testament prophets preached God's Word, declaring God's will in reference to particular situations. Most of them were prophets of moral and social righteousness. Thus, when under the inspiration of the Holy Spirit one proclaims the Word of God with power and authority, indicating its relevance to specific human problems, personal and social, one may be said to be doing prophetic preaching. Paul says that prophecy edifies, encourages, consoles, convicts, and instructs (1 Corinthians 14:3, 24-25, 31). Good preaching does the same. This does not mean, however, that in Paul's understanding prophecy is simply preaching. It is possible, too, that under a particular inspiration of the Spirit preaching may become prophecy, in Paul's meaning of the word. We must remember, however, that when Paul speaks of prophecy, he is speaking of something much more direct, spontaneous, and informal than that which now normally goes under the banner of preaching.

How did it come about that prophecy in the Pauline sense virtually disappeared from the life and experience of the church? It is clear that the acceptance of a canon of New Testament Scriptures both restricted the sphere of prophecy and reduced the need for it. But even before this, prophecy had virtually disappeared. The Montanist crisis of the second century (cf. chapter 2) sounded the death knell of prophecy. The Montanists literally got carried away with trances, visions, and other ecstatic experiences. They believed that these gave them an inside track to the mind of God, which no one else had. Unwilling to confine themselves to the apostolic witness to the gospel, they made claims to new revelations. They believed they had a hot line to heaven and the only way for anyone to stay up to date was to stay tuned in with them. What if the Montanists had been less heretical and arrogant on the one hand and the church had been more forbearing and willing to apply scriptural tests to the authenticity of prophecy on the other? How different things might have been in the history of the church! Now the struggle to regain a scriptural position is an uphill battle.

116

There are dangers with this view of prophecy, tremendous dangers! There is the danger of someone speaking when God has not spoken to that person. There is the peril of playing God and of proud and unbalanced people trying to exercise authority over others for personal advantage. There is the risk of new heresies arising, such as those of the Montanists or the Mormons. There is the danger of absolutizing the relative and giving too much significance to inspirations of this type.

But there are dangers on the other side as well. The chief one is that of quenching the Spirit, of not speaking when God has spoken (1 Thessalonians 5:19-21). There is also the hazard of programming everything so precisely that spontaneity is stifled, of having an atmosphere in which it simply never occurs to the average Christian that one might be the medium through which God would speak a word for the upbuilding of other members of the body.

Somewhere in the total experience of the congregation there should be a place for prayer and praise, for testimony, and, if the Spirit so directs, for prophecy in the Pauline sense. When and if such spontaneous prophecy occurs, the kind of tests which the charismatics have delineated should be clearly taught and strictly observed.

Healing

Within the charismatic movement there is a strong emphasis placed upon healing. Gifts of healing are among the charisms listed by Paul in 1 Corinthians 12:8-10. The fact that the noun "gifts" *(charismata)* is plural here is taken by charismatics to mean that various kinds of gifts are indicated.

Charismatics frequently point out that, strictly speaking, no one can claim the gift or gifts of healing. Those who are healed are really the recipients of the gift. Those who lay hands upon them and pray are simply channels for the work of the Spirit. If God so chooses, he can use any member of the body of Christ as a channel of healing for others. Nevertheless, within the Christian community, particularly among charismatics, we are told, there are those who are used with a fair degree of frequency as channels of healing. These people are often said to have a ministry of healing. Many of them, perhaps most, object to being called "faith healers." For example, the late Kathryn Kuhlman, who was called a "veritable one-woman shrine of Lourdes," said again and again that she had never healed anybody. She ascribed to God all healing that happened in services which she conducted.[5]

Charismatics frequently point out that other gifts often operate in close conjunction with the gifts of healing. Most frequently mentioned among these are the word of knowledge, faith, and discerning of spirits. By a word of knowledge, supernaturally given, sometimes charismatics are able, they say, to recognize the nature of the ailment and its cause so they can pray effectively for the sick person. Some charismatics claim that through a word of knowledge they are often given impressions which tell them someone is being healed of such and such a malady. The gift of faith, a strong conviction that God is actually going to heal, is healing, or has healed someone, frequently manifests itself along with the gift of healing. By the gift of discerning of spirits, we are told, those who are being used as channels of the healing gifts are able sometimes to detect whether the ailment is related to the presence of an unclean spirit. In such cases, so they say, the basic need is for deliverance, and the procedure to be followed is different from that used in ordinary healings.

In the history of Pentecostalism various disputes have arisen as to whether the use of doctors and nurses is legitimate. Nowadays, most main-line Pentecostals use doctors from time to time, while still holding that God can and often does heal without the use of medical means. Most charismatics say there is no conflict between the use of doctors and medicines on the one hand and prayer for direct healing on the other. Nevertheless, there are some "faith healers" who from time to time tell those whom they pronounce healed to stop their medication. Most charismatics who are used in this type of ministry, however, advise those whom they deem healed to go to a doctor to receive confirmation of the healing and instructions as whether to discontinue medication. They regard this counsel as not simply a matter of expediency or wisdom, but as one having a biblical basis, for Jesus instructed the lepers whom he had healed to show themselves to the priest (Luke 17:14).

While charismatics cite various Old Testament texts to support a doctrine of healing (Exodus 15:26; 23:25; Psalm 103:3; Isaiah 53:4-5), their main appeal is to the ministry of Jesus, the practice of the apostles, and the instructions given in James 5:14-16. Charismatics say we do not have to be in doubt as to whether God wants to heal. We know he does because of the attitude of Jesus. Whenever Jesus met sickness, he dealt with it as an enemy which he had come to destroy. He once referred to a woman, whose back was so bent that she could not straighten up, as a daughter of Abraham whom Satan had bound for eighteen years (Luke 13:16). Peter declared that Jesus "went about doing good and healing all that were oppressed by the devil" (Acts 10:38). Charismatics frequently point out that there is no record in the Gospels of anyone coming to Jesus for healing who went away unhealed. When a leper knelt before him and said, "Lord, if you will, you can make me clean," Jesus stretched out his hand and touched him, saying, "I will; be clean" (Matthew 8:2-3).

118

Most Christians, we are told, have no doubt about God's ability to heal, but they often have doubts about whether he wants to heal in their particular case. When asked what Jesus would do if he were here in the flesh, they usually brighten up and say: "Why, he would heal me." Charismatics then point out that Jesus is the revelation of God, and that if Jesus would heal them, so would God. In line with this belief, charismatics often say that one should not add the phrase, "if it be thy will," when praying for healing. This is a faith-destroying phrase, they say. Since we already know God's will, we don't need this proviso. If one is not sure about God's will in the matter, some suggest, one might pray for healing "according to your will."[6]

Charismatics point out that when Jesus sent his disciples out on their missionary journeys, he instructed them to heal the sick and in doing so to say, "The kingdom of God has come near to you" (Luke 10:9; cf. 9:2). The disciples carried out this commission. Following the descent of the Holy Spirit at Pentecost, the apostles continued to heal in Jesus' name. Even those who were not apostles were used in a healing ministry (Acts 8:7). Charismatics stress that, according to the book of Acts, healing and evangelism were coordinated in an approach to the total needs of people (e.g., Acts 3–4; 14). The apostles healed the sick, and the healings that took place helped to spread the gospel.

Special stress is laid upon James 5:14-16. Charismatics frequently carry out these instructions to the letter. They see in the words about sins being forgiven as well as the sick being healed an indication that there is often a close connection between sickness and sin (cf. Mark 2:1-12). They often give contemporary illustrations of how resentment or bearing a grudge has blocked physical healing so that the elimination of the spiritual problem resulted in the restoration of physical health. Usually the anointing with oil and the praying for the sick follow a period in which faith-building promises and teachings from the Bible are given. A few drops of olive oil on the forehead are usually used in the anointing. The laying on of hands is sometimes understood as a way of helping the patient release his or her faith, and sometimes as an expression of love, concern, and identification with the patient.

There are various approaches to healing in the charismatic movement, but the two most prominent ones may be described as follows. The first approach may be summarized in three points. First, complete healing is God's will for you. In support of this, many of the passages which we have already considered are introduced. Second, Jesus made provision for your complete healing in the atonement. Isaiah says, "with his stripes we are healed," and Peter quotes this in his first epistle (Isaiah 53:5; 1 Peter 2:24). Matthew quotes Isaiah 53:4 with reference to Jesus: "Himself took our infirmities, and bare our sicknesses" (Matthew 8:17, KJV). Since Jesus bore our infirmities and diseases for us, we do not need to bear them. Third, claim your healing by faith. Let your faith unite with that of those who are laying hands upon you and praying for you. In this way the circuit is closed, and the healing power of God is released. Praise God for his healing even though your symptoms may continue for a time.[7]

The second approach is not as easy to describe, because it is more complex. It in no way sets healing through prayer over against healing through medical means. It recognizes that there are many facets to health, and many ways by which God heals. It says that in the past the church has not discharged its responsibility in the healing ministry because of views overemphasizing disease as God's judgment on sin on the one hand and the disciplinary value of suffering on the other. Like the first approach, it represents God as on

119

the side of health, but it is not quite as dogmatic in its affirmations. This approach describes salvation in terms of wholeness—body, mind, and spirit—and underscores the biblical view of the essential unitary nature of human personality. It recognizes that there is often a direct relation between sin and disease but deals with this problem on a case by case basis, without setting it forth in terms of a fixed formula. It emphasizes the importance of faith but warns against faith in faith. Our faith is in the God of love revealed in Jesus Christ. It admits that God often heals through prayer when the patient does not have faith and sometimes when no one in particular does. Faith is a gift of God, and should not be understood as something we manufacture. There is a mystery in God's healing work, and we should resist the temptation of universalizing any one procedure into a universal law.[8]

This approach recognizes four basic kinds of sickness. The first is sickness of spirit caused by personal sin. A second type is emotional sickness or anxiety related to emotional hurts of the past. A third is physical sickness caused by disease or accidents. A fourth type is demonic oppression caused by evil spirits. A different type of prayer approach is indicated in connection with each type of illness. This approach claims that at times all four types are entwined in the health problems of one patient. It notes that, because of differences in personality and the way different people relate to others, some people are able to minister to certain individuals more effectively than others. Often the best results are achieved through a prayer team. This approach stresses the importance of the prayer team being concerned about the health of the patient, not about its reputation in the healing ministry. It praises God for victories, but recognizes that many are not healed. It stresses the importance of not saddling the patient with a sense of guilt for lack of faith when the desired results are not apparent.

Charismatic prayer meetings and charismatic literature are full of testimonies of miraculous healings in direct answer to prayer. Nevertheless, in most quarters of the movement there is a frank admission that not all for whom prayers are offered receive healing. Oral Roberts, who is internationally famous for his ministries of evangelism and healing, is often quoted as saying that he has prayed for more people who were not healed than perhaps any man alive. Various reasons why people are not healed are offered. Some tend to reduce the problem to unconfessed sin or a lack of faith on the part of the patient. Others enumerate long lists of possible reasons healing has not occurred. Many admit that they cannot explain it.

Appraisal of Healing

Most of us brought up within traditional Protestant churches have deep-seated prejudices against anything remotely resembling "faith healing." For many of us the problem is related to the view that "the age of miracles is over," if, indeed, it ever really existed. We have been nourished on a world view that thinks in terms of cause and effect in an almost endless regress, and we have our doubts as to whether, in our day at least, God ever breaks into this "closed system." To be sure, we pray for the sick, and sometimes they get well. But then we wonder if they wouldn't have gotten well anyway. Perhaps prayer did speed the recovery along, but we are not sure whether God did it or whether it was just the psychological effect of prayer in the life of the patient. At any rate, we have our doubts about the type of dramatic healings the charismatics talk so much about.

Then, too, many of us have seen the movies *Elmer Gantry* and *Marjoe*. Though *Elmer Gantry* was admittedly fiction, *Marjoe* (1972) was not. Marjoe Gortner produced the film about himself. After exploiting the revivalism-healing racket for all it was worth (and it obviously was a racket in his case), he cleaned up on it all in a daring exposé that netted him untold profits. We are willing to admit that Marjoe's case is somewhat extreme, but it tends to confirm the suspicions that we've had all along. All of this healing bit is just a big hoax. It is too spectacular, too sensational, and too many of the healing evangelists have simply exploited the sense of futility and desperation of sick people to line their own pockets. And, not a few of them, we suspect, have been leading double lives.[9]

With thoughts and attitudes like these in the back of our heads, it is not easy for many of us to examine the evidence impartially. But this is the task set before us. How are we to evaluate the claims about healing that come forth from the charismatic movement?

There is much truth in many emphases concerning healing in the charismatic movement. God is a compassionate God. Jesus is on the side of health and healing. Sickness like sin is an intruder and not a part of God's ideal plan for us. The Bible does think of salvation in terms of wholeness and does not divide a person into compartments. It lends no support to the idea of saving souls, while showing a complete indifference to the concrete needs of a person in his or her total existence. Jesus did heal the sick, and so did the apostles. Nevertheless, charismatics tend to be too simplistic, to make too many sweeping generalizations, to ignore or pass over too lightly too many other important aspects of the subject.

Jesus came into a world in which a pat formula held sway: If

121

someone is righteous, that one will prosper; if one is a sinner one will suffer. Jesus' contemporaries found support for this kind of thinking in various passages in their Bible, the Old Testament (Exodus 15:26; 23:25; Deuteronomy 30:15-18). Human experience, however, did not always confirm this faith. Some of the Psalms (e.g., 37, 73) come to grips with the problem, and their solution is a "wait and see" attitude. The intent of the Book of Job is to repudiate this interpretation, but the point is somewhat weakened by the complete restoration of the good fortunes of Job in the last chapter of the book. The stories of Jesus' healing the paralytic in Capernaum (Mark 2:1-11) and the lame man at the pool of Bethesda (John 5:1-14) suggest that he recognized that there is sometimes a definite causal connection between sin and sickness. However, Jesus rejected the popular assumption that when one suffers, this suffering is always related to one's own sin or the sins of one's parents. He refused to attribute the affliction of the man born blind either to the man himself or to his parents but spoke instead of the glory of God that would be revealed through his being made whole (John 9:1-7).

Jesus believed that suffering could be redemptive, and he set about to make it so. He seems consciously to have defined his mission in terms of the fulfillment of the role of the Suffering Servant of the Lord in the latter part of Isaiah (particularly Isaiah 53).[10] The fact that Jesus, the spotless Son of God, suffered the cruel death on the cross is the strongest possible refutation of the theory that if one is a great sufferer, he is *ipso facto* a great sinner. The direction of New Testament thought is not focused backward to the cause of suffering but forward to its positive use. Since our Lord, though the Son of God, "learned obedience through what he suffered" (Hebrews 5:8), the disciplinary value of suffering in developing strong character is established (Hebrews 12:5-11).

This fact, however, should not lead us into a theology that glories in suffering as if it is always sent from God and is an unmitigated blessing. Doctors and research scientists dedicate their lives to the eradication of disease as a dread enemy. The church must not glorify it as a benign friend! Rather, we ought to join with them in the battle against it, using all of the spiritual resources at our disposal in the fight. At this point the charismatic movement has something valid to say to us. Too often the church has encouraged an attitude of placid acceptance of disease on the part of the patient rather than standing alongside of him or her in the struggle against it.

Psychosomatic medicine has increased our awareness that there is often a close relationship between psychic states and physical

122

health. Envy and hate are destructive in their influences upon the body. Joy and peace are therapeutic. A deep experience of worship and praise sometimes brings healing at every level—physical as well as spiritual. But this is not always the case. It would be a vast oversimplification to say that good physical health and spiritual health always go together. Just as there are many physically healthy people who are not partakers of Christ's salvation, there are also many radiant Christians, enjoying the closest imaginable fellowship with Christ, whose lives are wracked by physical infirmities. When we flatly equate physical health with spiritual health, we sow the seeds of needless spiritual anguish in the lives of many dedicated Christians whose bodies are already burdened with intense pain.

We distort the biblical witness when we judge spiritual health by body temperature. Physical health may accompany salvation in this life, but this is not always so, nor is it necessarily the case. Implying that it is falls into the fallacy of equating salvation with prosperity, and adversity with sin.

Jesus healed the sick, but he did not heal all the sick. It is true that there is no record of his having sent anyone away unhealed who came to him for healing. However, there were many sick people at the pool of Bethesda that day when Jesus healed the man who had been an invalid for thirty-eight years, but Jesus seems to have healed only one out of all this pitiable group (John 5:1-16). To be sure, God is on the side of health, but does this assurance give us a solid basis for assuming that it is his will for every sick person to be healed? Death still remains as a fact of experience, and though Paul speaks of it as "the last enemy" (1 Corinthians 15:26) and declares that ultimately it will be destroyed, it holds sway now in accord with God's permissive will.

The problem with most charismatic interpretations of this subject is that they are too categorical, too unconditional. They commit with reference to disease the same error the perfectionists commit in relation to sin. They affirm for time what is only intended for eternity. The perfectionists affirm that because Christ redeems us from sin and some day we will be free of it, we can be and ought to be completely free of it now. The charismatics assume that the power which raised Jesus from the dead and will one day remove all sickness, suffering, and death should heal us from all sickness now. The resurrection power is at work in the world today, but we live in a state of tension between the already and the not yet.[11] We are not in a position to dictate to God, and seeking his will is always our responsibility as Christians. Thus, in praying for healing, it is good to

123

use the words "according to thy will," admitting our limitations.

Frequently, through his grace and mercy, God saves us from our sicknesses as well as our sins, but this is not always the case. Paul's thorn in the flesh was not removed, despite his repeated prayers (2 Corinthians 12:7-9). And yet Paul's prayer was answered in that God supplied "grace abounding." It is true that we do not know what the "thorn" was, and any interpretation is nothing more than a conjecture. Many think it was some kind of illness, but charismatics usually reject this kind of interpretation. Often they suggest that it refers to harassment by Paul's enemies. This is a possible interpretation, but the words "my power is made perfect in weakness" do not support this view. Timothy suffered from stomach troubles and frequent ailments (1 Timothy 5:23). Moreover, Paul left Trophimus ill at Miletus (2 Timothy 4:20). Surely all of those men were of strong faith, and their physical infirmities are in no wise to be interpreted as due to some deficiency in their spiritual lives. Christlikeness, not physical health, is the goal of the Christian life (Ephesians 4:13; Romans 8:29), and sometimes physical infirmities are the disciplinary measure that God uses to stimulate the development of strong character.

124

How shall we evaluate the two approaches to healing that we have recognized in the charismatic movement? The first approach bristles with problems. It affirms that complete health is God's will for all. However, in the light of the facts we have already considered, how can we be sure that complete health is the will of God for every person with whom we pray?

This approach sees healing as grounded in the atoning death of Christ. This is a typical approach in Pentecostalism and one that is very common throughout the charismatic movement. Matthew 8:17 says that Jesus "took our infirmities and bore our diseases." But the context makes clear that Jesus bore our infirmities and diseases, not by dying on the cross for them, but in his ministry of healing through which, out of sympathy and love, he bore them away. First Peter 2:24 quotes Isaiah 53:5: "By his wounds you have been healed." But again the context is important. The first part of this verse in First Peter says that Christ bore our sins, not our diseases, in his body on the cross, and the following verse speaks of the wandering sheep returning to the shepherd. Peter obviously understood the words "By his wounds you have been healed" to mean you have been healed from your sins, for you have returned to the Shepherd.

This theory presupposes that sickness and disease need atonement. If this is the case, "then *sickness implies a clouded conscience and broken fellowship with God.*"[12] This saddles us with the theory which sees an inevitable relationship between sickness and sin, a view which Jesus repudiated, as we have already seen. Moreover, this theory misconceives the gospel because no such view was propounded by the apostles. There is no evidence that it was a part of the proclamation *(kerygma)* of the early church. Paul says: "Christ died for our sins in accordance with the scriptures" (1 Corinthians 15:3). There is not the slightest evidence, however, that he also taught and believed: "Christ died for our sicknesses in accordance with the scriptures."

The first approach to healing may result in recovery of health for some, but it sows the seeds of guilt and despair for those who are not healed. When healing does not occur, the reason given is unconfessed sin or lack of faith on the part of the patient. When healing occurs, the healing evangelist gets credit because he or she helped supply the faith that was needed. In this approach the patient bears the responsibility when he or she is not healed, because he or she cannot close the circuit. This leaves the person trying to manufacture faith, trying desperately to claim healing, despite all the evidence that he or she has not been healed.

The logical conclusion of this view is that faith should demonstrate itself by foregoing medication, and this leads to the setting of healing by prayer over against healing with medicine. If one really has faith, one ought to be able to claim healing and give up medicine. Sometimes these conclusions are in fact drawn, and with disastrous consequences.

The second approach has real possibilities for the life of the church. It is not simplistic and thus avoids reducing everything to a pat formula. It works in close cooperation with the best medical and psychiatric help available. It does not burden the patient with guilt if healing does not occur. It bathes one in love, so that, whatever the outcome, one is drawn nearer to God.

The first approach is typified by Kenneth Hagin, a Baptist who joined the Assemblies of God and later became an independent evangelist. The second is represented by Francis MacNutt, a Catholic charismatic. The first approach emphasizes faith, but in such a way as to make it a law. The second stresses grace in such a way as to demonstrate Christ's love. Thus in these two approaches, typified by these two men, you have a Protestant preaching law (in effect, at least) on the one hand, and a Catholic demonstrating grace on the other.

Morton Kelsey, in one of the most significant books on healing to appear in recent years, shows how the church, through the influence of philosophies foreign to the New Testament, gradually moved away from a New Testament position on healing. It replaced the message of God's love with a view of his judgment and the disciplinary value of suffering. It shut God out of his universe with an alien concept of natural law.[13] Now signs are beginning to emerge that the church is once again recognizing its indispensable role in the ministry of healing. Psychosomatic medicine has made us aware that there are many disorders that have their roots in spiritual problems, and the charismatic movement is causing us to reexamine the biblical witness in regard to the matter of healing.

Francis MacNutt sees a hopeful step toward the recovery of a scriptural position in the Catholic Church's restoration of the sacrament of "anointing of the sick." This Catholic sacrament started out as anointing of the sick on the basis of James 5:14-16 and Mark 6:13. During the Middle Ages it evolved into the sacrament of "supreme unction" to be administered only to the dying to prepare their souls for death. Now the Church is returning to the biblical base from which it started, and the purpose of the sacrament is being defined in terms of "Anointing the Sick" for the purpose of healing.[14] Surely this is a move in the right direction.

126

The church needs to avoid the extremism of the ultraconservative wing of the charismatic movement while appropriating the type of faith so widespread in this movement that God often heals the sick in direct answer to prayer. It needs to affirm that all healing is divine healing, that which occurs through medical means no less than that which comes as a direct answer to prayer. God, in answer to prayer, uses medical means and natural causes to speed the healing process.

In the Old Testament we find references to rollers or splints for broken limbs (Ezekiel 30:21), to balm used as a sedative for pain (Jeremiah 51:8), and to a cake of figs used as a plaster for a boil (Isaiah 38:21). In the New Testament Jesus refers to the use of oil and wine for wounds, probably viewing wine as an antiseptic and oil as a soothing agent (Luke 10:34). Paul urges Timothy to use wine for the sake of his stomach and his frequent ailments (1 Timothy 5:23). Jesus himself sometimes touched the patients whom he healed or used saliva in the healing process. James counsels the use of oil along with prayer and confession of sin (James 5:13-16).

Some of the most helpful words on this in ancient writings are found in the apocryphal book of Ecclesiasticus:

> Honour the doctor for his services,
> for the Lord has created him.

His skill comes from the Most High,
and he is rewarded by kings. . . .
The Lord has created medicines from the earth,
and a sensible man will not disparage them. . . .
by using them the doctor relieves pain
and from them the pharmacist makes up his mixture. . . .
My son, if you have an illness, do not neglect it,
but pray to the Lord, and he will heal you. . . .
Renounce your faults, amend your ways,
and cleanse your heart from all sin. . . .
Then call in the doctor, for the Lord has created him;
do not let him leave you, for you need him.
There may come a time when your recovery is in their hands;
then they too will pray to the Lord
to give them success in relieving pain
and finding a cure to save the patient's life.
—Ecclesiasticus 38:1-13 (NEB)

Protestants, unlike Catholics, do not recognize this passage as belonging to the canon of the Scriptures. However, this should not keep us from recognizing the value of the commonsense approach that is set forth here. Obviously, the writer saw no conflict between the use of doctors and medicine on the one hand and prayer on the other. Such an approach to sickness and healing on the part of the church will allow it to relate to the medical profession, not as competitors, but as part of the healing team. In this way, special divine resources for healing, which might otherwise go untapped, can be brought to bear upon the patient's health.[15]

127

Deliverance from Demonic Oppression or Possession

Deliverance is not one of the gifts of the Spirit listed in 1 Corinthians 12, but it plays such an important part in the charismatic movement that it calls for special treatment. Charismatics often testify that along with a deepened awareness of the presence and power of the Holy Spirit there comes a new recognition of the reality of Satan and the need of many for deliverance from demonic oppression. Charismatics view the Christian life in terms of spiritual warfare against the wiles of the devil and the demonic hosts in league with him (Ephesians 6:10-18). They support this interpretation by pointing to the life of Jesus. They remind us that after being anointed with the Spirit, Jesus was plunged into the wilderness for a firsthand encounter with the devil (Matthew 4:1-11; Luke 4:1-13). Emerging victorious from this contest, he entered the synagogue in Nazareth and read from the scroll of Isaiah (61:1-2). In doing so, he declared himself to be anointed by the Spirit of the Lord, among other things, "to proclaim release to the captives" and "to set at liberty those who are oppressed" (Luke 4:18). Thereupon, he embarked upon a ministry that involved not only preaching and teaching but healing the sick and casting out demons as well.

Charismatics describe the casting out of demons as "deliverance ministry," borrowing the term from Jesus' reference to "deliverance to the captives" (Luke 4:18, KJV). They prefer the term "deliverance" to "exorcism," because in certain church circles (Roman Catholic and Anglican) exorcism connotes a formal ecclesiastical prayer to free a person from evil spirits. According to church law, exorcism can only be done by a priest and with the consent of the bishop. Deliverance, on the other hand, is more informal. It involves the liberation of those who are oppressed by evil spirits. It can be effected through the ministry of lay people as well as clergy. A distinction is usually made also between demonic possession and demonic oppression. When the term "possession" is used, it normally means that the individual's personality is completely submerged and taken over by an evil spirit alien to the person. Such cases, we are told, are rare. In cases of demonic oppression it is not the whole personality, but only certain areas of one's life that are controlled by demons. Charismatics say that such cases are much more common.

Though deliverance is not treated by Paul as one of the gifts of the Spirit, it is closely related to the gifts. Some charismatics think of it as one aspect of healing. Others relate it to miracles and discerning of spirits (1 Corinthians 12:9-10).

Charismatics involved in the deliverance ministry take quite seriously, even literally, all that the Bible says about Satan, demons, and the realm of the occult. They believe that before the creation of men and women there was a fall in the heavenly realm. Lucifer, an archangel of God, fell because of pride (Isaiah 14:12-15; Ezekiel 28:11-18). Evidently a host of lesser angels were involved with him in the rebellion (2 Peter 2:4; Jude 6), for Jesus speaks of "the devil and his angels" (Matthew 25:41). The devil and his angels were expelled from heaven and thrown down to earth (Revelation 12:9). In the Garden of Eden the devil in the form of a serpent seduced Eve, and she disobeyed God and so did Adam (Genesis 3). Thus, they say, humanity came under the subjection of the devil, who became "the god of this world" (2 Corinthians 4:4; cf. John 12:31; 16:11).

Charismatics quote passages from the Bible to support the idea that the heathen sacrificed to demons and not to God (Deuteronomy 32:17; 1 Corinthians 10:20). When the Israelites entered the land of Canaan, they found all kinds of idolatrous, immoral, and occult practices connected with the worship of the people of the land. They were strictly forbidden to imitate them in any of these practices. Charismatics emphasize that all forms of occult practice—divination, soothsaying, necromancy, witchcraft, sorcery, and the use of charmers, mediums, and wizards—were placed out-of-bounds for Israel (Deuteronomy 18:10-14; Leviticus 19:26). Violations of these prohibitions were even punishable by death (Exodus 22:18). None of these channels was needful for the Israelites, we are told, because God had provided adequate channels for making his will known (Isaiah 8:19-20).

Charismatics remind us that the Bible represents the devil as a liar and the father of lies (John 8:44). He uses all kinds of deceit in extending his sway over people, even at times disguising himself as an angel of light (2 Corinthians 11:14). Charismatics emphasize that the Bible represents Satan as a defeated foe. "The reason the Son of God appeared was to destroy the works of the devil" (1 John 3:8). Through his death and resurrection, Christ has won the decisive victory over the devil and all the evil powers associated with him (John 12:31-33; 1 Corinthians 2:8; Colossians 2:14-15; Ephesians 1:21-23).

Jesus cast out demons (Mark 1:23-26, 34, 39; 3:10-11; 5:1-20; 9:14-29) and commanded his disciples to do the same (Mark 3:13-15; 6:7; Luke 10:17), charismatics remind us. The early church obeyed this command (Acts 16:16-18), and even some who were not apostles were engaged in this ministry (Acts 8:6-8). In casting out demons, the apostles used the name of Jesus. When some Jewish exorcists (evidently non-Christians) imitated Paul in using the name of Jesus in attempting to cast out demons, they failed miserably (Acts 19:11-16).

A number of charismatics who are deeply involved in deliverance ministry, particularly Don Basham, a Protestant, and Francis MacNutt, a Roman Catholic, say that they did not choose this ministry for themselves but that they were led into it by the Spirit of God in answer to human need. As they applied scriptural principles in dealing with people who were demonically oppressed, they experienced an amazing degree of success in effecting deliverance for the captives. The New Testament then became their textbook on deliverance, and, they say, in case after case they discovered details of the New Testament stories of demon possession and how deliverance is effected to be verified in life.

On the basis of scriptural study and experience charismatics involved in deliverance ministry set forth a number of statements concerning demons and the means by which they can be cast out.[16] These may be summarized as follows: Demons recognize the lordship

129

of Christ. Though they are disobedient spirits, they are ultimately subject to his authority (Mark 1:24-25; 5:7-8; Ephesians 1:15-23, especially verse 21). Therefore, in dealing with those oppressed by demons, one must take authority over the demons and command them in the name of Jesus Christ to come out (Luke 10:17; Acts 16:16-18). Christians can be oppressed by evil spirits, though most charismatics are doubtful that a true Christian can ever be fully possessed by them. Scripture is not very clear on this point, they say, but the fact that Paul lists discerning of spirits among the gifts suggests that spirits other than the Holy Spirit may operate in the lives of Christians. Many of those who need deliverance, according to charismatics, are in fact Christians, and many of them are Christians claiming to have had the experience of baptism in the Holy Spirit.

Many engaged in this ministry find that it is helpful to ask the demons to name themselves (Mark 5:9). The demons are often reluctant to do this. However, when one serving in the authority of Jesus insists that they do so, we are told, frequently they speak through the one in whom they dwell in a voice distinctly different from the natural voice and give their names as "lust," "gluttony," "anger," and the like. Sometimes they say they are not going to leave, because "this is my house." Often there is more than one demon (Mark 5:9) in a person at one time, we are told. One charismatic reports a woman who was delivered of forty-one separate demons, each one having identified itself before being driven out.[17] Demons often empower those in whom they dwell with physical strength far exceeding anything that is natural or normal (Mark 5:4; Acts 19:1-17). Thus, in the deliverance ministry it is best for a group to work together, and often strong men are needed, we are told. Some charismatics think that it is important to bind the demons with a word before casting them out (Matthew 12:29; 16:19; 18:18). Some charismatics say that often the demons will not respond to a command in Jesus' name to leave if they think that the one in whom they are dwelling really wants them to stay. For this reason, they say, it is frequently necessary for the person being delivered to renounce the evil spirit dwelling within. If the one seeking deliverance has had any contact in the past with any form of the occult, it is particularly important, charismatics insist, for that person to confess this and openly and positively renounce these practices.

Most charismatics involved in this ministry recognize the danger of one going overboard and seeing demons everywhere, even where they do not exist. Misguided fanatics can do a lot of damage to very sensitive people in this way, they admit. For this reason the gift of discerning the spirits is especially important, they say. Some charismatics often used in the deliverance ministry concede, however, that the genuine gift of discernment of spirits, apart from guesswork, is relatively rare. These people emphasize the importance of experience, sound judgment, common sense, and psychological insight.

It is especially easy to confuse demon oppression with carnality, many charismatics admit. Many of the things which "demon chasers" often attribute to demons really have their roots in the works of the flesh, they say (Galatians 5:19-21). Nevertheless, such attitudes as lust, anger, jealousy, and even experimenting with the occult can begin as works of the flesh. They can be nourished, however, to the point that an unclean spirit of the same disposition takes control. The important thing, then, is to keep the moral walls guarding the inner citadel of the personality in a good state of repair (Proverbs 25:28). The method by which this is done, they say, is the crucifixion of the old person, and yielding oneself completely to the lordship of Christ rather than to the appetites of the flesh (Romans 6; Galatians 5).[18]

Charismatics often emphasize the importance of commanding the evil spirits not only to leave but also never to return (Mark 9:25). Some say the demons should be sent to the abyss or pit, while others say that the best thing is to send them to the Lord Jesus for him to dispose of them as he sees fit. Those who take the latter approach often warn against the danger of "exorcists" becoming infected with the same kind of mean spirit that they are seeking to combat.

Once the demons are driven out, we are told, care must be taken to keep them from returning. The life must not be left empty (Matthew 12:43-45) but should be filled by the Holy Spirit. Any behavior patterns which allowed the demons' entrance in the first place should be broken. Any broken spots in the walls of the moral life should be repaired. The one who has been delivered and filled with the Spirit should be taught to praise the Lord, to nourish his or her spirit on the Word of God, and to live in constant fellowship with other Christians as a part of a warm Christian community.

Effective ministry to those suffering demonic oppression, we are told, usually involves the following elements. The first step is a prayer for protection for the oppressed, all of the afflicted's relatives, all in the house, and all involved in this ministry. Next, the spirits are asked to identify themselves, after which they are usually bound by a word before they are cast out. Then a follow-up ministry along the lines we have discussed is begun to make sure that the person who has been freed from demons does not become a victim again.

Appraisal of Deliverance

For some Christians this whole discussion may seem like a return to the superstitions of the Dark Ages and to the witch-hunts of Salem. "Can these people really be serious?" they may be wondering. The answer is "Yes, they are quite serious!"

Back in the forties when I was a seminary student, the Christian world was beginning to awaken to the dreadful reality of radical evil. World War II had the effect of causing some theologians to accept with all seriousness the existence of a personal devil. There were some who spoke of the demonic element in human society, though there is little evidence that they had reference to fallen angels who gave their allegiance to Satan. Many of us were aware that in lands like China and Africa missionaries sometimes reported experiences that seemed like modern counterparts to biblical exorcism. Nevertheless, if someone had suggested a study of biblical demonology, it would have seemed to most of us as merely an academic exercise without any relevance to life in America in the twentieth century. How different things are today!

During the sixties and the seventies we have witnessed a revival of the occult throughout the world on a scale unparalleled in modern times. Episcopal Bishop James A. Pike, who in 1963 denounced glossolalia in Christian circles as "heresy in embryo, embraced spiritualism a few years later following the death of his son. In 1967 Pike participated in a televised seance led by Arthur Ford, one of the best-known mediums of our day. Pike helped popularize spiritualism with his book *The Other Side* (1969), published in the same year that his tragic death occurred in the wilderness near the Dead Sea. Jeane Dixon became world famous following her prediction of the death of President Kennedy. By 1972, it was reported that astrology had become a 200 million dollar annual business in Ameica, with 71 percent of the daily newspapers of the country carrying horoscopes in their columns each day.[19] For many it started as a game, but, increasingly, large numbers of péople adopted the practice of consulting their horoscopes before making major decisions.

Thousands of young people began experimenting with marijuana, LSD, and other hallucinogenic drugs. A great interest was shown in Zen Buddhism, Yoga, oriental mysticism, and transcendental meditation. The bizarre elements in the Sharon Tate murder and the weird hold of Manson over his so-called "family" rocked the nation. The movie *Rosemary's Baby* helped popularize Satanism. Satanism came out into the open with Anton LaVey, leader of the Church of Satan, serving as its high priest. In 1971 another lesser figure in the

132

movement led a "Crusade for Satan" in a dozen major American cities.[20] In 1974 *The Exorcist* broke box-office records. Other movies of the same type were then produced. There is little wonder that Hal Lindsey's book *Satan Is Alive and Well on Planet Earth* (1972), written from the standpoint of ultraconservative, noncharismatic Christianity, became a best seller almost overnight.

All of this shows that the questions which the charismatics raise with regard to the devil and demons are of more than academic interest in today's world. What are we to make of the biblical interpretation of charismatics on these points? The proof-text method which they use is certainly questionable. Isaiah 14:12-14 is a dirge against the king of Babylon, and Ezekiel 28:11-18 is a lamentation over the king of Tyre. Still, it is difficult to deny that these passages have overtones which suggest the origin of satanic evil, and 2 Peter 2:4 and Jude 6 strengthen this interpretation.

The charismatic interpretations that we have considered show no awareness of how the concept of Satan entered biblical thought. In early biblical literature there is the tendency to see God as the instrumental cause of all that happens. Thus the Lord (Yahweh) is interpreted as having incited David to take a census of Israel, though David is later punished for having done so (2 Samuel 24). The ethical problem is solved in 1 Chronicles 21 by a later writer who attributes to Satan what Second Samuel had ascribed to God.

133

Most critical Bible scholars are agreed that Satanology, demonology, and angelology were relatively late developments in the faith of Israel. The people of Israel received their strongest impetus in this direction following their contact with Persian dualism during the period of the Exile. Many scholars even question whether there is any reference to Satan in the account of the Fall in Genesis 3. In answer, it may be said that the names "Satan" and the "devil" are not used, but it cannot be denied that the serpent has the role of the adversary (literal meaning of Satan), who opposes God and suggests rebellion against him to man. Moreover, in later biblical literature the serpent is clearly identified with the devil or Satan (Revelation 12:9; 20:2).

The influence of Persian dualism upon biblical angelology, Satanology, and demonology can hardly be denied. However, the distinctive character of the biblical interpretations also needs to be highlighted. Judaism, especially in the interbiblical period, accepted these elements into its faith, but in such a way as in no wise to compromise its fundamental monotheism. There is no teaching of a bad god to be set alongside of the good god. In Jewish thought the devil exists only because God permits his existence. He and his demonic cohorts are powerful, but they are not all powerful. They were admitted into biblical faith because they fill a profound need, that of explaining the persistence and power of evil in a world created by God and declared by him to be good.

The New Testament sets forth God and Satan as the heads of two warring kingdoms, but it leaves no doubt about the outcome of this struggle. God's kingdom will triumph, and people are offered "a choice between a Kingdom that is destined for victory and one that is doomed to destruction."[21] Jesus routs the kingdom of Satan in his exorcism of demons (Matthew 12:28), but he wins the decisive battle against all of the Satanic forces through his death and resurrection (John 12:31-33; 1 Corinthians 2:8; Colossians 2:12-15; Ephesians 1:15-22; Hebrews 2:14-16). If these views are correct, though one may quibble with the charismatics here and there about their interpretation of specific passages, one cannot fault them biblically on their basic understanding of the existence of Satan and evil spirits.

The philosophical question still remains. What are we to make of all of this in an age of science and technology? Can we accept as fact the existence of a sinister spiritual power called Satan and that of evil spirits or demons in league with him? With regard to this question there are four main approaches.

One approach is to interpret all of this as part of a mythological world view, a three-storied view of the universe, which modern science makes untenable. According to this three-storied view, above the world are God and his angels, and below the earth is the underworld with the devil and his demons. In between is the earth on which humanity dwells. From time to time there are interventions from God and the angels from above and from the devil and the demons from below. Rudolf Bultmann, the leading exponent of this view in our day, saw no possibility of supernatural intervention of any kind into the closed universe of cause and effect in which we live. Not only did he regard the idea of the devil and demons as mythological, but he treated the doctrines of the incarnation, the atonement, the resurrection, and the Second Coming of Christ as falling into the same category. According to him, the task of theology is that of interpreting the meaning of existence enshrined in each of these mythological conceptions.[22]

There are many who do not go all of the way with Bultmann in his understanding of the mythological but nevertheless find his approach very helpful. They think that it frees them from a literalness in biblical interpretation which would make faith in a scientific and secular age virtually impossible. This is certainly a plus in regard to the prescientific view of a three-storied universe. I find this approach unsatisfying, however, because of the anti-supernaturalistic presuppositions which underlie it. It appears to rule out the possibility of miracles before considering the evidence.

A second approach, and one which is closely related to the first, recognizes the dreadful reality of evil and even uses the category of the demonic but does not accept the existence of evil spiritual beings with separate centers of consciousness. This view has been championed most forcefully by Paul Tillich. Tillich regarded the demonic as the necessary symbol for the combination of the creative and the destructive which permeates human existence individually and all the structures of society collectively. When the demonic manifests itself in personality, a "being which has power over itself is grasped by another power and thereby divided." The state of being grasped by the demonic is the opposite of the state of grace. This first state results in the weakening of being, disintegration, and decay. The second has a fulfilling and form-creating effect. On the collective level Tillich saw capitalism and nationalism as two demonic powers which surpass all the rest in the sinister combination of the creative and the destructive.[23] This approach has the advantage of treating evil in all of its forms, personal and corporate, with complete seriousness, while avoiding the problems which many see in a literal approach to the biblical materials on this point. It leaves us, though, with no explanation of the origin of the demonic in a good world created by God.

Another approach is to suggest that Jesus, and perhaps the apostles as well, did not really accept the reality of the devil, demons, and the like, but that they simply accommodated themselves to the thought patterns of the people of their day for the sake of communication. For example, those who take this view argue that the most effective way for Jesus to deal with the problems of those who thought they were demon possessed was not to deny the existence of demons but to heal these deluded people by a command for the demons to come out. It seems to me that this is an attempt to avoid a modern problem. There would be nothing morally reprehensible about Jesus meeting people on their own ground in this way in order to help them. The fact of the matter is, however, that there is no evidence at all that this is what Jesus did or that he himself did not hold the same view in these matters as his contemporaries.

A fourth approach is that of recognizing the existence of the devil and demons. I follow this approach for two reasons.

135

First, I believe in the basic reliability of the biblical view of the nature of spiritual reality. As I see it, this view is not a part of an outmoded cosmology, the three-storied universe of which some theologians speak. Rather, it has to do with the basic structures of spiritual reality—God and the devil, good and evil. According to the Gospel accounts, Jesus recognized Satan and the demons for what they are, and the demons recognized him for who he is (Mark 1:21-28; 5:6-7). Paul lists the discerning of spirits as one of the gifts of the Spirit (1 Corinthians 12:10; cf. 1 John 4:1-2). The Bible treats the crucifixion of Jesus as the point at which the devil's hatred of God achieved its supreme and most direct manifestation. At the same time it represents it as the event which assures Satan's defeat. Satan and the powers of darkness in the biblical revelation constitute the indispensable backdrop to the victory of Christ secured through the cross and the resurrection.

Second, I do not believe that evil can be explained adequately as simply the absence of good, as darkness is the absence of light. There is an aggressiveness in evil that this view does not explain. Take, for example, the atrocities of Hitler and the attempt of the Nazis to exterminate the Jews or the murders associated with the "Manson family."

How does it happen that in the midst of a scientific technological revolution which exceeds anything our world has ever known before we have the greatest explosion of the occult on the one hand and of charismatic Christianity on the other that has taken place in centuries? Ours is a culture which a few years ago was talking about "the death of God" and of "religionless Christianity." Could it not be that the human heart is so made that it can never be satisfied when no room is left for the transcendent, mystical element in experience? Pushed out in one way, this longing reasserts itself in another. The same dynamics which spawned the new outbreak of the occult in our day may perhaps be understood as in some measure at work in other contemporary phenomena, such as the Jesus movement and the charismatic movement.

The view which I have defended should never be allowed to stand without three extremely important words of caution. The first word of caution is the recognition that this view may be used as a substitute for accepting responsibility for one's own failures. Like Flip Wilson's Geraldine, many of us find it quite easy to say: "The devil made me do it!" This type of an attempt to shift responsibility for one's own sin and failures to a sinister evil force outside us is as old as the Adam and Eve story (Genesis 3:13). The Bible will not tolerate any such escape. It accepts the reality of the devil and his angels, but it never treats temptation as irresistible (1 Corinthians 10:13). It always treats people as responsible for their own sin. In the epistle to the Romans Paul grapples seriously with the problem of evil, but he speaks directly of Satan only once (Romans 16:20) and of the demonic only once (Romans 8:38-39). Moreover, the book of James treats sin as arising, not from outside a person, but from within as one is "lured and enticed by his own desire" (James 1:13-15).

A second word of caution is that we need to be on our guard against overzealousness in demon chasing. Some people can recognize demons in every closet and under every bed. Some "demon chasers" have told the helpless victims of such dread diseases as leukemia and cancer that they could be healed if they would just renounce the demons they were harboring. There is the tendency on the part of some to ascribe all psychic disorders to demon possession. This simplistic view leaves no room for psychiatry or the insights of modern psychology. While these disciplines cannot be trusted to have all the answers, they certainly have some. If all mental disorders were of this kind, all that would be necessary in order to clear the wards of mental hospitals would be to turn a few experienced exorcists loose on them. In some charismatic treatments of the deliverance ministry one gets the impression that for every demon that is exorcised five more may be conjured up. While proclaiming deliverance, these people represent a mentality which may become an expression of a primitive type of bondage. It appears that anyone who specializes in this type of ministry should be an expert in counseling and should have an understanding of the basic insights of modern psychology.

A final word of caution is that we cannot emphasize too strongly Christ's victory over all the evil powers. Whatever these powers may be, real or imagined, they have been defeated in Christ. He is victor! He is King of Kings and Lord of Lords. No power in the universe can separate us from him (Romans 8:38-39). A concentration upon the demonic can open the door to all kinds of fears and anxieties that may be as destructive as any supposed demons. Concentration upon Christ and his victory can give us deliverance from all our fears.

While recognizing the reality of Satan and the demonic powers, we should join in this old hymn of the church in celebrating Christ's victory over them.

> Christian, dost thou see them on the holy ground,
> How the powers of darkness compass thee around?
> Christian, up and smite them, counting gain but loss;
> In the strength that cometh by the holy cross.[24]

CHAPTER 6

Other Gifts and Features of the Charismatic Movement

In addition to the remaining five spiritual gifts listed by Paul in 1 Corinthians 12:8-10, there are some other aspects of the charismatic movement that we should consider before moving on to a final evaluation in the last chapter. These other elements include the emphases in the charismatic movement on love, praise, and the return of Christ as well as the distinctive features of the movement within the Roman Catholic Church.

139

Other Gifts

Most of the five gifts out of the nine that Paul mentions in 1 Corinthians 12:8-10 have already been referred to in some other connection.

The Word of Wisdom

Charismatics usually understand "the word of wisdom" as having reference to a divinely inspired utterance given to a Christian in a difficult or dangerous situation by which the difficulty is solved or the opposition is silenced. It does not refer to a permanent endowment but to special wisdom that is given to different members of the body of Christ in different situations.

An Old Testament example of the word of wisdom is found in the way Solomon solved the problem of discovering who was the true mother of the child whom two women claimed as belonging to them (1 Kings 3:16-27). It was expected that the spirit of wisdom would rest upon the Messiah (Isaiah 11:2). Jesus demonstrated this gift again and again. One of the best-known examples of it occurred when he silenced his opponents who were asking whether it was lawful to pay taxes to Caesar by saying: "Render to Caesar the things that are Caesar's and to God the things that are God's" (Mark 12:17). Jesus promised his disciples that in times of testing they would be given wisdom which their adversaries could not withstand (Luke 21:12-15; 11:11-12). This was demonstrated in the case of Stephen, who at the time of his martyrdom spoke words which may have been instrumental in the conversion of Saul of Tarsus. Paul said that all of the treasures of wisdom and knowledge are hidden in Christ (Colossians 2:2-3).

The Word of Knowledge

"The word of knowledge" is understood by most charismatics as referring to a divine disclosure of facts to a Christian which could not have been known through natural means. Charismatics distinguish it sharply from such psychic phenomena as mental telepathy or extrasensory perception. Since they recognize only two sources of supernatural knowledge or power, they say that that which does not have its origin in God comes from Satan. There are many Old Testament examples to which they refer in illustrating the meaning of this gift (1 Samuel 9:15-20; 10:21-23; 2 Samuel 12:7-13; 2 Kings 5:20-27; 2 Kings 6:8-23). Jesus demonstrated such supernatural knowledge when he spoke to Nathanael about having seen him under the fig tree (John 1:48) and when he told the Samaritan woman she had had five husbands and was then living with a man who was not her husband (John 4:18). It was probably through a word of knowledge that Peter saw through the hypocrisy of Ananias and Sapphira (Acts 5:1-11). This gift is often helpful, we are told, in getting to the root of spiritual problems or in diagnosing health disorders.

Faith

Charismatics understand the gift of faith as referring neither to the faith which is the condition of salvation nor to that which is the fruit of the Spirit (Galatians 5:22). Rather, they think of it as the faith that moves mountains (Matthew 17:20; 1 Corinthians 13:2), which looks to God to perform that which, humanly speaking, would be impossible. This kind of faith was demonstrated by Jesus when at the graveside of Lazarus he thanked God for having already heard his prayers (John 11:41-42). It is the kind of faith, we are told, which often accompanies the gift of healing as, for example, when Peter

140

commanded the lame man to stand (Acts 3:1-10). It was demonstrated by Elijah when before the prophets of Baal on Mount Carmel he called on God to answer with fire from heaven (1 Kings 18:20-40).

Miracles

Charismatics understand miracles as events that seem to contradict the so-called laws of nature. Examples of miracles in the life of Jesus are seen in his turning water into wine (John 2:1-12), in his walking on the water (Matthew 14:25-33), his feeding the multitudes (Mark 6:30-44; 8:1-10), and his stilling the storm at sea (Mark 6:45-52). Miracles are seen in the lives of the apostles when Peter is delivered from prison by an angel (Acts 5:17-25; 12:1-17) and later when an earthquake opens prison doors for Paul and Silas (Acts 16:25-40).

Discerning the Spirits

The gift of "discerning of spirits" is interpreted by most charismatics as the divinely bestowed ability within certain situations to distinguish between the divine and the demonic. Jesus could recognize the source of the inspiration of those possessed by demons even though at times they might be telling the truth, as when they called him "the Holy One of God" or "Son of the Most High God" (Mark 1:24; 5:7). Paul later showed the same kind of discernment in a similar situation (Acts 16:16-18). Charismatics regard this gift as particularly important as an aid in distinguishing between true and false prophecy and in recognizing demon oppression.[1]

141

Appraisal of the Other Gifts

Charismatics have made some important contributions to our understanding of these gifts. The real problem lies not so much in their interpretation of them as in the unusually high importance which they attach to them. A hankering after miracles permeates the charismatic movement. Many charismatics acknowledge this but think that it is a reaction against the skepticism concerning the power of God to work miracles that permeates traditional Christianity. They believe that our skeptical age requires signs and wonders, demonstrations of the Spirit and of power (Romans 15:19; 1 Corinthians 2:4).

Jesus did not perform his miracles as demonstrations to compel faith but as acts of mercy to meet human need. At the same time, the miracles did manifest the power of God and the reality of the kingdom he proclaimed (Matthew 11:2-6; 12:28). Jesus did not trust himself to those who believed simply because of the signs he did (John 2:23-25). He refused to perform a miracle, like a magician doing his act, even when he might have saved his own life by dazzling Herod with a demonstration of power (Luke 23:6-12).

Jesus told the Pharisees, "A wicked and adulterous generation seeks for a sign" (Matthew 16:4), and he refused to show them a sign in response to their request. Jesus knew, however, that they did not want to believe. The miracles he had performed were not done in private, but in public. Even when they saw his miracles, they put the wrong construction upon them, interpreting them as signs of the power of Satan (Beelzebub) rather than of God (Mark 3:20-27).

Charismatics would argue on the other hand that the important thing is not so much that miracles evoke faith as that they flow forth from faith. This is a good argument. Doubtless if there were more faith, there would be more miracles. Jesus certainly implied as much when he spoke of the faith that moves mountains. Yet, what shall we say of a faith that is built on miracles and has come to expect them? Is this a higher type of faith than that of a Christian in whose life miracles do not flow so freely? This is not necessarily so. To a large degree miracles are beyond our control. We may thwart them, but we cannot always bring them forth at will. No one can, for we are not talking about magical tricks but supernatural demonstrations of the power of God. What happens to a faith that is built on miracles when and if the miracles stop? If God can give them, he can also take them away. God wants us to believe in him whether we see miracles or not.

Charismatics are to be criticized for a tendency to exaggerate the miraculous, for undue credulity that will believe any kind of miracle tale, and for silence in the face of deception. A case in point is the type of stories told in Mel Tari's book *Like a Mighty Wind*.[2] In this book, tales are related that parallel all of the most amazing miracles in the life of Jesus—walking on water, turning water into wine, feeding a large number of people adequately with very meager provisions, and even raising the dead. There can be no doubt that truly wonderful miracles have occurred in Indonesia in recent years in connection with the revival there. However, when noncharismatic Christians earnestly seeking the truth have tried to find out what happened, according to the most reliable reports that I have read, they have not been able to verify any of the spectacular miracles reported above.[3] I may have overlooked it, but nowhere do I remember reading of charismatics raising their voices in protest against this type of deception. I do not doubt God's ability or willingness to perform miracles in our day, but I do cherish honesty. I think charismatics are doing their own cause harm by their strange silence about such things.

The More Excellent Way

Charismatics are quite mindful of the context of Paul's great discourse on love, 1 Corinthians 13. It comes in between the two chapters in which he is discussing spiritual gifts. They see this chapter not as a detour from the main theme but as inseparably connected with it. They understand love not as an alternative to the gifts but as the principle for applying them. The more excellent way of which Paul speaks (12:31) is that of letting love express itself through the gifts, rather than making the gifts an end in themselves.[4] While urging the Corinthians to desire spiritual gifts, they say, he enjoins them to make love their aim (12:31; 14:1).

The love of which Paul speaks is *agape,* the kind of sacrificial love which God expressed toward us in Christ. Charismatics frequently point out that Paul is not treating love as one of the *charismata,* the highest and most important of all. They have no doubt that the love of which Paul speaks has its source in the Father, is manifested in the Son, and comes to us through the Holy Spirit (Romans 5:5-8). Love, they say, is never mentioned by Paul as a *charisma* of the Spirit, but it heads the list when he mentions the fruit of the Spirit (Galatians 5:22). "Gifts can be given in an instant; fruit takes time to produce."[5]

Does Paul teach that the gifts apart from love are valueless? This is the usual interpretation of 1 Corinthians 13:1-3. On this point charismatics are not in complete agreement. Some say that Paul is not saying that the gifts apart from love are valueless. They may accomplish worthy ends and bring blessings to the recipients of them. But when they are exercised apart from love, they are of no value to the one who so uses them. On the other hand, there are charismatics who think the basic question is whether the recipient of the gift encounters the risen Lord in the gift or simply the person exercising it. Seen from this standpoint, agape love is indispensable. "When gifts are no longer an expression of Christ's actions," says Bittlinger, "they are not only useless but harmful in their effect. They are counterfeits which offer my neighbor nothing, but positively deceive him."[6]

Charismatics recognize the nature of love as it is expressed in 1 Corinthians 13:4-7 as a description of the character of Jesus Christ. They also understand Paul as saying that love is absolute, while the gifts are relative (1 Corinthians 13:8-13). Prophetic utterances and words of knowledge will pass away, and tongues will cease. Intended

143

for the protection and edification of the church on earth, the gifts will no longer be needed when the church is with its Edifier. Love, on the other hand, will abide throughout eternity, for God is love (1 Corinthians 13:8-13; 1 John 4:8, 16).

Countless are the testimonies of charismatics who speak of the baptism in the Spirit as a baptism of love. They speak of being overwhelmed with the consciousness of God's love for them and of a welling up within their hearts of love for God and for their fellowmen. Presbyterian charismatic Leonard Evans sounds love as the central theme of the gospel. He bears witness again and again to how his marriage, his life, and his ministry as a pastor were transformed by a discovery of the centrality of love. He declares that love to God is manifest in one's love to one's neighbor. "God is the infinite faucet of love," he says. "By faith, we hook the hose of our life up to him. Then we make the mistake of trying to shoot the water back to the faucet, rather than to our fellow man."[7]

The charismatics have many good insights to share about the role of love. They are correct in maintaining that Paul does not set forth love as an alternative to the gifts. Rather, his point in this passage is that love is the motive and the atmosphere in which God intends the gifts to operate. Some scholars think that Paul had written his great hymn of love prior to writing First Corinthians, but in writing to the church in Corinth, he polished it and inserted it in this place because of its obvious appropriateness for the situation. Whether this be true or not, it must certainly be admitted that chapter 13 is admirably suited to its context. Love not only provides the standard for testing and measuring the gifts, but it is the indispensable means of maintaining unity in the body as well.

In my judgment, charismatics are also correct when they say that Paul does not treat love as one of the *charismata.* Most commentaries are agreed on this point. First Corinthians 14:1 in the *New English Bible* reads: "Put love first; but there are other gifts of the Spirit at which you should aim also, and above all prophecy." The insertion of the word "other" before "gifts" in this passage is unjustified. This is an interpretation of the text, not a translation.

Does Paul say that the gifts are valueless apart from love? Those who say "no" are correct as far as the literal words are concerned. The gifts that Paul mentions here—tongues, prophecy, knowledge, the faith that moves mountains, liberality, and martyrdom—with the single exception of martyrdom—are all mentioned elsewhere in his letters. Paul discounts not the gifts, but the exerciser of them when love is lacking. He says: "I am a noisy gong or a clanging cymbal . . . I am nothing . . . I gain nothing" (1 Corinthians 13:1-3). It is conceivable that through the gifts help could be rendered without love. The recipient of another's liberality could be benefited by it even though the giver had no love. However, Paul is evidently writing to discourage the use of gifts apart from love. Doubtless, he believed that great havoc had been wrought in the church at Corinth by this very thing.

There are some who think that Paul had both a positive and a negative picture before him when he wrote 1 Corinthians 13:4-7. The positive picture was the character of Christ. Thus, one could read: "Christ is patient and kind; Christ is not jealous or boastful." The negative picture, according to this view, was that manifest in the tongues speakers at Corinth. This would mean that he was saying: "Tongues speakers are impatient and unkind . . . tongues speakers are arrogant and rude. . . ." In answer, we should say clearly that this is speculation. The character of Jesus is certainly portrayed in verse 4-7, but we cannot be certain that Paul made this a conscious portrayal. It is possible that Paul had tongues speakers in mind when writing these verses, but this is nothing but conjecture. What is certain is that no matter what side of the fence we may stand on with regard to the charismatic movement, we had better be extremely cautious about ascribing such qualities as impatience and unkindness, jealousy and boastfulness, arrogance and rudeness to those on the opposite side. In doing so we will very likely be taking on those same characteristics ourselves!

A great deal of love is manifest within the charismatic movement. Often there is hugging and kissing, usually men with men and women with women, but sometimes between the sexes. Sometimes love can be conveyed by touch more effectively than in any other way. However, there are obvious dangers here, and charismatics need to be mindful of them and on their guard. Such manifestations can in some cases incite the carnal nature.

Sometimes those not involved in the charismatic movement think that charismatics tend to limit the manifestations of their love to those of like mind. Charismatics, on the other hand, often feel that those outside the movement do not have an abundance of love for them. We need to be very careful in judging others in such matters. In the final analysis, love is a matter of the heart, and only one who sees the heart, as God does, is in a position to judge.

Within the charismatic movement there are people with various hobbyhorses. With some people it is tongues; with others it is healing, exorcism, or praise; with still others it is love. If one is going

145

to ride a hobbyhorse, whether one bears the label of charismatic or not, one can find no better one than love.

The Centrality of Praise

Praise occupies a central place in the lives of most charismatics. This is true to such a degree that the phrase "Praise the Lord" has been called "the hallmark" of the charismatic movement. Praise is understood as the highest form of worship. We are to praise God not only for what he has done and the blessings he has bestowed, but above all for who he is. He is worthy of all glory, honor, adoration, and praise. Praise is the means, we are told, by which God transforms us into the likeness of his Son. Countless are the testimonies of lives that have been transformed through praise. Through it often the emotions are cleansed, old hurts are healed, and even physical healings are accomplished.

Most of the choruses that serve such an important function in charismatic prayer meetings are heartfelt expressions of praise. During the singing of these choruses charismatics often lift their hands as an expression of adoration and worship. The stress that many charismatics place upon tongues is related to praise. They claim that through the exercise of tongues they are able to praise the Lord in a way that transcends the limitations of ordinary human speech. Moreover, praising the Lord in this way, they say, primes the pump, so to speak, and enables them to express their adoration in praise more fully, freely, and spontaneously in their own languages.

Among charismatics, no one has emphasized praise more strongly than Merlin R. Carothers. As an ex-convict who was converted to the Lord, called to the gospel ministry, and "baptized in the Spirit," Carothers attributes the tremendous dynamic which his ministry displays to some lessons he says the Lord taught him about praising him for all things. Most of Carothers' books, all of which have been published by Logos International, bear praise titles: *Prison to Praise* (1970), *Power in Praise* (1972), *Answers to Praise* (1972), *Praise Works!* (1973), and *Walking and Leaping* (1974). The first four books have sold over four million copies, and all of these books year after year remain on the best-seller lists of religious publications.

Carothers insists that as Christians we should praise God for all things, no matter how adverse the circumstances. He cites case after case of how he has applied this formula in his own life and recommended it to others with marvelous results. He calls upon a man whose wife is about to divorce him to praise the Lord for this fact. He does the same to a wife whose husband has fathered a child out of wedlock by another woman, and to all kinds of people who have just lost loved ones through such dread diseases as cancer or through such adverse circumstances as the carelessness of a drunken driver. He maintains that praising God for all things is God's will for us and what Scripture tells us to do (1 Thessalonians 5:16-18; Ephesians 5:20).

Carothers' rationale for this position is that God is a loving Father who has the hairs of our head numbered and is not unmindful when a sparrow falls (Matthew 10:29-30). Nothing can happen to us which God does not permit (even though Satan may be the instrument by which it occurs), and he will permit nothing that is not for our good (Romans 8:28). Therefore, we should trust God and praise him not only *in* all things but *for* all things.

Jehoshaphat praised the Lord when he was surrounded by what seemed like an impossible host of enemies, and the Lord gave him and his army a mighty victory without their having to fight (2 Chronicles 20:1-23). Paul and Silas praised the Lord when they had been beaten and placed in stocks in prison, and the Lord sent an earthquake and delivered them (Acts 16:19-34). Carothers maintains that we are to praise God neither because of any expectation concerning the good effects to come from it nor because we think that if we do so, God is going to change the situation so drastically that what we had regarded as adversity becomes a blessing. Rather, we are to praise God for all things simply because we believe he loves us and therefore we can trust him. No matter what the problem, he insists, we should pray like this: "Lord, I don't understand this problem, but I believe that you love me and that you have sent this for my good, so I praise you for it." Carothers relates the praise of which he speaks to joy in the Lord, and says that where there is joy and praise, anxiety and grumbling must flee.

By way of appraisal, we should say that in the Christian life praise is no side issue. It is certainly one of the most important keys to triumphant Christian living. The charismatic movement is to be commended for its recognition of this important point. The Bible is full of prayers of praise, and the charismatic movement (but here it is not alone) has rendered a tremendous service to Christendom by setting many of these prayers to music and helping them to win acceptance and wide use in the churches. Worshipful adoration of the living God is the highest function of the Christian in this life. It cleanses, liberates, transforms, and motivates for service to others. The book of Revelation leads us to believe that praise will engage our time and energies throughout eternity to the glory of God.

147

There can be no doubt that Carothers' books have been a blessing to many. The testimonies that he relates of how applying praise in difficult situations has brought newness of life are not to be disparaged or passed over lightly. For example, he tells of a wife who had been praying for years for her alcoholic husband, but when she started praising the Lord that he was just as he was, within a day or so he was converted and healed of his alcoholism. In this sense "praise works." Nevertheless, Carothers' view is quite extreme. Extremism of nearly every kind turns some people on and some off. Some receive Carothers' approach as a message of hope, others as a slap in the face.

One gets the impression from reading *Prison to Praise* that Carothers was led to this emphasis upon praising God for everything from a subjective experience, conversations which he had with God.[8] Then, as he started studying the Scriptures, he found confirmation for it everywhere. Carothers quotes a lot of Scripture to support his position, but it is doubtful if his interpretation is sustained by more than one verse of the Bible. That one verse is Ephesians 5:20, which does say that we are to give thanks for everything. First Thessalonians 5:18 says that we are to give thanks in all circumstances. In 2 Corinthians 12:9-10 Paul praises God for his weaknesses through which God's power is revealed, but he does this only after he has prayed to God three times for the removal of his "thorn in the flesh" and gotten God's answer that the "thorn" serves a divinely appointed purpose in his life. We are not told that Jehoshaphat praised God for the circumstances that he faced or that Paul and Silas praised God because they had been beaten and placed in prison. In both of those cases the most that can be argued is that they praised God in those circumstances.

148

There is an important difference between the King James Version and the Revised Standard Version in Romans 8:28. The KJV reads: "all things work together 'for good," while the RSV has "in everything God works for good. . . ." The manuscripts are divided upon this point.[9] The KJV would suggest that everything that happens to a Christian is according to God's plan, while the RSV rendering would suggest that no matter what happens to a Christian, God is able to bring good out of it.

In my view, it is biblical to praise God in all things, but Carothers' emphasis upon praising God for all things is a distorted one. In the first place, it represents a distorted view of divine providence. It confuses God's permissive will with his intentional will. It is obvious that everything that happens is according to God's permissive will, or it would not have happened. It does not follow, though, that whatever happens is according to God's intentional will. God intends for us to obey him, but he permits us to disobey. We are not then to blame God for our disobedience. Even so, God is not helpless, and when we turn to him even within the worst messes that our sins bring upon us, he is able to bring forth good. This kind of distinction saves us from having to judge the character of God by all of the terrible things we see happening in the world and leaves us free to see in God the loving Father revealed in Jesus Christ.

In the second place, Carothers' view represents a distorted view of prayer. The Bible shows us that there is a place for various forms of prayer—praise, thanksgiving, confession, petition, and intercession. Logically speaking, Carothers' view reduces all prayer to praise. There is no room for petition or intercession, for one can hardly thank God in sincerity that everything is just as it is and then proceed to ask him to bring about changes in these things. If one did so, it would mean that any thanksgiving that one might offer would be on the basis of anticipated changes in the circumstances rather than on the basis of existing conditions. This is what Carothers specifically says praise should not be.

Even within the charismatic movement there are many who think Carothers' interpretations are extreme and who reject them.[10] It needs to be made crystal clear that the options are not between Carothers' view of praise and no praise at all. Rather, a third option needs to be emphasized, that of thanking God in all circumstances, but not necessarily for all circumstances. This, I believe, is the view that has the fullest claim to biblical support.

Expectation of the Early Return of Christ

Many Protestant charismatics have taken over from Pentecostalism the expectation of the early return of Christ. The full gospel, according to the Full Gospel Business Men's Fellowship International, is belief in Jesus Christ as Savior, Healer, Baptizer in the Holy Spirit, and the soon-coming King. The expectation of the early return of Christ is widespread in conservative Christianity and is by no means limited to Pentecostal and Neo-Pentecostal circles. However, what is distinctive in Pentecostal and Neo-Pentecostal interpretations is the tendency to treat the charismatic renewal itself as evidence of the proximity of Christ's return. Baptist charismatic Jamie Buckingham writes:

> What is the charismatic renewal? In a word, it is the supernatural visitation of the Holy Spirit, preparing the church for the coming again of the Lord Jesus Christ. As in New Testament times the gifts are being restored. The

church is being perfected without spot or wrinkle, to the virginal purity of a bride adorned for her husband. It is the answer to the prayer "thy kingdom come on earth as it is in Heaven"—the ushering in of the Kingdom because the King is coming.[11]

Among Pentecostals, references to the "former rain" or "early rain" and the "latter rain" (Joel 2:23; James 5:7) are frequent. They interpret the outpouring of the Holy Spirit at Pentecost as the "former rain" and the restoration of the gifts of the Spirit which is occurring in the Pentecostal movement as the "latter rain," the prelude to the Second Coming. In between are the intermittent showers which keep the grain alive until the time of the harvest. This explains, they think, why the gifts poured out so profusely upon the early church never completely died out in the history of the church. But now as we approach the end once again, these gifts are being poured out in profusion.

Many Protestant charismatics have adopted this Pentecostal interpretation of last things. Some charismatics also interpret the explosion of the occult that we are witnessing in this generation as a sign of the end of time. "We are living in days when Satan is pouring out his spirits as well as Jesus Christ the Holy Spirit"[12] (Revelation 9:20; 16:13-14; 18:2). Many of the "Jesus People" who moved from the realm of the occult to acknowledge the lordship of Jesus Christ are convinced that this is the last generation that will inhabit the earth. The King is at hand, they believe, and many of them, with all of the urgency imaginable, are seeking to win converts for Christ before the Lord returns.

Many in Christianity in whom the hope of Christ's imminent return burns brightly speak of a great tribulation that is coming upon the earth. Many believe that the church will escape the tribulation coming upon the world because they expect the church to be caught up (raptured) to meet the Lord in the air. There are other Christians, however, who interpret the Scriptures to mean that even the faithful must go through the great tribulation before the Lord comes. Protestant charismatic Corrie ten Boom with her background of years in a Nazi concentration camp for helping the Jews during World War II takes this position. She believes that the outpouring of the Holy Spirit all over the world is intended to make Christians strong so they can endure the tribulation coming upon the church before the return of the Lord Jesus Christ.[13]

Catholic charismatics tend to look upon the predictions of the early return of Christ as belonging to a fundamentalist type of thinking which they cannot accept. Cardinal Suenens, warning against "irresponsible apocalyptic forecasts," calls our attention to the words of Jesus that knowledge of the end of time is a secret of the Father. He counsels keeping in our hearts a living hope while striving to make the world a better place in which to live.[14]

Questions which the charismatics raise at this point could carry us deeply into a consideration of eschatology, the doctrine of last things. Only a brief treatment of some of the salient issues is in order.

A number of different approaches are possible to the doctrine of the Second Coming of Christ. There are many who regard the hope of the Second Coming as a light that failed. They take the position that since over nineteen centuries have passed since this hope was first expressed and Christ still has not returned, there is no reason for us to be concerned about it now. Some reinterpret the doctrine to mean not a cataclysmic coming of Christ at the end of history but a progressive coming as his teachings are disseminated throughout the earth and the principles of love, justice, and brotherhood which he championed win wider and wider acceptance. Others look for a literal, personal, visible, imminent return of Christ, and they formulate charts depicting the details of events preceding, during, and following his advent. Not satisfied with any of these views, I want to make some basic affirmations concerning the subject.

First, the expectation of the Second Coming of Christ is a hope which the church can ill afford to surrender. It rests upon the affirmation: Jesus is Lord! If he is really Lord, he is Lord of time and eternity, of individual lives and of all history. As history had a beginning, it will also have an end. Christ is going to bring to perfection that which he undertook when he came the first time. General MacArthur, pushed out of the Philippines during World War II, left with the promise: "I will return." He did return! The promise of Christ's return is no less certain.

Second, it will be a personal return, recognizable by all (Luke 17:24), though the exact form that it will take defies human understanding. The Bible uses images of this world to describe things that relate to the other world. It describes heaven as having streets of gold and gates of pearl. These are generally taken as symbols expressing that which is of highest value. Likewise the biblical images of the sounding of a trumpet and Christ appearing on the clouds of heaven are to be taken seriously, but not necessarily literally.

Third, from the perspective of the New Testament we have been living in the last days since Pentecost (Acts 2:17; Hebrews 1:2; 1 Peter 1:20; 1 John 2:18). There are passages in the New Testament, however, in which "the last time" refers to the end of the world (1

Peter 1:5) and "the last day" to the final resurrection (John 6:39-40). Pentecostals take some words from Joel and James and without regard to the context of those passages draw up a chart of future events. Joel treats a devastating locust plague as the judgment of the Lord upon Israel. He promises, however, that if Israel will repent, God will bless the land with renewed productivity. In that context he refers to the early and latter rain (Joel 2:23). James also refers to the early and latter rains (James 5:7-9) but in a different connection. He is writing to encourage patience in view of the delay in the coming *(parousia)* of the Lord. In doing so he points to the example of the Palestinian farmer waiting patiently in the long interval between the early rains of October and November and the late rains in April and May. He is suggesting that there is a similar interval between the Lord's sowing and the Lord's harvest. Therefore, James urges his readers to emulate the Palestinian farmer in showing patience.[15]

The passage in Joel is followed by the promise of the universal outpouring of God's Spirit (Joel 2:28-32), the passage quoted by Peter at Pentecost. In order for it to fit properly into the Pentecostal interpretation, the reference to the early and latter rain (Joel 2:23) should follow the promise of the outpouring of the Spirit. There is no specific reference to the work of the Spirit in the passage in James. If one is seeking to provide a chart of future events on the basis of scattered references in the Bible taken from their context, the Pentecostal interpretation along these lines has as good a claim to validity as most, and a better claim than some. However, I am skeptical of this whole line of approach.

Fourth, we should avoid forecasting the time of the coming of the Lord and making our plans and conducting our activities on the basis of those forecasts. Scripture warns us against this (Mark 13:33; Acts 1:7). Moreover, history shows us the folly of it. In the past many have made such predictions and have been proven wrong. Failure to prepare for one's life work on the basis of an anticipated early return of the Lord seems to me to be extreme and shortsighted.

Fifth, we need to live in anticipation of our Lord's return and daily be engaged in the faithful performance of the tasks he has given us to do. The Bible counsels watchfulness and prayer in anticipation of the Lord's coming (Matthew 25:13; Mark 13:33; Luke 21:36), but it chides idleness (2 Thessalonians 3:6-12). There should be an attitude of expectancy, but preparation for the long haul. Many evangelicals in whom the hope of the Lord's early return burns brightly find this hope to be a strong incentive for evangelism. Many of them, however, manifest an indifference to social problems. The personal and social dimensions of Christian responsibility need to be held together in anticipation of the Lord's coming and our accountability before him in the judgment.

Distinctives of the Charismatic Movement in Roman Catholicism

When Catholics first began to share the Pentecostal experience, they started calling themselves Catholic Pentecostals. Later they began speaking about the charismatic movement within the Catholic Church. Now the accepted term is the charismatic renewal within the Catholic Church or the Catholic charismatic renewal. Already, in various connections we have called attention to some points of view of Catholic charismatics, but it should be of help to summarize some of the distinctives of the Catholic charismatic renewal. Roman Catholic charismatics seek to relate their experience to the whole body of Catholic tradition and practice, and they very consciously attempt to keep the charismatic emphasis within the broader perspective of the whole church.

Relation to Catholic Tradition

Those who are active in the Catholic charismatic renewal are striving earnestly to baptize the distinctive emphases of the renewal into the best of Catholic dogma, tradition, and piety. They have expressed uneasiness about the term "baptism in the Spirit" and have suggested other terms such as "manifestation of baptism" and "renewal of the sacraments of initiation." For the most part they have rejected the two-stage theology that is characteristic of Pentecostalism and much of the charismatic movement within Protestantism. They see the Pentecostal experience as rooted in the sacraments of initiation, some Catholics emphasizing baptism, others confirmation, some both.

153

Catholic charismatics stress the positive things that Vatican II teaches about the spiritual gifts. They declare that the church and the charisms go together and maintain that the church cannot really fulfill its function in the world without them. At the same time they tend to play down the newness of the movement, refusing to claim that charismatic manifestations within the life of the church began with the current Catholic charismatic renewal.

Many Catholic theologians involved in the charismatic renewal have been combing the writings of Catholic mystics through the ages seeking points of contact for the renewal and ways of interpreting the renewal that are in keeping with accepted norms of Catholic piety.

Catholic charismatics seek to demonstrate by word, attitude, and deed that they are not a "foreign body" within the Catholic Church but that they remain loyal Catholics. They maintain that their charismatic experience has given them a deepened appreciation for the mass and for the liturgy of the church. They are zealous in attending confession, mass, and in performing all of the functions expected of a good Catholic.

One of the ways Catholic charismatics show that they remain loyal Catholics, even though a new dimension has been added, is by demonstrating their devotion to Mary. Catholic charismatic Cardinal Suenens relates that he received a standing ovation from the twenty thousand assembled at the International Catholic Charismatic Conference in 1973 when he spoke of Mary as a secret of holiness. He devotes a chapter of his book *A New Pentecost?* to a discussion of "The Holy Spirit and Mary." He expresses an awareness that many Protestants think Catholics ascribe to Mary much that should be ascribed to the Holy Spirit. He sees Mary as a model of complete submission to the Holy Spirit and even speaks of Mary illumined by the Spirit as "the first charismatic." He makes no reference to the Catholic dogma of the Assumption of Mary.

154   Cardinal Suenens says: "The Son born of her is and remains the Son of the Father and the Son of Mary." He says that just as a river leads us to the sea, Mary cannot fail to lead us to Jesus. He calls Mary "the Christian *par excellence.*" The Spirit who fills Mary, according to the cardinal, is the Spirit of the Son. Therefore, Mary is not a screen concealing the Lord from us. He maintains that Mary is a guarantee of true humanity in that she prevents us from attempting "to keep God at a distance by denying his closeness to us." Her influence is also an important guard against the inhumanities of technology and war and can soften the rigidity of institutions and bureaucracies. He speaks of her also as the guarantee of humility and of balance and wisdom.[16]

Catholic charismatics go to great pains to demonstrate their submission to authority within the Catholic Church. They avoid being secretive; they praise the pope and the reforms of Vatican II; and they welcome the participation of members of the hierarchical structure in their charismatic meetings. When charismatics encounter the opposition of their bishops in regard to the way they conduct their prayer meetings, they usually seek to conform to the restrictions imposed until more understanding is achieved. Often this approach of submission to authority has resulted in the restrictions being relaxed or removed, we are told.[17]

Leaders of the charismatic movement within the Catholic Church frequently warn other charismatics of the danger of Catholics taking into the Catholic Church "cultural baggage" from Pentecostalism or Protestant fundamentalism. While not criticizing these within the context of those groups, they maintain that this "cultural baggage" is completely out of place within Catholicism. One of the most capable theologians involved in the Catholic charismatic renewal, J. Massingberd Ford, offers a number of suggestions along these lines. She warns against the non-Catholic view of claiming assurance of salvation. In support of the view that one cannot be sure of one's salvation until one reaches heaven, she quotes 1 John 1:10 and Philippians 2:12. She says we should avoid the Montanist mistake of speaking of ourselves as "Spirit-filled," "for no one is 'Spirit-filled' except Jesus and his Blessed Mother." She warns also against interpreting tongues as a necessary sign of being baptized in the Spirit. Maintaining that the sacraments of baptism and confirmation are the prime source of the Holy Spirit, she insists that anyone who has been baptized has the Holy Spirit.

Ford counsels Catholic charismatics against being overdemonstrative in an emotional way, cautioning them to be sensitive to the feelings of others. Though she does not object to Catholic charismatics laying hands on people for whom they pray as an expression of faith and supporting love, she objects to talking about "praying over people" or "laying hands on people." Her concern is to avoid anything that sounds like magic. She says that no one should be allowed to feel out of place if one disagrees with the practice of placing the hands on someone and praying for that person. Ford warns also against charismatics using phrases like "we" and "they" as the Montanists did. Meetings should be conducted in such a way that one who does not speak in tongues will not feel out of place.

Ford disagrees with a practice common among Protestant charismatics of omitting the phrase "if it is your will" while praying for the sick. Praying in the name of Jesus means, as she understands it, praying according to the character of Jesus. This means, of course, praying for God's will to be done. She warns that talking about devils or demons is misleading and frightening for an outsider. Never should we attribute a physical disease to a devil, she says. She regards this as a primitive way of thinking. She disagrees with the way many fundamentalists use Scripture, and she insists that "good and sure academic progress in biblical scholarship" should be combined with spirituality.

Ford objects strongly to Catholics seeking re-baptism, saying

155

that the Holy Spirit is not concerned about the amount of water used in baptism. Finally, she warns Catholic charismatics against becoming *"pushy pentecostals."* She advises speaking with discretion and joy about God's gifts to us, saying that we must never give the impression that we are better Christians than others.[18]

Relation to the Whole Church

There is a strong emphasis upon Christian community in the Catholic charismatic renewal. Often this takes the form of a covenant community in which the members live together in households and commit themselves to each other economically as well as spiritually. A number of these have sprung up in various places, but the best-known one is probably "The Word of God Community" in Ann Arbor, Michigan.

Along with this emphasis upon community, the leaders of the Catholic charismatic renewal define the goals of the movement in terms of the charismatic renewal of the whole church. The aim of the renewal is fullness of life in the Spirit for all of God's people. Catholic charismatic Stephen Clark suggests that the renewal needs an approach to baptism in the Spirit and spiritual gifts that integrates these elements fully into the Christian life, while keeping the focus of renewal upon the Lord, not upon these.[19] Catholic charismatics think that at some point in the future the church may be so renewed that a separate movement is no longer needed. All are agreed, however, that the renewal has a long way to go before this point is reached.

There is a strong ecumenical emphasis within the Catholic charismatic renewal. Many Catholic charismatics feel a spiritual oneness with Protestant charismatics, and a good many of them participate gladly from time to time in ecumenical charismatic meetings that are dominantly Protestant. They recognize that this type of ecumenical fellowship is possible for Catholics only because of Vatican II which committed the Catholic Church to ecumenism. While attending these meetings, most Catholic charismatics maintain their love for the Catholic Church and loyalty to its traditions. At the same time, in these meetings they usually avoid reference to anything that is distinctively Catholic, such as the veneration of Mary or obedience to the pope and constituted Catholic authority.

Appraisal of the Catholic Charismatic Renewal

The leadership within the Catholic charismatic movement has been extremely strong from the beginning. Many of the leaders have been university and seminary professors who have guided the movement in such a way as to help it win acceptance within the Catholic Church and to integrate it into the best traditions of Catholic life. The growth of the movement in a short period of time has been no less than phenomenal. Far from being a disruptive force within the Catholic Church, as has sometimes been the case with the charismatic movement in Protestantism, it has proved itself to be a tremendous power for spiritual renewal within the life of the church. For this reason, we can accept Stephen Clark's statement that "the charismatic renewal in the Catholic Church has emerged as one of the most vital occurrences in contemporary Christianity." [20]

It is truly remarkable that Catholics have received anything so obviously Protestant in its origins. It is also easy to understand why Catholic charismatics have been unwilling to accept Pentecostalism in unaltered form but have sought to stamp a Catholic image upon it. No doubt this accounts, at least in a measure, for the fact that Catholic charismatics have been so eager to show that they are still loyal Catholics, though their Christian life has taken on a charismatic dimension. They operate within the framework of authoritarian church structures which, if they so desired, could at any time curb the renewal and greatly limit its influence. This is not to suggest that in their zeal for their church charismatics are acting out of expediency rather than out of conviction. They remain committed Catholics, despite some emphases that seem quite evangelical. They have been trained to think of obedience to God as being expressed through obedience to recognized church authorities. Sacramental worship has been and continues to be a vital part of their experience.

Some Protestant charismatics raise the question as to whether Catholic charismatics have not been too eager to become respectable too quickly. Taking note of the tremendous growth of the movement within the Catholic Church, they want to know why Catholic charismatics are not speaking out on such issues as the Catholic doctrine of papal infallibility, the church's opposition to Catholics joining in non-Catholic Communion services, the church's position on birth control in the light of the world food problem, and Vatican politics. They are not suggesting that Catholic charismatics should defy their leaders or insult the pope but that they should make their voices heard on these issues. [21]

In my view this is an issue that Catholics themselves will have to settle. The conflict between the concern for numerical expansion and the need to take a prophetic stance on relevant issues is one that confronts the Christian movement at all times. It would appear that with Catholic charismatics it is a question of priorities and methods.

157

They have been concerned to demonstrate that they are not a "foreign body" within the Catholic Church. They have stated their goal as charismatic renewal which will revitalize the life of the whole church. So far they have steered clear of becoming a pressure group and have sought to work as leaven within the existing structures. If Catholic charismatics should follow the policy that their Protestant charismatic friends are suggesting, they would doubtless incur the wrath or suspicion of the hierarchy and lose much of their appeal across the full spectrum of Catholic life. It is not for us who sit on the outside to pose the issue in terms of truth versus popularity. The type of spiritual renewal which the movement is helping to bring about within Catholicism is desperately needed. This also is an aspect of Christian truth that needs to be recovered. Tremendous changes have taken place within Catholicism since the early sixties. Big battles are still being fought between the progressive and conservative forces. Our task as Protestants is not to throw stones at the Catholics but to put our own house in order.

It is easy for us as Protestants to take a judgmental stance toward Catholic charismatics. We wonder why, if they really have the Holy Spirit and are reading the Bible, they can fail to see things our way. But Catholic charismatics remain Catholics. Doctrinal differences between us remain. We should rejoice, however, in the evidences that the Lord whom we know to be at work in our lives and within our churches is also at work in their lives and within their churches.

By and large, Catholic charismatics have handled the charismatic element more effectively than Protestant charismatics. I find myself in agreement with most of the suggestions that J. Massingberg Ford makes to Catholic charismatics, except in the places where she expresses something that is distinctive in Catholicism. The common-sense approach that she recommends is highly commendable, and it is to be hoped that the charismatic movement within Protestantism will move more in these directions.

CHAPTER 7

Summary
and
Conclusion

Even if you are one who always scans the closing pages of a detective story to find out the villain's identity before reading the story, I strongly recommend that you not read this chapter until you have read the rest of the book. This is not a detective story, and we are not dealing with villains, but the statements made here are based on the argument advanced throughout the book. Reading this section without first reading the preceding chapters would be like trying to erect a roof in midair without a structure below to support it.

General Observations

Let us begin this final chapter by attempting to sum up the positive elements in the charismatic movement in light of the criticisms which have been raised.

Fellowship and Vitality

Those within the charismatic movement bear witness to a sense of being accepted and loved. They feel that in this group there are those who care about their vital needs—physical, financial, and spiritual. Along with this warmth of fellowship is an amazing vitality. Taken as a whole, this type of Christianity embracing classical Pentecostalism and Protestant and Catholic Neo-Pentecostalism has for some years been the fastest growing type of Christianity in the world. Because of its tremendous vitality, if for no other reason, traditional Christianity cannot afford to ignore it. However, the very feeling of warmth within the fellowship of the charismatic movement and the sense of power and growth have led to a kind of spiritual pride on the part of some. They look at those within the more traditional churches where this warmth and growth are less evident and are tempted to pride themselves on their new experience of spiritual vitality. Charismatics tend to judge noncharismatics by terming them "unspiritual." Noncharismatics judge charismatics by accusing them of spiritual pride. Both groups need to remember the words of our Lord, "Judge not, that you be not judged" (Matthew 7:1). Likewise, Paul counseled: "Who are you to pass judgment on the servant of another? It is before his own master that he stands or falls" (Romans 14:4). Rather than judging other groups, both sides of the dispute need to be more aware of and sensitive to their own shortcomings.

A Sense of Expectancy

A note of victory pervades the charismatic movement. Charismatics say that the presence of the risen Christ in their lives makes it possible for them to triumph over all the evil powers that would hold them in bondage. Because of this confidence, they are expectant that God's Spirit will work new things in their lives. They anticipate messages from God through prophecy or tongues and interpretation, or through Bible study and prayer. They expect that they will see sick people healed and lost people saved. They expect others to experience "the baptism of the Spirit," and they look for direct answers to specific prayers.

160

Spontaneity

In charismatic worship, there is a freedom for all to participate. Anyone who feels so led, as time permits, has an opportunity to give a testimony, lead in prayer, speak a word of prophecy, minister to others in praying for the sick, or praise the Lord in heartfelt song. This sense of spontaneity, coupled with the expectancy that God will make himself known in new ways, sometimes leads to an unwillingness to make any plans without some specific effort to find the leading of the Spirit. In this effort, there is always the danger of attributing to God decisions that come from one's own subjective consciousness. This attitude can produce an arrogant self-righteousness in which the possibility of human error is not admitted. On the other hand, too many Christians lead their lives in such a way that they leave God little room for making his will known.

Emotional Expression

Emphasis is placed upon praise, joy, and love. One can raise one's hands in worship, clap, shed tears, show love for a brother or sister in Christ, express love to God in prayer, and say "Hallelujah," without fear of being regarded as disruptive. At the same time, there is often a distrust of the intellect, even an anti-intellectualism among charismatics. They think of experiences like speaking in tongues as ways in which the Holy Spirit is able to bypass the censor of the faculties of reason. But where there is this mistrust of reason, as tainted by the fall, there is strangely little or no mistrust of emotions which would seem to be equally liable to the taint of sin. Even so, the way in which emotions are expressed varies a great deal among charismatics, depending upon the cultural and religious background of the people involved.

Bible Study

Most charismatics read their Bibles regularly, and they often carry a Bible around with them. In the charismatic movement there are many teachers who give a great deal of their time to leading group Bible study. But frequently doctrine tends to be based more upon experience than upon careful study of the Bible. Thus, there is often a need to relate the experience to the whole faith of the church and the correction of the norm of Scripture.

161

Simplicity of Expression

Much charismatic literature is a model of simplicity. Because their faith is so closely related to contemporary experience, charismatic writers are able to express it in everyday language. However, along with this simplicity comes the danger of oversimplification and lack of perspective. There is frequently a distorted emphasis upon speaking in tongues, healing, and exorcism.

Ecumenical Appeal

Just at a time when doctrinal and structural ecumenism seems to be mired down, the charismatic movement is offering a demonstration of a different kind of ecumenism. Despite the wide differences that continue to exist in doctrine and church polity among the various communions of Christendom, Protestants of all kinds, Roman Catholics, and main-line Pentecostalists are meeting together to worship and praise God. This new unity that is emerging is not the result of planning and organization but seems to be occurring spontaneously. Even so, one of the most persistent charges brought against the charismatic movement is that it is divisive. Much of the disunity that occurs in connection with the movement is due to extremism on both sides, a misguided zeal on the part of some charismatics and an overreaction on the part of some noncharismatics. Another factor is the division which something new creates over against the inertia of the status quo.

Renewal of Spiritual Life and Witness

The charismatic movement is one of the factors which directly or indirectly is stimulating the Christian movement as a whole to a deeper concern about renewal and spiritual vitality. As people experience a new depth of the work of the Spirit in their lives, they are motivated to tell others about Jesus with a new boldness. This witness is directed largely toward the conversion of individuals, but it sometimes contributes to the solution of social problems as well. Teen Challenge, under the leadership of David Wilkerson, has helped to turn the tide against the drug culture. Many families within the charismatically renewed Episcopal Church of the Redeemer in Houston, Texas, have opened their homes to people within the community who have deep personal or social problems. In Ireland, charismatic Protestants and Catholics are working to reduce tensions in that troubled land.

A Growing Consensus

162

There is an ever-increasing number of noncharismatics who are listening intently to the interpretations offered by charismatics and in the light of what they have heard are going to the Scriptures not with the intention of refuting the charismatics but with the idea of investigating the biblical material firsthand to see if those things are so (Acts 17:11). On the other hand, within the charismatic movement there is a growing number of charismatics who are listening to the constructive criticisms of the movement being offered by noncharismatics not so much with the intention of offering rebuttals as with the desire to profit by the criticisms received and help correct the movement's mistakes. Thus, from two sides lines are converging so that a constructive dialogue is in progress and one may perhaps even speak of a consensus developing between certain progressive charismatics and certain open-minded noncharismatics.[1] Some of the chief points of the consensus that appear to be emerging are these.

The Holy Spirit as the Channel of Blessing

All the blessings that God has for us he has prepared for us in Christ, but they are mediated to us through the Holy Spirit. We cannot program the work of the Holy Spirit. All of the treasures in

Christ that the Christian will ever know in this life are latent in the experience of becoming a Christian. The appropriation of these, however, may come gradually, but this process may be accelerated through post-conversion crisis experiences. The presence of the risen Christ in our lives should be known through experience. Crisis experiences are never intended as a substitute for growth in the Lord, but only as a stimulus to growth. The important question has to do not with the number or dramatic character of the experiences that we have had but with the quality of our daily walk with the Lord.

Gifts of the Spirit in the Churches

The churches of New Testament times were thoroughly charismatic. There is no sound biblical basis for relegating the gifts of the Spirit mentioned in 1 Corinthians 12:8-10 to the apostolic age and treating them as if they had no relevance for our day. The either/or of the gifts of the Spirit versus the fruit of the Spirit is unscriptural and must be rejected in favor of a both/and position which is open both to the gifts and to the fruit but gives the primacy to the fruit.

Acceptance of Tongues

Speaking in tongues is to be accepted as one of the *bona fide* gifts of the Spirit, but care is to be taken that an unscriptural evaluation not be placed upon it. This gift may legitimately be used in worship services in which there is an openness to the gifts, according to the guidelines given by Paul in 1 Corinthians 14. The chief value of tongues is in the enrichment of the personal devotional life. Esteeming tongues as a sign of deep spirituality is to be avoided.

Fullness of Life in the Spirit

The chief concern of charismatic and noncharismatic Christians alike should be the fullness of life in the Spirit. Christians should be open to any method that God may choose to use to promote genuine spiritual renewal according to New Testament standards. Genuine renewal should be carried on within the context of Christian community. We should be on our guard against both spiritual pride and spiritual complacency. Since the purpose of the gifts is the building up of the Christian community, we should be very careful about any use of them that promotes discord. Preserving unity, however, though exceedingly important, is secondary to following the leadership of the risen Lord. Great concern should be given to the development of New Testament churches in which the members can express Christ and minister freely to one another.

Witness to Christ

Attention should always be focused on the goal of bearing effective witness to Christ in the world. There is a deepening concern for wedding a warm evangelistic witness to legitimate social concerns. In its quest for social justice the church must take care that it does not lose its savor. There is a need for divine guidance in the quest for balance between the personal and the social dimensions of the gospel.

A Summary Evaluation

In the Introduction I proposed three criteria for evaluation of the charismatic movement to be employed throughout the subsequent discussion of it. What may we say of the charismatic movement in summary in the light of these criteria?

Is It Scriptural?

Does a practice or belief employ sound principles of biblical interpretation and present a gospel that is in accord with the central teachings of Scripture? No simple "yes" or "no" answer is possible. Some emphases are well grounded scripturally; others are not.

164 This movement has forced Christendom to focus attention on certain long-neglected areas of Scripture, particularly the gifts and their relevance for our day. In doing so I believe it has rendered an invaluable service for the whole church. Long ago the English nonconformist, John Robinson, wrote, "I am very confident the Lord has more truth and light to break forth out of his Word." I believe that God has been using the charismatic movement in helping some of this light to break forth.

I have called attention in a number of places to some of the doubtful methods of biblical interpretation frequently employed, such as using the proof-text method of scriptural quotation that ignores both the contexts of the passages quoted and other passages that do not support the conclusions suggested, basing doctrines on inferences from narrative sections in Acts, claiming the Lord's endorsement of tongues on the basis of Mark 16 without reference to the textual problem involved. There are a number of places in which it seems to me the conclusions of many charismatics are not well founded scripturally—the interpretation of baptism in the Spirit as a post-conversion experience, the interpretation of tongues as the initial evidence of baptism in the Spirit, and the grounding of healing in the atoning death of Christ, to mention only a few.

Is It Christ-Centered?

Does a practice or belief focus the spotlight upon the Christ revealed in the Scriptures or does it let other emphases steal the limelight? Again a simple answer is difficult. Sometimes the spotlight is focused on the Holy Spirit, and the experience of salvation through Jesus Christ is made to seem only a pale shadow of the overpowering experience of the Holy Spirit that comes later. There are within mainline Pentecostalism some non-Trinitarian, Jesus-only groups. Still most charismatics are Trinitarian and testify to a deepened love for Jesus and gratitude for Christ's atoning death that has come through their charismatic experience. Many noncharismatics feel that both within the charismatic movement and the Jesus movement emphasis that should be placed upon the lordship of Christ is placed upon devotion to Jesus. Most charismatics would answer that there is no conflict, but that the name "Jesus" lends itself to worship and devotion more readily than the titles "Christ" and "Lord." In the interest and devotion of charismatics very often the most neglected member of the Trinity is the heavenly Father.

What Practical Effects Does It Have?

What kind of influence does a practice or belief have upon **165** individuals, churches, and society as a whole? Should we talk about charismatic renewal or about charismatic confusion?

There is little room for doubt that the charismatic movement is being used as an instrument for renewal both on a personal and a corporate level within the Roman Catholic Church. The matter is not so clear among Protestants. Among Protestants it appears to be both an instrument for renewal and a cause of confusion. It can hardly be disputed that under the influence of the charismatic movement many Protestants have experienced personal, spiritual renewal. The renewing force, of course, is not the movement itself but the Spirit of God working through the movement. Many Christians have come to a deeper sense of the reality of God. They have found new joy in the Lord and their lives overflow with praise. Their prayer lives have deepened, and they have a new depth of conviction in their faith. They have a greater love for the church and a stronger desire to share their faith in the Lord. Likewise many churches have been renewed in their worship, in their fellowship, and in their evangelistic outreach through the influence of the charismatic movement.

There can also be little doubt that another effect of the movement has been confusion. Many Christians under the influence of this movement have become proud and condescending. They have become very critical of the institutional church and the Christians in it. Under the influence of such people many churches have been torn with strife and often church splits have resulted.

How may we account for this difference between the effects of the movement in Catholicism and Protestantism? Part of the explanation may be the kind of fanatical opposition that it has often incurred among Protestants. More fundamental than this, however, I believe, is the difference in the way the movement has been handled by Catholic and Protestant charismatics. From the first, in Catholicism many able theologians have been actively involved. Protestant charismatics have had few first-rate theologians to help give guidance to the movement. Catholic charismatics have been careful to baptize the charismatic element into the best traditions of their church. Protestants, on the other hand, have often brought much of Pentecostal doctrine and practice undigested into their churches with the result that the charismatic dimension has appeared as a "foreign body" incompatible with the basic faith and practices of the denominations involved. Catholic charismatics have taken particular pains to demonstrate their love for their church and appreciation of its traditions. Protestant charismatics, on the other hand, have often been critical of the institutional church and frequently have manifested an attitude of superiority toward other Christians.

It is too early to evaluate the impact of the movement upon society as a whole. The success of various forms of Pentecostalism in dealing with people addicted to drugs is impressive. Traditional Christianity often, but not always, shuns people with particular problems like addiction to narcotics, alcoholism, deep-seated personality problems, and sexual perversion for fear of the bad influence such people will have in the churches. Often charismatics show a particular compassion for such people with the conviction that the Lord can deliver them from these forms of bondage and bless their testimonies as a result. Even so, up to this point, those involved in the movement seem to demonstrate more zeal in ministering to the victims of society's ills than in dealing effectively with the roots of the problems by seeking to bring about changes in society.

Possible Approaches

As I see it, the possibilities for the future with regard to the relationship between traditional Christianity and charismatic Christianity, particularly with reference to Protestantism, may be summarized in six words: exclusion, indifference, toleration, separation, conversion, and reconception.

Exclusion. Charismatics may be excluded from traditional churches either by being frozen out of them or being put out. In some places this has happened and is still happening. In such churches the charismatic movement is usually caricatured, with only the negative side being recognized. Often such churches emphasize the work of the Holy Spirit but in such a way as to exclude the charismatic dimension. Members are constantly warned against the dangers "on the other side of the fence."

Indifference. Some pastors and churches are simply ignoring the movement. In some cases this attitude is based on a lack of awareness. In other cases it is a calculated strategy based on the assumption that if you ignore the "problem," it will go away.

Toleration. The presence of charismatics in a church is tolerated as long as they do not actively try to win others to their point of view. Sometimes it becomes a matter of mutual toleration, with neither group very happy about the presence of the other, but neither group trying actively to remove the other. Sometimes this approach results in the charismatics becoming dissatisfied and leaving of their own accord.

167

Separation. Some charismatics are voluntarily separating themselves from the traditional churches and forming their own churches. These are frequently called "house churches" because usually they begin in a home. Often there is no membership roll, but these "house churches" perform the functions of the traditional churches including the administering of baptism and the observance of the Lord's Supper. Among those who identify themselves with these "house churches" are those who have been forced out or frozen out of the traditional churches. Many have become tired of simply being tolerated by these churches. All of them come together seeking the freedom and spontaneity in worship and the warmth of fellowship that they desire. At the present time these churches are independent bodies with no particular relation to one another. Usually the members of any particular "house church" have various denominational backgrounds. In the future new Neo-Pentecostal denominations may result from them.

Conversion. Sometimes by the conversion of its members to their point of view and by bringing in others from the outside charismatics take over a church. Usually there are some who cannot go along with the trend in the church and as a result of their dissatisfaction move to another church. This type of conversion seldom takes place when the pastor is not an active charismatic. Sometimes the conversion moves in the opposite direction. Charismatics themselves begin to raise questions about some of the excesses they see in the movement and some of the doctrinal interpretations common to it. Finding their emotional needs satisfied in some warmhearted, traditional church, they no longer identify themselves with the movement. I know of no instance, however, in which a whole church that had been strongly charismatic has been converted to a more traditional position.

Reconception. In the light of the challenge presented by the charismatic movement, the churches as local bodies and the various communions as denominational entities may go to the Scriptures for a fresh study and then seek to reconceive themselves in the light of any new light which might come to them from God's Word. They may seek to incorporate anything in the movement that conforms to sound scriptural norms while avoiding anything that does not.

A Way Forward

All six of these approaches are being employed somewhere at the present time with reference to the charismatic movement. Doubtless for some time to come, in various places all six will continue to be used. In many places the second approach, that of ignoring the movement, is untenable. There are still areas of the world, however, in which the influence of the charismatic movement is negligible, if not almost unknown. Churches that take the second approach are the most vulnerable when problems arise because they do not know what they are dealing with.

The approach which many traditional churches welcome most is the fourth one, separation. The voluntary separation of charismatic Christians from the traditional churches often gives these churches a sense of relief, for, as they see it, their separation "takes the bee out of their bonnet." They reason also that the charismatics will be happier in a church with people of similar convictions. The approach of exclusion is not a happy one and is usually carried on in a spirit of confrontation in which genuine Christian love is often conspicuous by its absence. The approach of toleration, live and let live, works in some cases. Often, however, an element of tension arises in the fellowship, and neither group is very happy about the presence of the other. It is not likely that at any time in the near future traditional churches as a whole will be converted to charismatic Christianity or that charismatic churches as a whole will be reconverted to traditional Christianity.

It seems to me that a more serious consideration should be given to the sixth approach, reconception. This is not a new approach in facing current challenges. Most American churches have been following this approach in recent years in some measure in regard to their stance toward social problems. Though many lament the fact that in social issues the church has often lagged far behind society as a whole, nearly all would admit, I believe, that progress has been made.

If we would follow the reconception approach, we need to ask ourselves what the appeal of the charismatic movement is, what there is in it that causes many people to get so excited about it that often they become dissatisfied with the style of traditional church life.

What is needed most of all is a fresh study of the Scriptures that will lead us to incorporate what is positive in the movement while eliminating what is negative. Traditional Christianity is in great need of spiritual renewal. The situation varies with individuals and from church to church, but much of the excitement with the gospel which Christians in New Testament days had is not clearly in evidence in traditional Christianity. Much of the appeal of the charismatic movement is that, despite all of its aberrations, it seems to have recovered much of the vitality of the early church. Traditional Christianity needs the vitality, not the aberrations. Many noncharismatic churches are already experiencing renewal through a new emphasis upon the work of the Holy Spirit. The Holy Spirit, working according to scriptural norms, will not lead us away from Christ but will give us a renewed sense of Christ's presence among us.

All over the world, but particularly in the United States, the foundations of family life are collapsing on an unprecedented scale. Basic principles of personal morality are being flouted as never before by people who call themselves Christians. Often the church is silent in the face of social injustice and oppression, and frequently it seems more concerned about preserving its own status than in fostering justice and combating oppression. In the face of racial strife, religious animosities, the population explosion, world hunger, the ecology crisis, the problems of the inner city, wars here and there, and the constant threat of thermonuclear war the church seems quite powerless, if not irrelevant. Yet Jesus said of his disciples that they were the salt of the earth and the light of the world. Surely in our day God is calling us to repentance. Lukewarmness among those who bear the name of Christ is as unpalatable to our Lord today as when he addressed the church of Laodicea with the words: "Because you are lukewarm, and neither cold nor hot, I will spew you out of my mouth" (Revelation 3:16). God wants us to be vessels for noble use, "consecrated and useful to the master of the house" (2 Timothy 2:21). The command to evangelize the world has not been revoked. We cannot fulfill this commission in our own strength. We do not know when our Lord will return, but we need to be engaged faithfully in the task that he has committed to us with all the power that he has promised us. May God help us to be open to all that he has *for* us so we may be effective channels for all that he wants to do *through* us!

Notes

INTRODUCTION

[1] Frank Stagg, *The Holy Spirit Today* (Nashville: Broadman Press, 1973), pp. 24, 26.

[2] Kilian McDonnell, "The Catholic Charismatic Renewal: Reassessment and Critique," *Religion in Life,* vol. 44, no. 2 (Summer, 1975), p. 138.

[3] Positive assessments of the movement: Robert E. Terwilliger, "The Charismatic Christ and Christian Theology," Michael Ramsey, Robert E. Terwilliger, A. M. Allchin, *The Charismatic Christ* (New York: Morehouse-Barlow Co., 1973), p. 68; David J. du Plessis, "The New Pentecost," *Logos Journal,* vol. 3, no. 2 (Mar.-Apr., 1974), p. 51; Ralph Martin, "God Is Restoring His People," *Logos Journal,* vol. 4, no. 2 (Nov.-Dec., 1974), p. 51; John A. Mackay, *Ecumenics: The Science of the Church Universal* (Englewood Cliffs, N.J.: Prentice-Hall, Inc., 1964), p. 198.

[4] This resolution was adopted in November, 1975, almost unanimously by some 500 messengers representing 230 Baptist churches in the Union Association, Houston, Texas, according to Dan Martin, "Charismatics Condemned in Houston," *The Religious Herald,* vol. 148, no. 43 (November 13, 1975), p. 7.

[5] Negative assessments of the movement: James C. Logan, "Controversial Aspects of the Movement," *The Charismatic Movement,* ed. Michael P. Hamilton (Grand Rapids: Wm. B. Eerdmans Publishing Co., 1975), p. 43; Robert L. Hamblin, *The Spirit-Filled Trauma* (Nashville: Broadman Press, 1975), p. 90; Donald W. Burdick, *Tongues: To Speak or Not to Speak* (Chicago: Moody Press, 1969), p. 87; W. A. Criswell, *The Holy Spirit in Today's World* (Grand Rapids: Zondervan Publishing House, 1966), p. 225; Donald G. Bloesch, "The Charismatic Revival: A Theological Critique," *Religion in Life,* vol. 35, no. 3 (Summer, 1966), p. 374.

[6] Kilian McDonnell, "Catholic Pentecostalism: Problems in Evaluation," *Dialog,* vol. 9 (Winter, 1970), pp. 35-54.

CHAPTER ONE
PROFILE

[1] John Stevens Kerr, *The Fire Flares Anew* (Philadelphia: Fortress Press, 1974), p. 4.

[2] James W. Jones, *Filled with New Wine: The Charismatic Renewal of the Church* (New York: Harper & Row, Publishers, 1974), p. 101.

[3] Lesslie Newbigin, *The Household of God* (London: SCM Press, 1953), p. 30.

[4] Quoted by Frederick Dale Bruner, *A Theology of the Holy Spirit* (Grand Rapids: Wm. B. Eerdmans Publishing Company, 1970), pp. 32-33.

[5] Quoted by John L. Sherrill, *They Speak with Other Tongues* (New York: McGraw-Hill Book Company, 1964), p. 25. Even as early as 1955 Van Dusen had expressed similar views. See Henry P. Van Dusen, "Caribbean Holiday," *The Christian Century,* vol. 72, no. 33 (August 17, 1955), pp. 946-948.

[6] Quoted by Sherrill, *op. cit.,* p. 27.

[7] David du Plessis, *The Spirit Bade Me Go* (Plainfield, N.J.: Logos International, 1970), pp. 10-11, 113. See also Michael Harper, *As at the Beginning* (Plainfield, N.J.: Logos International, 1971), pp. 13-20, 51-59.

[8] David du Plessis, "The New Pentecost," *Logos Journal,* March–April, 1974, p. 2.

[9] Demos Shakarian, "We Are Not Interested in Starting New Churches," *Voice,* December, 1975, p. 31. Reprinted from the November, 1974, issue of *Voice* by popular demand. The story of Demos Shakarian and the FGBMFI is now available in book form. See *Demos Shakarian* as told to John and Elizabeth Sherrill, *The Happiest People on Earth* (FGBMFI, 836 S. Figueroa, Los Angeles, CA 90017).

[10] See Dennis J. Bennett, *Nine O'clock in the Morning* (Plainfield, N.J.: Logos International, 1970), pp. 1-65; Harper, *op. cit.,* pp. 60-64; Morton T. Kelsey, *Tongue Speaking: An Experiment in Spiritual Experience* (Garden City, N.Y.: Doubleday & Company, Inc., 1964), pp. 98-102; Harper, *op. cit.,* pp. 64-69.

[11] David Wilkerson, *The Cross and the Switchblade* (Westwood, N.J.: Fleming H. Revell Company, 1963).

[12] Pat Robertson, *Shout It from the Housetops* (Plainfield, N.J.: Logos International, n.d.), written with the assistance of Jamie Buckingham.

[13] Synesio Lyra, Jr., "The Rise and Development of the Jesus Movement," *Calvin Theological Journal,* April, 1973, p. 40; Lowell D. Streiker, *The Jesus Trip—Advent of the Jesus Freaks* (Nashville: Abingdon Press, 1971), p. 9, as quoted by Lyra, *op. cit.,* p. 50. The best-researched book on the Jesus movement is Ronald M. Enroth; Edward E. Ericson, Jr.; C. Breckinridge Peters, *The Jesus People: Old Time Religion in the Age of Aquarius* (Grand Rapids: Wm. B. Eerdmans Publishing Company, 1972).

[14] The conservative figure is cited by Kilian McDonnell, "The Catholic Charismatic Renewal: Reassessment and Critique," *Religion in Life,* vol. 44, no. 2 (Summer, 1975), p. 143. The larger figure is given by Ralph Martin, "God Is Restoring His People," *Logos Journal,* Nov.-Dec., 1974, p. 50.

[15] Quoted in Edward D. O'Connor, *The Pentecostal Movement in the Catholic Church* (Notre Dame, Ind.: Ave Maria Press, 1971), pp. 292-293.

[16] John Patrick Bertolucci, "Pentecost in Rome '75: A Catholic View," *Logos Journal*, July–August, 1975, pp. 42-43.

[17] Quoted by O'Connor, *op. cit.,* p. 287.

[18] Léon Joseph Cardinal Suenens, *A New Pentecost?* (New York: The Seabury Press, Inc., 1974), p. 31.

[19] *Ibid.,* p. 30.

[20] See Kevin and Dorothy Ranagham, *Catholic Pentecostals* (Paramus, N.J.: Paulist Press Deus Books, 1969), p. 9. and Doug Wead, *Catholic Charismatics: Are They for Real?* (Carol Stream, Ill.: Creation House, 1972), p. 110. Having originated among some laymen and priests in Mallorca, Spain, the movement came to America in 1957, and spread rapidly. There has been some tension between the two movements, as the charismatic movement has tended to supplant the cursillo one. The organizational structure that the movement provided and the familiarity with spiritual experience which it encouraged caused many leaders in this movement to become leaders and organizers of charismatic prayer cells.

[21] J. Rodman Williams, "A Profile of the Charismatic Movement," *Christianity Today,* vol. 19, no. 11 (February 28, 1975), p. 10.

[22] J. Rodman Williams, *The Era of the Spirit* (Plainfield, N. J.: Logos International, 1971), p. 13.

[23] *Christianity Today,* February 28, 1975, p. 10.

[24] The discussion of "baptism" is also based on the *Christianity Today* article.

[25] Williams, *The Era of the Spirit,* p. 24.

[26] *Ibid.,* p. 28.

[27] *Ibid.,* p. 33.

[28] Interesting descriptions of charismatic prayer meetings may be found in James W. Jones, *Filled with New Wine,* pp. 7-12, and in Erling Jorstad, ed., *The Holy Spirit in Today's Church* (Nashville: Abingdon Press, 1973), pp. 29-44. See also James Cavnar, "Dynamics of the Prayer Meeting," in Kevin and Dorothy Ranagham, *As the Spirit Leads Us* (Paramus, N.J.: Paulist Press, 1971), pp. 60-77.

CHAPTER TWO
HISTORICAL BACKGROUND

[1] E. Glenn Hinson, "A Brief History of Glossolalia," Frank Stagg, E. Glenn Hinson, Wayne E. Oates, *Glossolalia* (Nashville: Abingdon Press, 1967), pp. 48-56. Irenaeus (late second century) and Origen (early third century) reflect a hazy aquaintance with glossolalia as a contemporary phenomenon, but both Chrysostom (347–407) and Augustine (354–430) write as if it had not occurred since early times.

[2] Morton T. Kelsey, *Tongue Speaking: An Experiment in Spiritual Experience* (Garden City, N.Y.: Doubleday & Company, Inc., 1964), pp. 41-47, especially pp. 43, 46.

[3] George H. Williams and Edith Waldvogel, "A History of Speaking in Tongues and Related Gifts," *The Charismatic Movement*, ed. Michael P. Hamilton (Grand Rapids: Wm.B. Eerdmans Publishing Company, 1975), p. 71.

[4] Cf. Thomas S. Kepler, comp., *The Fellowship of the Saints: An Anthology of Christian Devotional Literature* (Nashville: Abingdon Press, 1948).

[5] Williams and Waldvogel, *op. cit.*, pp. 71-73.

[6] Henry P. Van Dusen, *Spirit, Son and Father* (New York: Charles Scribner's Sons, 1958), p. 82.

[7] George H. Williams, *The Radical Reformation* (Philadelphia: The Westminster Press, 1962), pp. 49, 133.

[8] Williston Walker, *A History of the Christian Church* (New York: Charles Scribner's Sons, Revised Edition, 1959), p. 420.

[9] Hinson, *op. cit.*, p. 63.

[10] E. S. Waterhouse, "Pietism," James Hastings, ed., *Encyclopaedia of Religion and Ethics* (Edinburgh: T. & T. Clark, 1956), vol. 10, pp. 6-9; Walker, *op. cit.*, p. 445.

[11] John Greenfield, *Power from on High* (London: Marshall, Morgan & Scott, Ltd., 1931), pp. 13-30. The idea behind the prayer meeting was that just as in the days of the old covenant the fire was never permitted to go out on the altar (Leviticus 6:12-13), even so in a congregation which is the temple of the living God "the intercession of his saints should incessantly rise up to him like holy incense" (p. 28).

[12] Quoted by Hinson, *op. cit.*, p. 64.

[13] Williams and Waldvogel, *op. cit.*, p. 80.

[14] Hinson, *op. cit.*, pp. 61-62. See also Gordon Strachan, "Theological and Cultural Origins of the Nineteenth Century Pentecostal Movement," Thomas A. Smail, ed., *Theological Renewal* (London: Fountain Trust, 1975), pp. 17-24. A not-so-sympathetic treatment of what is called "the Irvingite departure" is to be found in Ronald Knox, *Enthusiasm* (New York: Oxford University Press, 1961), pp. 550-558.

[15] Vinson Synan, *The Holiness-Pentecostal Movement in the United States* (Grand Rapids: Wm. B. Eerdmans Publishing Company, 1971), p. 13.

[16] Frederick Dale Bruner, *A Theology of the Holy Spirit* (Grand Rapids: Wm. B. Eerdmans Publishing Company, 1970), p. 38; Synan, *op. cit.*, p. 19.

[17] H. Shelton Smith, Robert T. Handy, Lefferts A. Loetscher, *American Christianity: An Historical Interpretation with Representative Documents*, vol. 2 (1820-1960) (New York: Charles Scribner's Sons, 1963), pp. 20-24.

[18] Bruner, *op. cit.*, p. 42.

[19] *Ibid.*; Synan, *op. cit.*, p. 52.

[20] James D. G. Dunn, *Baptism in the Holy Spirit*, Studies in Biblical Theology Second Series, 15 (Naperville, Ill.: Alec R. Allenson, Inc., 1970). Torrey is credited with having most clearly crystallized the distinction: "The Baptism with the Holy Spirit is not for the purpose of cleansing from sin, but for the purpose of empowering for service." Quoted from R. A. Torrey, *The Baptism with the Holy Spirit* (1896), p. 14, by James D. G. Dunn, "Spirit-Baptism and Pentecostalism," *Scottish Journal of Theology*, vol. 23, no. 4 (November, 1970), p. 400. The contributions of A. J. Gordon, F. B. Meyer, A. B. Simpson, and Andrew Murray also deserve mention.

[21] Michael Harper, *As at the Beginning* (Plainfield, N.J.: Logos International, 1971), p. 26.

[22] The story is related in Michael Harper, *op. cit.*, pp. 25-27; Nils Bloch-Hoell, *The Pentecostal Movement* (New York: Humanities Press, 1964), pp. 19-29; John Thomas Nichol, *The Pentecostals* (Plainfield, N.J.: Logos International, 1966), pp. 26-29; and John L. Sherrill, *They Speak with Other Tongues* (New York: McGraw-Hill Book Company, 1964), pp. 30-36.

[23] Nichol, *op. cit.*, pp. 32-33.

[24] Synan, *op. cit.*, p. 110.

[25] For a description of the persecution see Sherrill, *op. cit.*, pp. 46-51 and Nichol, *op. cit.*, pp. 70-73. Some of the reasons for the persecution were unbridled emotionalism, an excess of glossolalia, and abuse of prophecy, intense anti-intellectualism, immoral behavior on the part of some Pentecostals, and a supercilious attitude toward fellow Christians on the part of many involved in the movement. Cf. Nichol, *op. cit.*, pp. 74-80.

[26] Cf. Walter J. Hollenweger, *The Pentecostals*, translated from the German by R. A. Wilson (Minneapolis, Minn.: Augsburg Publishing House, 1972), pp. 22-24, 323; Nichol, *op. cit.*, pp. 88-92.

[27] See Prudencio Damboriena, *Tongues As of Fire: Pentecostalism in Contemporary Christianity* (Washington and Cleveland: Corpus Books, 1969), p. 142.

[28] Kilian McDonnell, "The Spirit and Pentecostalism," Daniel Callahan, ed., *God, Jesus, and Spirit* (New York: Herder and Herder, 1969), p. 305.

[29] William R. Read, Victor M. Monterroso, and Harmon A. Johnson, *Latin American Church Growth* (Grand Rapids: Wm. B. Eerdmans Publishing Company, 1969), p. 318.

[30] Bruner, *op. cit.*, p. 24.

[31] The historian is David Barrett, according to Walter J. Hollenweger, "Pentecostalism and the Third World," *Dialog*, vol. 9, no. 2 (Spring, 1970), p. 126.

[32] David du Plessis, *Pentecost Outside Pentecost* (Dallas: Privately Printed, 1960), p. 6, as quoted by Bruner, *op. cit.*, p. 22.

[33] This paragraph is based on Read, Monterroso, and Johnson, *op. cit.*, pp. 313-325; Walter J. Hollenweger, "Pentecostalism and the Third World," *Dialog*, vol. 9, no. 2 (Spring, 1970), pp. 122-129; and C. Peter Wagner's well-researched and highly readable *Look Out! The Pentecostals Are Coming* (Carol Stream, Ill.: Creation House, 1973).

[34] Read, Monterroso, and Johnson, *op. cit.,* pp. 318-319.

[35] Emilio Castro, "Pentecostalism and Ecumenism in Latin America," *The Christian Century,* vol. 89, no. 34 (September 27, 1972), p. 956.

[36] The distinction between sects and churches has been generally accepted among sociologists since Ernst Troeltsch formulated it in his monumental work *The Social Teaching of the Christian Churches* (New York: The Macmillan Company, 1950, first published, 1912; first English edition, 1931). Liston Pope gives a list of twenty-one specific aspects for evaluating a group's movement from the sect type to the church type, *Millhands & Preachers* (New Haven: Yale University Press, 1942), pp. 122-124.

CHAPTER THREE
BAPTISM IN THE HOLY SPIRIT

[1] Quoted by Michael Harper, *Power for the Body of Christ* (London: The Fountain Trust, 1964), p. 22.

[2] *Ibid.*

[3] Not all Neo-Pentecostals agree. For different interpretations see Howard M. Ervin, *These Are Not Drunken, As Ye Suppose* (Plainfield, N.J.: Logos International, 1968), pp. 46-47, and Thomas A. Smail, *Reflected Glory: The Spirit in Christ and Christians* (London: Hodder and Stoughton, 1975), p. 145.

[4] John A. Schep, *Baptism in the Spirit* (Plainfield, N.J.: Logos International, 1972), p. 21.

[5] Harper, *op. cit.,* p. 12.

[6] Dennis and Rita Bennett, *The Holy Spirit and You* (Plainfield, N.J.: Logos International, 1971), pp. 26-27.

[7] Thomas A. Smail, *op. cit.,* pp. 41-50, especially pp. 46, 48.

[8] *Theological and Pastoral Orientations on the Catholic Charismatic Renewal,* prepared at Malines, Belgium (Notre Dame, Ind.: The Communications Center, 1974), p. 63 (hereafter referred to as Malines Document); Leon Joseph Cardinal Suenens, *A New Pentecost?* (New York: The Seabury Press, Inc., 1974), p. 224.

[9] J. Rodman Williams, *The Pentecostal Reality* (Plainfield, N.J.: Logos International, 1972), pp. 72-73; Michael Harper, *Walk in the Spirit* (Plainfield, N.J.: Logos International, 1970), p. 23; Bennett, *op. cit.,* pp. 36-77.

[10] David du Plessis, *The Spirit Bade Me Go* (Plainfield, N.J.: Logos International, 1970), p. 70; Bennett, *op. cit.,* p. 34.

[11] Arnold Bittlinger, "Baptism in Water and in Spirit: Aspects of Christian Initiation," Kilian McDonnell and Arnold Bittlinger, *The Baptism in the Holy Spirit As an Ecumenical Problem* (Notre Dame, Ind.: Charismatic Renewal Services, Inc., 1972), pp. 11-12, 19-20.

[12] Suenens, *op. cit.,* p. 80.

[13] Malines Document, pp. 30-31, 33; Kilian McDonnell, "The Baptism in the Holy Spirit as an Ecumenical Problem," Kilian McDonnell and Arnold Bittlinger, *op. cit.,* pp. 32-34; Simon Tugwell, *Did You Receive the Spirit?* (New York: Paulist Press,

1972), pp. 84-93, 117; Suenens, *op. cit.,* pp. 80-81. For Catholic charismatic interpretations that are nearer typical Protestant Neo-Pentecostal ones, see Ralph Martin, "Baptism in the Holy Spirit: Pastoral Implications," Kilian McDonnell, ed., *The Holy Spirit and Power: The Catholic Charismatic Renewal* (Garden City, N.Y.: Doubleday & Company, Inc., 1975), pp. 91-104; and Stephen B. Clark, *Baptized in the Spirit* (Pecos, N.M.: Dove Publications 1970), pp. 1-76. Clark discusses baptism in the Spirit largely as a second stage of Christian experience, but he says that normally "a person should be joined to Christ and baptized in the Spirit at the same time" (p. 58).

¹⁴ David M. Howard, *By the Power of the Holy Spirit* (Downers Grove, Ill.: Inter-Varsity Press, 1973), p. 36.

¹⁵ Michael Green, *I Believe in the Holy Spirit* (Grand Rapids: Wm. B. Eerdmans Publishing Company, 1975), pp. 141-142. I am indebted in this section thus far to ideas from Anthony A. Hoekema, *Holy Spirit Baptism* (Grand Rapids: Wm. B. Eerdmans Publishing Company, 1972), pp. 15-24; John R. W. Stott, *The Baptism and Fullness of the Holy Spirit* (London: Inter-Varsity Press, 1964), pp. 1-21; Green, *op. cit.,* pp. 123-147; and Howard, *op. cit.,* pp. 22-31. For a helpful, scholarly exegesis of 1 Corinthians 12:13 consult James D. G. Dunn, *Baptism in the Holy Spirit,* Studies in Biblical Theology, Second Series, 15 (Naperville, Ill.: Alec R. Allenson, Inc., 1970), pp. 127-131. Dunn steers his course between the Pentecostal, Neo-Pentecostal interpretations, on the one hand, and sacramental interpretations that regard the passage as speaking of water baptism on the other. Likewise Karl Barth interprets baptism with the Holy Spirit as related to the beginning of the Christian life, speaking of it as the "divine preparation of man for the Christian life in its totality." Karl Barth, *Baptism As the Foundation of the Christian Life, Church Dogmatics* (Edinburgh: T. & T. Clark, 1969), vol. 4, book 4, p. 31.

¹⁶ Stott, *op. cit.,* pp. 26-27.

¹⁷ *Ibid.,* p. 25; cf. Dale Moody, *Spirit of the Living God* (Philadelphia: The Westminster Press, 1968), p. 138; Dunn, *op. cit.,* p. 54.

¹⁸ These three points are given by Stott, *op. cit.,* pp. 32-33. See Moody, *op. cit.,* p. 138, for an insight into the meaning of the present tense of the verb.

¹⁹ Stott, *op. cit.,* p. 10; James H. McConkey, *The Threefold Secret of the Holy Spirit* (Chicago: Moody Press, 1897), pp. 25-26. Dunn will not call the disciples "Christians" before Pentecost; cf. *Baptism in the Holy Spirit,* pp. 38-54.

²⁰ Käsemann thinks that they were simply disciples of John the Baptist, not Christians at all. Ernst Käsemann, *Essays on New Testament Themes,* Studies in Biblical Theology, First Series, 41 (Naperville, Ill.: Alec R. Allenson, Inc., 1964), pp. 141-142. It should be pointed out, however, that some scholars believe that the disciples mentioned in Acts 19:1-7 were Christians who had an inadequate understanding of the Christian faith. See Ernst Haenchen, *The Acts of the Apostles: A Commentary* (Philadelphia: The Westminster Press, 1971), pp. 554-557.

²¹ See Green, *op. cit.,* p. 139.

²² Dunn, *Baptism in the Holy Spirit,* p. 5.

²³ John Taylor, *The Go-Between God* (Philadelphia: Fortress Press, 1972), p. 120; Smail, *op. cit.,* p. 43.

²⁴ Ernst Haenchen thinks Luke placed the coming of the Spirit on the day of Pentecost because he had adopted the tradition of the forty days and simply wanted to

177

date the Spirit's descent to coincide with the next feast. Ernest Haenchen, *op. cit.*, pp. 172-175. Dunn gives good reasons for believing that the dating of the Spirit's descent at Pentecost is historically reliable. James D. G. Dunn, *Jesus and the Spirit* (Philadelphia: The Westminster Press, 1975), pp. 140-142.

[25] Smail, *op. cit.*, p. 106.

[26] Edward Schweizer, article on "Pneuma" in *Theological Dictionary of the New Testament*, ed. Gerhard Friedrich (Grand Rapids, Mich.: Wm. B. Eerdmans Publishing Co., 1968), vol. 6, p. 410.

[27] Moody, *op. cit.*, pp. 69, 72; Richard B. Rackham, *The Acts of the Apostles* (Grand Rapids: Baker Book House, 1964), pp. 117, 159; F. F. Bruce, *Commentary on the Book of Acts*, The International Commentary on the New Testament (Grand Rapids: Wm. B. Eerdmans Publishing Company, 1956), pp. 183, 229; T. C. Smith, "Acts," *The Broadman Bible Commentary* (Nashville: Broadman Press, 1971), vol. 10, p. 70.

[28] Taylor, *op. cit.*, p. 202. In this context Taylor speaks only of the second blessing theology with no reference to the idea of recurring Pentecosts.

[29] Bittlinger, *op. cit.*, p. 20; cf. also R. E. O. White, *The Biblical Doctrine of Initiation* (Grand Rapids: Wm. B. Eerdmans Publishing Company, 1960), p. 108.

[30] Stott, *op. cit.*, p. 14; cf. Moody, *op. cit.*, p. 64.

[31] Frank Stagg, "The Holy Spirit in the New Testament," *Review and Expositor*, Spring, 1966, pp. 142-144. Throughout this paragraph I am indebted to insights found in Stagg's article.

[32] Bruner says: "Baptism becomes baptism of the Holy Spirit" (Frederick Dale Bruner, *A Theology of the Holy Spirit* [Grand Rapids: Wm. B. Eerdmans Publishing Company, 1970], pp. 168-169). Throughout Bruner's book there is the tendency to interpret the mere fact that one has received baptism as evidence that one has received the Holy Spirit. The Catholic view, of course, is that the Spirit is bestowed through the sacraments of initiation.

[33] Markus Barth, *Ephesians: Translation and Commentary on Chapters 4-6, Anchor Bible* (Garden City, N.Y.: Doubleday & Company, Inc., 1974), vol. 34a, pp. 468-469. This view is expressed more fully in Barth's earlier book, *Die Taufe— ein Sakrament?* (Zurich: EVZ, 1951). Barth's distinguished father agrees; cf. Karl Barth, *op. cit.*

[34] Words by Henry H. Tweedy, 1935. *The Baptist Hymnal* (Nashville: Convention Press, 1975), No. 264.

CHAPTER FOUR
GIFTS OF THE SPIRIT AND SPEAKING IN TONGUES

[1] Michael Harper, *Walk in the Spirit* (Plainfield, N.J.: Logos International, 1968), pp. 79-80; cf. Arnold Bittlinger, *Gifts and Graces* (Grand Rapids: Wm. B. Eerdmans Publishing Company, 1968), pp. 20-21.

[2] For the first position, see James W. Jones, *Filled with New Wine* (New York: Harper & Row, Publishers, 1974), pp. 46-47.; Agnes Sanford, *The Healing Gifts of the Spirit* (Philadelphia: A. J. Holman Company, division of J. B. Lippincott Company,

Notes

1966), p. 141. For the second view, see Thomas A. Smail, *Reflected Glory: The Spirit in Christ and Christians* (London and Toronto: Hodder and Stoughton, 1975), p. 16.

[3] Michael Harper, Editorial in *Renewal*, August–September, 1973, p. 3.

[4] Arnold Bittlinger, "Die Bedeutung der *Charismen* für den Gemeindeaufbau," in *Die Bedeutung der Gnadengaben für die Gemeinde Jesu Christi*, Oekumenische Texts und Studien, 33 (Marburg: Oekumenischer Verlag Dr. R. F. Edel, 1964), p. 10.

[5] Don Basham, *A Handbook on Holy Spirit Baptism* (Springdale, Pa.: Whitaker House, 1969), p. 43.

[6] Larry Christenson, *Speaking in Tongues* (Minneapolis: Dimension Books, 1968), p. 124.

[7] Malines Document, pp. 17-18, 42, 47, 53, 61.

[8] Léon Joseph Cardinal Suenens, *A New Pentecost?* (New York: The Seabury Press, Inc., 1974), pp. 109-110, 132.

[9] Cf. John F. Walvoord, *The Holy Spirit* (Wheaton: Van Kempen Press, Inc., 1954), pp. 163-188; cf. J. Dwight Pentecost, *The Divine Comforter* (Westwood, N.J.: Fleming H. Revell Company, 1963), p. 166; W. A. Criswell, *The Holy Spirit in Today's World* (Grand Rapids: Zondervan Publishing House, 1966), pp. 220-222.

[10] Benjamin B. Warfield, *Counterfeit Miracles* (New York: Charles Scribner's Sons, 1918), pp. 3-31. Also, see Anthony A. Hoekema, *Holy Spirit Baptism* (Grand Rapids: Wm. B. Eerdmans Publishing Company, 1972), pp. 55-78; and Anthony A. Hoekema, *What About Tongue-Speaking?* (Grand Rapids: Wm. B. Eerdmans Publishing Company, 1966), p. 110.

[11] James D. G. Dunn, *Jesus and the Spirit* (Philadelphia: The Westminster Press, 1975), p. 254. Italics in the original.

[12] Malines Document, pp. 6, 37, 41-42, 52-53.

[13] Christenson, *op. cit.*, p. 22.

[14] Basham, *op. cit.*, p. 82.

[15] The following question whether real languages are involved: Malines Document, p. 53; and Suenens, *op. cit.*, p. 99. James W. Jones will not go beyond saying that it sounds like a foreign language. He thinks that the question is not really important, since the purpose of the gift is not to communicate knowledge but to give the Holy Spirit freer reign in one's life. Jones, *op. cit.*, p. 52.

[16] For stories of tongues that were recognized as real languages see Howard M. Ervin, *These Are Not Drunken, As Ye Suppose* (Plainfield, N.J.: Logos International, 1968), pp. 127-128; Robert C. Frost, *Aglow with the Spirit* (Plainfield, N.J.: Logos International, Revised Edition, 1971), p. 45; Dennis and Rita Bennett, *The Holy Spirit and You* (Plainfield, N.J.: Logos International, 1971), pp. 86, 91-92; Dennis J. Bennett, "The Gifts of the Spirit," Michael P. Hamilton, ed., *The Charismatic Movement* (Grand Rapids: Wm. B. Eerdmans Publishing Company, 1975), pp. 22-30; John Sherrill, *They Speak with Other Tongues* (New York: McGraw-Hill Book Company, 1964), 89-103; Don Basham, *op. cit.*, pp. 94-97; and *The Miracle of Tongues* (Old Tappan, N.J.: Fleming H. Revell Company, 1973), pp. 34-121; Morton T. Kelsey, *Tongue Speaking: An Experiment in Spiritual Experience* (Garden City, N.Y.:

Doubleday & Company, Inc., 1964), pp. 152-157. However, the Malines Document says: "Whether tongues, in certain cases, is a true language or not remains to be seriously investigated" (p. 53).

[17] Malines Document, p. 52.

[18] *Ibid.*, pp. 41-42. Howard Ervin takes the hard-line, Pentecostal view, *These Are Not Drunken*, pp. 105-106. Don Basham's view is a little softer, but is close to Ervin's, *A Handbook on Holy Spirit Baptism*, pp. 78-80. At the opposite pole among charismatics are the following: Donald L. Gelpi (Catholic), *Pentecostalism: A Theological Viewpoint* (New York: Paulist Press, 1971), pp. 176-177, 195; Smail, *op. cit.*, p. 43; Sanford, *op. cit.*, p. 180. In between, moving from the right to left (hard-line toward liberal view) are the following: Christenson, *op. cit.*, pp. 54-56; Michael Harper, *Power for the Body of Christ*, pp. 33-38; Stephen B. Clark (Catholic), *Baptized in the Spirit* (Pecos, N.M.: Dove Publications, 1970), pp. 25-28; Kevin and Dorothy Ranaghan, *Catholic Pentecostals* (Paramus, N.J.: Paulist Press Deus Books, 1969), p. 193.

[19] Bennett in Hamilton, ed., *The Charismatic Movement*, pp. 18-19.

[20] Kevin and Dorothy Ranaghan, *op. cit.*, p. 206.

[21] Sanford, *op. cit.*, p. 164.

[22] For the first view see Basham, *A Handbook on Holy Spirit Baptism*, pp. 94-95. This view is defended by J. G. Davies, "Pentecost and Glossolalia," *Journal of Theological Studies*, New Series, vol. 3, no. 2 (Oct., 1952), pp. 228-231 and by Robert H. Gundry, "'Ecstatic Utterance' (N.E.B.)?" *Journal of Theological Studies*, New Series, vol. 17 (1966), pp. 299-307, especially p. 303. For the second view consult Frank Stagg, "Glossolalia in the New Testament" in Frank Stagg, E. Glenn Hinson, and Wayne E. Oates, *Glossolalia* (Nashville: Abingdon Press, 1967), pp. 25-44. For the third view see Dale Moody, *Spirit of the Living God* (Philadelphia: The Westminster Press, 1968), pp. 62-63; and Watson E. Mills, *Understanding Speaking in Tongues* (Grand Rapids: Wm. B. Eerdmans Publishing Company, 1972), pp. 26-76.

[23] Dunn, *op. cit.*, pp. 189-196, particularly p. 191.

[24] For an excellent brief summary of the textual evidence see Frank Stagg's treatment of the subject, to which I am heavily indebted. Stagg, Hinson, Oates, *op. cit.*, pp. 23-24.

[25] John P. Kildahl, *The Psychology of Speaking in Tongues* (New York: Harper & Row, Publishers, 1972), p. 47.

[26] For the best treatment of the subject available from a strictly linguistic point of view, consult William J. Samarin, *Tongues of Men and Angels* (New York: The Macmillan Company, 1972), especially chapter 5. Samarin finds no evidence for the belief popular among charismatics that tongues are real languages.

[27] For an interpretation in terms of Jung's view of the "collective unconscious" see Kelsey, *op. cit.*, pp. 188-199. For an emphasis upon the correlation between glossolalia and demonology consult James N. Lapsley and John H. Simpson, "Speaking in Tongues: Infantile Babble or Song of the Self? (Part II)," *Pastoral Psychology*, vol. 15, no. 146 (September, 1964), pp. 19, 24. For a discussion of the relation between glossolalia and infantile babble see Wayne E. Oates, "A Socio-Psychological Study of Glossolalia," Frank Stagg, E. Glenn Hinson, Wayne E. Oates, *Glossolalia*, pp. 76-99, especially pp. 84-93.

[28] For interpretations of glossolalia as essentially learned behavior see Kildahl, *op. cit.*, pp. 35-86 and especially an article by the same author in Michael P. Hamilton, ed., *The Charismatic Movement*, pp. 124-142.

[29] Kildahl, *op. cit.*, pp. 40, 44-45, 65.

[30] Kildahl in Hamilton, ed., *The Charismatic Movement*, p. 136.

[31] *Ibid.*, p. 137. A similar story is related by W. A. Criswell in his book, *The Holy Spirit in Today's World* (Grand Rapids: Zondervan Publishing House, 1973), pp. 219-220.

CHAPTER FIVE
GIFTS OF PROPHECY, HEALING, AND DELIVERANCE

[1] Cf. Dennis and Rita Bennett, *The Holy Spirit and You* (Plainfield, N.J.: Logos International, 1971), p. 99; Bruce Yocum, "Prophecy," *New Covenant*, vol. 2, no. 12 (June, 1973), pp. 26-27 and vol. 3, no. 1 (July, 1973), pp. 12-14; Michael Harper, *Prophecy: A Gift for the Body of Christ* (Plainfield, N.J.: Logos International, 1970, originally published 1964), p. 19.

[2] Bennett, *op. cit.*, p. 100.

[3] Don Basham, *A Handbook on Tongues, Interpretation and Prophecy* (Springdale, Pa.: Whitaker House, 1971), pp. 107-108.

[4] Kevin and Dorothy Ranaghan, *Catholic Pentecostals* (Paramus, N.J.: Paulist Press Deus Books, 1969), p. 174.

[5] Kathryn Kuhlman, *I Believe in Miracles* (New York: Pyramid Books, Pyramid Publications, 1962), and *God Can Do It Again* (Old Tappan, N.J.: Fleming H. Revell Company, 1973).

[6] MacNutt favors omitting "if it be thy will" in praying for the sick. If one cannot do this, he suggests the words "according to thy will." Francis MacNutt, *Healing* (Notre Dame, Ind.: Ave Maria Press, 1974), pp. 205-206.

[7] For an example of this approach, see Kenneth Hagin, *The Key to Scriptural Healing* and *Healing Belongs to Us* (Tulsa, Okla.: Kenneth Hagin Evangelistic Association, fifth ed., 1974).

[8] For an example of the second approach, see Francis MacNutt, *op. cit.* For his insights, MacNutt pays particular tribute to Tommy Tyson, Agnes Sanford, and Morton T. Kelsey.

[9] For an invaluable source of information concerning healing evangelists, see David Edwin Harrell, Jr., *All Things Are Possible: The Healing and Charismatic Revivals in Modern America* (Bloomington and London: Indiana University Press, 1975), particularly pp. 4, 138-144.

[10] I develop this idea much more fully in my book, *Interpreting the Atonement* (Grand Rapids: Wm. B. Eerdmans Publishing Company, 1966), pp. 33-38, 56-63.

[11] *Ibid.*, pp. 149-150.

181

[12] Rowland V. Bingham, *The Bible and the Body* (London: Marshall, Morgan and Scott, 1952), p. 59. Emphasis is made in the original.

[13] Morton T. Kelsey, *Healing and Christianity* (New York: Harper & Row, Publishers, 1973), pp. 8-32, 191-242.

[14] MacNutt, *op. cit.*, p. 9.

[15] Throughout this appraisal of healing I have drawn on materials from my article, "The Biblical Basis of Medical Missions," *The Commission,* vol. 31, no. 2 (February, 1968), pp. 9-12, and vol. no. 3 (March, 1968), pp. 20-23.

[16] Based largely on the following books: Don Basham, *Deliver Us from Evil,* (Washington Depot, Conn.: Chosen Books, 1972); Michael Harper, *Spiritual Warfare* (London: Hodder and Stoughton, 1970); and MacNutt, *op. cit.*

[17] Basham, *Deliver Us from Evil,* p. 144.

[18] Cf. Bob Mumford, "Flesh or Demons? Where's the Battle?", *New Wine: The Best of 1974,* pp. 10-14, 19.

[19] Cf. *The Weird World of the Occult,* compiled by Walker L. Knight (Wheaton, Ill.: Tyndale House Publishers, 1972), p. 16.

[20] *Ibid.,* pp. 22-23.

[21] T. W. Manson, *The Teaching of Jesus* (Cambridge: The University Press, 1948), p. 166.

[22] Rudolf Bultmann, "New Testament and Mythology," Hans Werner Bartsch, ed., *Kerygma and Myth* (London: S.P.C.K., 1953), pp. 1-44; and Rudolf Bultmann, *Existence and Faith* (Cleveland and New York: Meridian Books, imprint of World Publishing Company, 1960), pp. 289-296.

[23] Paul Tillich, *The Interpretation of History* (New York: Charles Scribner's Sons, 1936), pp. 77-122. There are similar interpretations of the demonic in other books by Tillich, such as *The Protestant Era* (Chicago: The University of Chicago Press, 1948) and *The Courage to Be* (New Haven: Yale University Press, 1952).

[24] *Hymnbook for Christian Worship* (Valley Forge: Judson Press, 1970), No. 248.

182

CHAPTER SIX
OTHER GIFTS AND FEATURES OF THE CHARISMATIC MOVEMENT

[1] My discussion of "other gifts" is based largely on Dennis and Rita Bennett, *The Holy Spirit and You* (Plainfield, N.J.: Logos International, 1971), pp. 124-168; Arnold Bittlinger, *Gifts and Graces* (Grand Rapids: Wm. B. Eerdmans Publishing Company, 1968), pp. 27-34, 40-42, 45-48.

[2] Published by Creation House, 1971.

[3] Cf. Edward E. Plowman, "Demythologizing Indonesia's Revival," *Christianity Today,* vol. 17, no. 11 (March 2, 1973), pp. 49-50.

[4] Larry Christenson, *Speaking in Tongues* (Minneapolis: Bethany Fellowship, Inc., 1968), p. 116; Bittlinger, *op. cit.*, pp. 74-75.

[5] Don Basham, "Gifts or Fruit?", *New Wine: The Best of 1975*, p. 23.

[6] Bittlinger, *op. cit.*, p. 81.

[7] Leonard Evans, "The Theology of the Love Commandment," *New Covenant*, vol. 3, no. 4 (October, 1973), p. 21.

[8] Merlin R. Carothers, *Prison to Praise* (Plainfield, N.J.: Logos International, 1970), pp. 58-63.

[9] While very strong manuscript evidence supports the translation in the RSV and makes clear what it is almost certain Paul wanted to say, the translation in the KJV is permissible in the light of Paul's conviction that Christ has overcome and is overcoming hostile forces (cf. Romans 8:35, 38-39). For support of the KJV translation consult C.K. Barrett, *A Commentary on the Epistle to the Romans* (London: Adam & Charles Black, 1957), p. 169. For support for the RSV translation consult John Knox, "Romans," in George A. Buttrick, gen. ed., *The Interpreter's Bible* (Nashville: Abingdon Press, 1954), vol. 9, pp. 524-525.

[10] A number of letters objecting to Carothers' interpretation have appeared in various issues of *Renewal*, the charismatic magazine published in England by Fountain Trust.

[11] Jamie Buckingham, "Charismatic Renewal," *Logos Journal*, vol. 3, no. 5 (September–October, 1973), p. 9.

[12] Michael Harper, *Spiritual Warfare* (London: Hodder and Stoughton, 1970), p. 42.

[13] Corrie ten Boom, "The Coming Tribulation," *Logos Journal*, vol. 4, no. 6 (November–December, 1974), p. 20.

[14] Léon Joseph Cardinal Suenens, *A New Pentecost?* (New York: The Seabury Press, Inc., 1974), p. 175.

[15] Dale Moody, *The Hope of Glory* (Grand Rapids: Wm. B. Eerdmans Publishing Company, 1964), pp. 226-227.

[16] Suenens, *op. cit.*, pp. 196-211, especially pp. 203, 205.

[17] Edward D. O'Connor, *The Pentecostal Movement in the Catholic Church* (Notre Dame, Ind: Ave Maria Press, 1971), pp. 166-171.

[18] J. Massingberg Ford, *The Pentecostal Experience* (New York: Paulist Press, 1970), pp. 48-58.

[19] Stephen B. Clark, *Where Are We Headed?* (Notre Dame, Ind.: Charismatic Renewal Services, Inc., 1973), p. 20.

[20] *Ibid.*, p. 5.

[21] Cf. an editorial, presumably by Michael Harper, in *Renewal*, no. 51 (June–July, 1974), pp. 2-4.

CHAPTER SEVEN
SUMMARY AND CONCLUSION

[1] Among noncharismatics I have in mind James D. G. Dunn, Michael Green, and to a lesser degree, John Taylor. On the charismatic side I have reference particularly to Thomas A. Smail. Since Smail is the editor of the British bimonthly charismatic magazine, *Renewal,* he is in a position to exercise great influence among charismatics. I certainly do not mean to imply complete agreement between progressive charismatics and open-minded noncharismatics, nor do I mean to suggest that the four men listed above would give assent to everything that I have stated in my discussion of this point. However, it does seem to me that a consensus is emerging along the lines that I have described. On the Catholic side this type of consensus between charismatics and sympathetic noncharismatics is set forth in the Malines Document.

Bibliography

SYMBOLS: P=Pentecostal; CP=Catholic Pentecostal; PP=Protestant Pentecostal; NPS=Non-Pentecostal, but sympathetic; NP=Non-Pentecostal

Basham, Don, *A Handbook of Holy Spirit Baptism*. Springdale, Pa.: Whitaker House, 1969. PP. Simple question-and-answer style. Conservative, charismatic point of view.

Bennett, Dennis and Rita, *The Holy Spirit and You*. Plainfield, N.J.: Logos International, 1971. PP. Readable treatment of charismatic theology. Dennis Bennett is the Episcopalian credited with having launched the charismatic movement.

Berkhof, Hendrikus, *The Doctrine of the Holy Spirit*. New York: John Knox Press, 1964. NPS. Perhaps the best treatment of the doctrine of the Holy Spirit from the perspective of systematic theology.

Bittlingei, Arnold, *Gifts and Graces*. Grand Rapids: Wm. B. Eerdmans Publishing Company, 1967. PP. *Gifts and Ministries*. Grand Rapids: Wm. B. Eerdmans Publishing Company, 1973. PP. Beautiful books by a German Lutheran charismatic scholar.

Bruner, Frederick Dale, *A Theology of the Holy Spirit*. Grand Rapids: Wm. B. Eerdmans Publishing Company, 1970. NP.

Scholarly refutation of Pentecostal theology, but has only limited application to the best in the charismatic movement.

Christenson, Larry, *Speaking in Tongues.* Minneapolis: Bethany Fellowship, Inc., 1968. PP.

Dunn, James D. G., *Baptism in the Holy Spirit.* Naperville, Ill: Alec R. Allenson, Inc, 1970. *Jesus and the Spirit.* Philadelphia: The Westminster Press, 1975. NPS. Solid biblical scholarship. The most important, relevant biblical studies available.

Ervin, Howard M., *These Are Not Drunken As Ye Suppose.* Plainfield, N.J.: Logos International, 1968. PP. Hard-line Pentecostal view by a Baptist preacher and teacher. Dense, pedantic style.

Ford, J. Massingberg, *The Pentecostal Experience.* New York: Paulist Press, 1970. CP.

Gelpi, Donald L., *Pentecostalism: A Theological Viewpoint.* New York: Paulist Press, 1971. CP.

Green, Michael, *I Believe in the Holy Spirit.* London: Hodder and Stoughton, 1975. NPS. Scholarly, but highly readable.

Hamilton, Michael, ed., *The Charismatic Movement.* Grand Rapids: Wm. B. Eerdmans Publishing Company, 1975. A helpful symposium representing various points of view.

Harper, Michael, *As at the Beginning.* London: Hodder and Stoughton, 1965. *Power for the Body of Christ.* London: The Fountain Trust, 1964. *Spiritual Warfare.* Plainfield, N.J.: Logos International, 1970. *Walk in the Spirit.* Plainfield, N.J.: Logos International, 1970. PP. Important books by an early leader of the charismatic movement in England.

Hoekema, Anthony A., *Holy Spirit Baptism.* Grand Rapids: Wm. B. Eerdmans Publishing Company, 1972. *What About Tongue Speaking?* Grand Rapids: Wm. B. Eerdmans Publishing Company, 1966. NP. Written with the intention of refuting the various claims of the charismatic movement.

Hollenweger, Walter J., *The Pentecostals.* Minneapolis: Augsburg Publishing House, 1972. P. Scholarly, sympathetic treatment of Pentecostalism by a former Pentecostal.

Jones, James W., *Filled with New Wine: The Charismatic Renewal of the Church.* New York: Harper & Row, Publishers, 1974. PP. An important, highly readable book by an Episcopal clergyman and religion professor.

Kelsey, Morton T., *Healing and Christianity.* New York: Harper & Row, Publishers, 1973. *Tongue Speaking.* New York: Doubleday & Company, Inc., 1964. Kelsey is an Episcopalian who is sympathetic to tongue speaking and who conducts healing services.

Kildahl, John H., *The Psychology of Speaking in Tongues.* New York: Harper & Row, Publishers, 1972. NP.

McDonnell, Kilian, and Bittlinger, Arnold, *The Baptism in the Holy Spirit as an Ecumenical Problem.* Notre Dame: Charismatic Renewal Services, 1972. Important essays by a Catholic observer and a Lutheran participant in the charismatic movement.

McNutt, Francis, *Healing.* Notre Dame, Ind.: Ave Maria Press, 1974. CP. A beautiful book.

Mills, Watson, *Understanding Speaking in Tongues.* Grand Rapids: Wm. B. Eerdmans Publishing Company, 1972. NPS.

Moody, Dale, *Spirit of the Living God.* Philadelphia: The Westminster Press, 1968. NPS. Solid, helpful biblical study.

Newport, John, *Demons, Demons, Demons.* Nashville: Broadman Press, 1972. NP.

Nichol, Thomas, *The Pentecostals.* Plainfield, N.J.: Logos International, 1971. P. Readable, historical treatment of Pentecostalism by the son of a Pentecostal preacher.

O'Connor, Edward, *The Pentecostal Movement in the Catholic Church.* Notre Dame, Ind.: Ave Maria Press, 1971. CP.

187

Ranaghan, Kevin and Dorothy, *Catholic Pentecostals.* New York: Paulist Press, 1969. CP.

Samarin, William H., *Tongues of Men and of Angels.* New York: Macmillan Publishing Co., Inc., 1972. NP. The most important linguistic study of tongues to date.

Schweizer, Eduard, article on "Pneuma" in the *Theological Dictionary of the New Testament, VI.* Grand Rapids: Wm. B. Eerdmans Publishing Company, 1968. NPS. Very important scholarly treatment of the biblical teaching on the Holy Spirit.

Sherrill, John L., *They Speak with Other Tongues.* Old Tappan, N.J.: Fleming H. Revell Company, 1965. PP. One of the most influential books in promoting the charismatic movement.

Smail, Thomas, *Reflected Glory.* Grand Rapids, Mich.: Wm. B. Eerdmans Publishing Comapny, 1976. PP. The most important theological work to come out of the charismatic movement.

Stagg, Frank; Hinson, Glenn; Oates, Wayne, *Glossolalia.* Nashville: Abingdon Press, 1967. NP. The historical section by Hinson is especially helpful.

Stott, John R. W., *The Baptism and Fullness of the Spirit.* Downers Grove: Inter-Varsity Press, 1964. Revised and enlarged edition entitled *Baptism and Fullness.* Downers Grove: Inter-Varsity Press, 1975. NP. One of the most influential, good-natured polemics against basic charismatic theology.

Suenens, Léon Joseph Cardinal, *A New Pentecost?* New York: The Seabury Press, Inc., 1974. CP. A very influential charismatic book by a cardinal of the Roman Catholic Church.

Taylor, John, *The Go-Between God.* Philadephia: Fortress Press, 1972. NPS. A book on the Holy Spirit with striking beauty and originality.

Theological and Pastoral Orientations on the Catholic Charismatic Renewal. Notre Dame: The Communications Center, 1964. Frequently referred to as the Malines Document. The most important treatment available on Catholic charismatic theology.

Tugwell, Simon, *Did You Receive the Spirit?* New York: Paulist Press, 1972. CP. Rejects baptism in the Spirit but affirms tongues.

Watson, David, *One in the Spirit.* London: Hodder and Stoughton, 1973. PP. A sane, well-balanced charismatic presentation.

Williams, J. Rodman, *The Era of the Spirit.* Plainfield, N.J.: Logos International, 1971. *The Pentecostal Reality.* Plainfield, N.J.: Logos International, 1972. PP. Important books by a Presbyterian charismatic theologian.

CHARISMATIC JOURNALS:

Logos Journal (Plainfield, N.J.)
New Covenant, Catholic (Ann Arbor, Mich.)
New Wine (Fort Lauderdale, Fla.)
Renewal (Central Hall, Durnsford Road, London, SW 19, England)

Index

190 **NAMES**

Aquinas, Thomas, 41

Basham, Don, 129
Bennett, Dennis, 23, 52, 59, 73, 109
Bennett, Rita, 59, 73, 109
Bernard of Clairvaux, 41
Bittlinger, Arnold, 59, 73
Bloesch, Donald, 13
Boardman, W. E., 46
Boom, Corrie ten, 150
Boone, Pat, 18, 19, 24
Bruner, Frederick Dale, 46
Buckingham, Jamie, 149
Bultmann, Rudolf, 134
Burdick, Donald W., 13

Calvin, John, 41
Carey, William, 43
Carothers, Merlin, 146-149
Cash, Johnny, 18
Christenson, Larry, 52, 88
Clark, Stephen, 157
Cornwall, Judson, 52
Criswell, W. A., 13

Dixon, Jeane, 12, 132
Dunn, James D. G., 67, 98-99
Du Plessis, David, 12, 20, 21, 50, 52, 59,

Evans, Leonard, 144

Finney, Charles, 45-46
Ford, Arthur, 132
Ford, J. Massingberg, 155, 158
Fox, George, 42
Francis of Assisi, 41

Gortner, Marjoe, 121
Graham, Billy, 113

Hagin, Kenneth, 125
Haines, Ralph E., Jr., 18
Hamblin, Robert, 13
Harper, Michael, 55, 57, 59, 81

Irving, Edward, 44

John XXIII, Pope, 28, 29, 58
Jordan, Clarence, 113

Kelsey, Morton, 125
Kennedy, John F., 132
Kerr, John Stevens, 18
Kildahl, John, 106
King, Martin Luther, Jr., 113
Kuhlman, Kathryn, 117

LaVey, Anton, 132
Lindsey, Hal, 133

Logan, James C., 13
Luther, Martin, 14, 42

MacArthur, Douglas, 151
Mackay, John, 13, 20, 21
MacNutt, Francis, 125, 126, 129
"Manson family," 132
Martin, Ralph, 13
McDonnell, Kilian, 11, 12, 14
Montanus, 39
Müntzer, Thomas, 41

Newbigin, Lesslie, 19, 20, 21

Ozman, Agnes, 47

Parham, Charles, 47
Paul VI, Pope, 28, 58
Peale, Norman Vincent, 113
Pike, James A., 132
Prince, Derek, 52

Ranaghan, Kevin, 52
Roberts, Oral, 25, 120
Robertson, Pat, 25
Ruffini, Cardinal, 29

Sanford, Agnes, 94, 106
Seymour, William J., 47-48
Shakarian, Demos, 22, 25
Sherrill, Elizabeth, 24
Sherrill, John, 24, 30
Sherrill, Lewis L., 24
Simpson, A. B., 106
Smail, Thomas A., 57-58
Smith, Hannah Whitall, 46
Smith, Joseph, 44
Smith, Robert Pearsall, 46
Stagg, Frank, 11, 73
Stanley, Ann Lee, 44
Suenens, Léon Joseph Cardinal, 27, 29, 58, 83, 150, 154

Tari, Mel, 142
Tate, Sharon, 132
Taylor, John, 72
Tertullian, 40
Terwilliger, Robert E., 12
Tillich, Paul, 135
Torrey, R. A., 47, 55

Van Dusen, Henry P., 20, 21

Wesley, John, 43, 52
Wilkerson, David, 24, 30
Williams, J. Rodman, 30, 31, 32, 35, 58
Wilson, Flip, 136

Young, Brigham, 44

Zinzendorf, Count, 43

SUBJECTS

Anabaptists, 41, 42
Anti-intellectualism, 10, 161
Azusa Street Revival, 48-49

Baptism in the Holy Spirit, 31-32, 45, 47-48, 53-77, 79, 80, 90, 100, 101, 130, 144, 164
  Catholic interpretations, 60
  how received, 58-59, 72-73
  in the New Testament, 60-64
  water baptism, 59, 73-75
Baptism—water baptism, 57, 59, 68, 73-75, 153, 155, 167
Biblical interpretation, 15, 98, 99, 155, 164

Calvary, 69, 70, 76
Catholic distinctives, 60, 82-83, 153-158, 165-166
Charismatic movement
  and the media, 23-25
  characteristics, 30-32, 159-162
  "charismatic," 11, 79, 80, 87
  charismatic prayer meeting, 32-38
  criteria of evaluation, 15, 164-166
  definition, 10
  growing consensus, 162-164
  in Protestantism, 18-26
  in Roman Catholicism, 26-30
  international character, 10, 19
  possible approaches to, 166-168
  summary evaluation, 164-166
  terms for, 10
Christian experience, 64-68, 71
Christological norm, 62, 67, 69-70, 165, 169
Church
  body of Christ, 72, 80, 86, 87
  institutional, 12, 166
Confirmation, 66, 68, 153, 155
Conversion-initiation, 67, 74
Cursillo movement, 29-30

Deliverance, 127-137
Demons, 127-137, 155
Devil, 127-137, 155
Discerning the spirits, 117, 128, 131, 141
Divisiveness, 13, 100, 161-162

Ecumenism, 19-21, 32, 88, 156, 161-162
Emotion, 10, 45-48, 155, 160-161
Exorcism—see Deliverance

Faith, gift of, 117, 140-141
Fellowship, 31, 159-160
FGBMFI, 22-23, 25, 149

191

German Pietism, 42, 44, 52
Glossolalia—see Tongues
God, the Father, 165

Healing, 117-127
  and the atonement, 119, 124-125, 164
  and faith, 120-121
  and medical means, 117-118, 125-127
  anointing the sick, 119, 126
Holiness movement, 46-47, 52
Holy Spirit—Spirit of God
  and Christian ethics, 76
  freedom of, 67-68, 106, 163
  fruit of, 80-81, 100, 143, 163
  fullness of, 62-64, 163
  gifts of, 80-149, 163
  work of, 71-72, 76, 162-163
House churches, 167

Interpretation of tongues, 92, 93-94, 101, 106-107

Jansenists, 42
Jesus Christ
  and healing, 118, 121-124
  and the Holy Spirit, 69, 169
  baptism of, 57, 64
  the Baptizer, 55, 56, 57, 58, 61, 64, 149
  character of, 76, 143
  Lamb of God, 57, 64
  lordship of, 67, 75, 77, 80, 129-130, 131, 137
  victor, 137
  virgin birth, 56, 64
Jesus Movement, 12, 25, 26

Keswick Convention, 46-47

Lord's Supper, 31, 167
Love, 76, 81, 82, 125, 143-145

Malines Document, 82, 90, 91
Methodism, 43, 45
Miracles, 75-76, 85, 128, 141-143
Montanism, 39-40, 116, 155
Moravians, 43, 44, 52

Neo-Pentecostalism—See Charismatic movement

Pentecost, 56, 57, 58, 60, 65, 69-72, 90, 103, 151, 152
Pentecostal experience, 68, 79
Pentecostalism, 10, 11, 47-52, 58, 80, 88, 91, 100, 104, 117, 149, 150, 157, 159
  and the charismatic movement, 51-52
  denominations, 49
  growth, 49-51, 159

history of, 47-52
  methods, 50-51
  prejudices against, 10, 14
  theology of, 11, 62, 98
Personal witness, 26, 32, 164
Praise, 31, 35-38, 93, 146-149
Prayer, 32-38, 93, 117, 118, 119, 120, 149, 160
Pride, 80, 96, 100, 105, 160, 165-166
Prophecy, 86, 92, 94, 97, 109-116
  dangers of, 116
  Paul's interpretation, 113-115
  tests of, 112
Providence, 148-149

Quakers—Society of Friends, 42

Renewal
  church, 13, 165, 169
  personal, 30-32, 68, 159-162, 165, 169
Revivalism, 45-46

Sacraments of initiation, 68, 153
Sanctification, 11, 45, 49
Satan, 12, 127-137
"Second Blessing," 45, 46-47, 57
Shakers, 44
Singing in the Spirit, 35
Social dimension, 76, 77, 166, 169
Spiritual gifts, 80-149
  and the body of Christ, 80, 85, 86, 87
  and spiritual power, 79, 80, 87
  Catholic views, 82-83
  how received, 80, 86
  lists of, 86
  names for, 80
  place of, 79-88
  subject to abuse, 81, 85-86
Spiritual power, 54, 57, 75-77, 170

Tongues, 31-32, 88-107, 163, 164
  and mental health, 104
  as a gift, 89, 90, 91, 92
  as a sign, 47, 48, 89-91, 97-101
  ecstatic speech, 88-89, 102-103
  for everyone, 93, 106
  in church history, 39-44
  in Corinth, 96-97
  in private worship, 96-97
  in public worship, 92, 96-97
  psychological views, 103-104
  real languages, 89, 95, 101-102
  terminology, 94
Trinity, 49, 55, 71, 165

Vatican II, 12, 28, 29, 154

Word of knowledge, 117, 140
Word of wisdom, 139-140

192